# The Bottom Rung

# The Bottom Rung

## African American Family Life on Southern Farms

Stewart E. Tolnay

University of Illinois Press

Urbana and Chicago

© 1999 by the Board of Trustees of the University of Illinois
Manufactured in the United States of America
1   2   3   4   5   C   P   5   4   3   2   1

This book is printed on acid-free paper.

Library of Congress Cataloging-in-Publication Data
Tolnay, Stewart Emory.
The bottom rung : African American family life on Southern
farms / Stewart E. Tolnay.
p.   cm.
Includes bibliographical references and index.
ISBN 0-252-02435-4 (cloth : acid-free paper)
ISBN 0-252-06745-2 (pbk. : acid-free paper)
    1. Afro-American families—Southern States—Social conditions.
2. Southern States—Rural conditions. 3. Farm life—Southern
States. 4. Afro-Americans—Southern States—Social life and
customs. I. Title.
E185.92.T65   1999
306.85'08996073075—ddc21
98-9085
CIP

# Contents

# Preface

This study resulted from the intersection of professional training and personal experiences. In 1981 my wife and I moved to Athens, Georgia, for my first academic position. Soon after arriving, a friend invited us to her home and property in rural Oglethorpe County. The property was part of a much larger piece of land that had been a cotton plantation, owned and operated by the most powerful man in the county. On a clear, cool, Georgia day, we took a short hike and came upon the remnants of an old sharecropper shack. Old newspapers, magazines, and medicine bottles still littered the inside of the cabin. They stirred my imagination and made me wonder about the families that had made this building their home throughout the years. Subsequently, any drive through the Georgia countryside was almost guaranteed to offer glimpses of other abandoned sharecropper cabins and to rekindle my curiosity about the family lives of southern farmers.

My interest in these families took an academic direction because of my graduate training in demography at the University of Washington, including my dissertation research on the history of African American fertility. So, I turned to the work of early depression-era scholars for more information about the lives of these folks who had largely disappeared from the southern countryside. This is when I became acquainted with Arthur Raper, Charles Johnson, Rupert Vance, T. J. Woofter, Hortense Powdermaker, Howard Odum, Margaret Hagood, Carter Woodson, and other contemporary students of the southern plantation society. The important insights that I gained from the excellent ethnographic work of these pioneers then led me to the many secondary sources that make up the vast literature on the history of the rural South.

In 1988 we left Dixie for Albany, New York, and my frequent visual reminders of the sharecropper families came to an end. They were replaced, however, by complementary experiences more typical of a new region. On a hot August day we made our first venture into New York City by taking the Metro-North train from Peekskill. That train route cuts through Harlem on its way to Grand Central Station and offers close-up views of the dilapidated housing conditions that many families must endure in that part of the city. Open windows on a hot, humid day, ubiquitous graffiti conveying messages I did not understand, abandoned automobiles in vacant lots where children should be playing, and groups of young men loitering in alleyways all made me wonder about the family lives of inner-city residents. Again, I turned to the work of earlier social scientists as I sought answers to the many questions that filled my head. I gained a better historical perspective by reading W. E. B. Du Bois, E. Franklin Frazier, St. Clair Drake, Horace Cayton, Charles Johnson, and others. For more "modern" insights I turned to the work of Elijah Anderson, William Julius Wilson, Nicholas Lemann, Daniel Patrick Moynihan, Douglas Massey, and Nancy Denton.

My geographic mobility as well as the literature I had surveyed prevented me from overlooking the important connections between the two social groups that had attracted my attention—southern sharecroppers and inner-city residents. Surely, many people I saw leaning from the windows of the Harlem tenement buildings had parents and grandparents who, years before, sat on the porch of a sharecropper cabin in the rural South during the heat of the summer. Thus, although the two societies, the rural South and the urban North, may seem as different as it is possible to be, there are strong social, cultural, and familial threads that bind them. Those threads account for my decision to examine both societies in the same book. Although my primary objective is to document fully the many dimensions of family life on southern farms, I am also interested in the experiences of the southern migrants who made their way to northern cities.

A colleague once noted, with only a slightly critical tone, "You always study things that are so far away from you, either in time or space." I guess I have done it again. Clearly, I have never been a southern sharecropper. Neither have I ever lived in an inner-city neighborhood of a large metropolitan area. To my knowledge, I have no African American ancestry. I hope, however, that I have been able to overcome these handicaps by providing a reasonably accurate portrayal of the family life of southern farmers as well as a balanced discussion of the forces affecting family life in northern cities.

This book is organized around seven chapters and an epilogue. The first six are concerned primarily with the rural South before World War II, especially between 1910 and 1940. The seventh chapter and the epilogue change the geographic focus to the urban North and the temporal focus to after the war. In all chapters, the major focus is on African Americans, with parallel information presented for whites in order to provide a comparative perspective. Chapter 1 offers a general overview of southern agriculture from the slavery period through the Great Depression. The experiences of African Americans and the implications of agricultural organization for the family-related behavior of southern farmers receive special attention. In the second chapter I describe how southern farm families made a living by depending on the labor inputs of husbands, wives, and children. Chapter 3 turns to marriage formation among southern farmers by examining the timing of first marriages and the universality of marriage. Sociological theory regarding marriage behavior is used to interpret the nuptiality patterns described in the chapter. Family-building is the subject of chapter 4, which documents the reproductive behavior of southern farm couples. Again, the childbearing patterns described are interpreted in light of relevant sociological theories about fertility. Chapter 5 explores the stability of farm families once they had been established. It considers the extent to which marital unions and the living arrangements of children were disrupted through death, divorce, and desertion. Chapter 6 takes up the topic of geographic mobility and examines the extent to which farm couples moved between 1935 and 1940 and the magnitude of off-farm mobility during the same period. Chapter 7 follows southern migrants to northern cities and challenges the widely held belief that they carried with them a dysfunctional family culture. Finally, in the epilogue, I propose parallels between the structural conditions that affected family behavior of southern sharecroppers earlier in the century and those that shape the family behavior of inner-city residents at the century's close. The appendix offers a detailed description of the census data used throughout the book, especially the public-use microdata samples for 1910 and 1940. Although it is not necessary to read the appendix to understand the book's substantive chapters, some readers may benefit from doing so after reading chapter 1 and before reading chapter 2.

## Acknowledgments

It is always humbling, when completing a project of this length and scope, to compile a list of the people and organizations that deserve thanks and credit. It is also distressing to think that someone who should be acknowledged will be left out. The following have made important contributions to this project but should be absolved of any responsibility for its weaknesses or shortcomings. Those are mine and mine alone.

I have enjoyed considerable financial support while working on the project. I am indebted to the National Science Foundation for three separate grants that supported this research, either directly or indirectly (SES-9121499, SBR-9529308, and SBR-9512290). Recent work on the project also benefited from support by the National Institute of Child Health and Human Development (1R01HD3436301A1). I am grateful to Jeanne Gullahorn, former vice president for research at the University at Albany, for "bridge support" during a brief but stressful period between grants. Without such financial support this project would have taken even longer— if it had been completed at all.

The bulk of the quantitative evidence presented in this book is based on data from the U.S. Census, specifically from public-use microdata samples. I owe great thanks to the staff of the Social History Research Laboratory at the University of Minnesota, especially Steven Ruggles, Russell Menard, and Matt Sobek, for creating the Integrated Public Use Microdata Series (IPUMS) that makes such census data much more accessible. They have performed a valuable service for social scientists, across many different disciplines, who will likely grow to appreciate the IPUMS as I have. For the more qualitative dimension of this book, I thank Deanna Pagnini for her generosity in sharing the oral histories from the Federal Writers' Project, which she had laboriously transcribed and made machine-readable.

The University at Albany libraries were helpful in obtaining some of the more obscure reference items through interlibrary loan. I also appreciate their willingness to loan my project a microfiche reader so we could examine the photographs of Dorothea Lange in a more relaxed fashion. Once the photographs to be included in the book were identified, the Prints and Photographs Division of the Library of Congress efficiently responded to inquiries and processed the order.

The text of this book has gone through many re-writes, each of which has benefited from the insightful comments of readers who were generous enough to provide comments, criticisms, and suggestions. Allen Ballard,

Orville Vernon Burton, Patty Glynn, and Elena Vesselinov read the entire manuscript and provided valuable feedback. Vernon Burton's extensive and insightful comments were especially useful during the preparation of the final draft. At various stages of the project, other colleagues read specific chapters or reacted to presentations I made based on the book. Kyle Crowder commented on an early draft of the epilogue (in addition to carrying out the analysis on the PSID data described in chapter 7). John Logan provided useful suggestions that led to the improvement of chapter 7. I appreciate the effort made by my friends and colleagues to make this a better book, and I am sure that they will understand when they discover that I have rejected, after careful consideration, some of their suggestions.

Laura Harris worked as my graduate assistant during much of this project and performed countless tasks quickly and cheerfully. She was especially helpful in identifying the interviews from the Federal Writers' Project that would be most relevant for the subjects addressed in this book.

I owe special thanks to Patty Glynn, my computer programmer and spouse. As the former, she is responsible for the extensive and complex computer work that lurks behind the quantitative side of this book. As the latter, she provided continual moral support throughout the lengthy preparation period. I am extremely grateful for both.

Finally, the reference to "the bottom rung" in the title refers primarily to the position that African American families occupied on the southern agricultural ladder. For most, the possibility of climbing that ladder was remote. Likewise, when southern black families moved to northern cities they also found themselves on the bottom rung of an occupational ladder. Above them on the higher rungs were native-born whites, foreign-born whites, and even northern-born blacks. Their relative location on these ladders has had profound effects on African American families, south and north.

# The Bottom Rung

# 1

# Black Farm Families in the American South and Beyond

This book offers an in-depth investigation of a population that is virtually extinct in American society: black farmers. More accurately, it is a study of the family life of black southern farm households during the first few decades of this century. I am especially interested in how these families were formed through marriage and childbearing; how they were dissolved through death, divorce, or desertion; how they educated their children or put them to work in the fields; how they moved in search of opportunity; and the possible legacy of those experiences for family life in northern cities. Much of my attention is focused on women and children, the often-forgotten members of these farm households. Southern farm women were the glue that held families together. Not only did they bear the children and shoulder a disproportionate share of child care and household duties but they also worked in the fields alongside their husbands. Farm children were considered by many to be an important economic asset because they could increase the size of the family work force, thereby increasing family income. Conversely, some farm couples eventually came to realize that too many children, especially if they attended school, could place a heavy burden on family finances. Still, the rural South was largely a patriarchal society, so farm fathers and husbands must also figure prominently in a portrait of southern farm households.[1]

Any investigation of black southern farm families that does not also consider the social environment and racial atmosphere within which they struggled for survival is woefully incomplete. Black farm families had to deal with all of the same risks and uncertainties of the agricultural way of

life that inflicted white farm families. They also faced a daunting set of
social constraints and obstacles that were unique to their race. Black land-
ownership was controlled through legal and extralegal mechanisms. Black
mobility was restricted through the crop-lien system and debt peonage,
which could tie landless farmers to the same landlord year after year.[2] Black
political participation was curtailed through anti-voting legislation, which
virtually every southern state had adopted.[3] Black schools were supported
at a fraction of the level of white schools—where they were available at
all.[4] In addition, whenever southern blacks fought against these deplorable
conditions, they had reason to fear the wrath of white lynch mobs that had
claimed more than two thousand black victims between 1882 and 1930.[5]

But why study the families of southern farm households? Black farmers
have largely disappeared, so any knowledge gained from such a study seem-
ingly has limited relevance for today's African American population, which
is disproportionately located in cities, including a large percentage in northern cities at that. Indeed, in 1994 there were only 2,906 black farm op-
erators or managers in the United States, about 0.02 percent of the entire
employed African American civilian labor force.[6] Even black lawyers out-
numbered black farmers by a margin of roughly ten to one. Wouldn't it
make ten times as much sense to study the family patterns of black attor-
neys? At least two compelling reasons justify an investigation of the family life of black southern farm households during the early decades of the
twentieth century.

The first reason is based on the assumption that there is inherent value
in improving our understanding of the past, especially when it adds to our
knowledge about a major American ethnic group over an extended period.
Given their modern demographic profile, it is easy to lose sight of the fact
that the history of African Americans has been, for the most part, the history of a population working in southern agriculture. Thus, historical
appreciation for the African American experience can be enriched by a
thorough investigation of the southern farm family.

The second reason relies less on the pure historical value of such an inquiry and more on its potential to cast needed light on the modern African American population. The current regional and residential distribution of that population is of relatively recent origin. Most black Americans
do not have to reach very far back in their family genealogies to locate
relatives, often parents or grandparents, with roots in the rural South. The
massive out-migration of blacks from the South between 1910 and 1970,
many of them from rural communities, swelled the population of African

Americans in northern cities. Consequently, contemporary black families, even if they live in Philadelphia, Chicago, or Los Angeles, are not too far removed from the social and economic milieu that prevailed in the rural South earlier in the century.

Is it possible for family forms and cultural traditions with connections to the southern countryside to be exhibited in the urban black community of today? Prominent African American scholars such as Charles Johnson, W. E. B. Du Bois, St. Clair Drake, Horace Cayton, and E. Franklin Frazier believed that the family patterns of northern, urban blacks during the first half of the century were influenced strongly by southern migrants. More recent scholars such as Daniel Moynihan and Nicholas Lemann have drawn from that earlier work to make the same general argument about more recent periods. Whether or not one accepts their conclusion, the potential for using historical evidence to provide insight into contemporary social patterns and problems is intriguing and challenging. Therefore, even though "black farmer" may be disappearing as an occupational group, it is possible that remnants of the structures and culture that grew up around that segment of society can still be detected. That brings me to the second focus of this book.

After describing family life on southern farms during the first four decades of this century, I will follow those families to northern cities, where millions moved during the Great Migration that began in 1915. Specifically, I will evaluate the conclusion reached by Johnson, Drake, Cayton, Frazier, Moynihan, Lemann, and others: Southern migrants had a destabilizing influence on family structure in the North. Doing so is a logical extension of my first objective because those social scientists claimed that southern migrants carried with them a "dysfunctional family culture"—like so much excess baggage. If such a dysfunctional culture existed, then evidence of it should be apparent in the family lives of southern farmers. Further, there should also be greater instability in the family patterns of southern migrants in northern cities than among the native-born populations of those cities. Although this journey begins in the bucolic southern countryside near the turn of the twentieth century, it concludes in the northern metropolises at the century's close.

## Blacks in Southern Agriculture

Some might argue that there was precious little to distinguish the lives of southern black farmers in 1940 from those of their great-grandparents who labored under the yoke of slavery. To be sure, neither population enjoyed true equality, opportunity, or freedom. The societal arrangements that imposed these limitations, however, were considerably different under slavery and freedom. The legal status of slaves was unambiguous. They were property, and slave masters enjoyed all of the rights of ownership, including the right to sell or abuse their property as they saw fit.[7] The phylogenetic status of slaves was somewhat less certain; some whites doubted their native abilities if not their very humanity.

The legal status of emancipated slaves changed from that of "property" to "freedmen." In principle, that transition granted them the ability to compete with whites (and each other) for all of the coveted resources southern society offered, including wealth, the vote, and a good name. Unfortunately, the phylogenetic status of southern blacks was virtually unchanged after emancipation. Many southern whites were not eager to share society's scarce resources with a population they viewed as inherently inferior and flawed.[8] They quickly erected new social barriers, epitomized by the web of Jim Crow restrictions that began taking shape during the late nineteenth century, to replace the legal constraints of slavery.[9] There is good reason to suspect that southern blacks were at greater risk of physical violence following emancipation. The freedom they had gained placed them in direct competition with whites, and they lacked the protective influence of an owner who at least appreciated their economic value.[10]

It is possible, however, to go too far in emphasizing the similarities in life chances available to these two generations of southern rural blacks—slaves and twentieth-century sharecroppers. To do so deprives intervening generations of the credit they deserve for the substantial progress they were able to achieve in the face of overwhelming obstacles.[11] Circumstances for rural blacks did change across the generations, and many of those changes had important implications for their demographic behavior. Despite the deliberate efforts of local and state governments to deny blacks access to high-quality schools and teachers, the level of literacy rose sharply—from 35 percent in 1890 to 78 percent in 1930.[12] Some rural blacks in the South were also able to circumvent the myriad impediments to land ownership. The number of black farmers who owned their property had increased by roughly 25 percent by the turn of the twentieth century.[13] Clearly, these accomplishments would have been impossible for the vast majority of rural blacks before the Civil War, when it was forbidden to teach slaves to read and write and land ownership for slaves was impossible.

## The Slavery Era

By the eve of the Civil War, southern agriculture had become extremely dependent upon slave labor to generate desired profits. There were roughly four million slaves in the South in 1860, with the bulk concentrated in the Black Belt region of South Carolina, Georgia, Alabama, Mississippi, and Louisiana.[14] Although we often think of southern slaves toiling in cotton fields, that characterization is not quite accurate for two reasons. First, slaves were also instrumental in the production of other crops such as rice, tobacco, and sugar cane. Second, a much smaller number were also involved in non-agricultural activities. Even on cotton plantations, the contributions of slaves to the southern agricultural economy transcended planting, chopping, and picking. House slaves took care of a wide variety of functions within the home of the owner's family, including preparing meals, cleaning, and caring for children. Artisan slaves contributed skilled labor to a wide variety of tasks such as carpentry, brick laying, and tool construction and maintenance. The varied experience gained by southern blacks during the slavery era undoubtedly eased somewhat their transition to independence by providing many of the skills required to operate their own farms. It is equally certain that the loss of their labor and experience was a severe blow to the viability of white-operated farms, especially the very large plantations that could not operate on family labor alone.[15]

Black families during slavery have been the subject of considerable debate. Some scholars have attributed many of the challenges that contemporary African American families face to a legacy of the slavery experience.[16] They point to conditions during the slavery era that were likely to lead to family instability and impermanence. For instance, owners were free to break up slave families by selling one or more members to another plantation. In addition, males in slave-owning families were notorious for seeking sexual gratification from female slaves. Naturally, these liaisons sometimes led to illegitimate births, often to young slave women with no mate. Finally, it has been claimed that slave owners engaged in deliberate and selective slave breeding in order to create a larger, more able, work force. It is easy to understand how these practices, operating in concert, might have led to high levels of single motherhood and broken families among southern slaves. Then, after emancipation, the southern rural black population would have inherited the family patterns that had been established during the slavery era, initiating the legacy of slavery that scholars believe extends into the modern era.

This Mississippi woman, born a slave, works in the cotton fields, much as her mother likely did before her. (Photo by Dorothea Lange, Library of Congress, LC-USF34-17325-C)

Other scholars deny that there is a historical connection between black families during slavery and contemporary black families. For support, they point to two pieces of evidence that they believe contradict the existence of a legacy of slavery. First, extensive investigation of plantation records during the slavery period has been used to show that family life was not as transitory and disorganized as has been claimed.[17] In fact, it is argued, slave families were able to maintain a remarkable degree of stability given the virtual powerlessness of slaves to combat threats to the integrity of their families. The historian Orville Vernon Burton acknowledges that owners had an economic interest in early and frequent reproduction by their slaves, which would increase the size of their captive labor force. He argues, however, that this economic interest motivated owners to encourage marriage and family stability among their slaves.[18] Second, statistical studies of free black families during the late nineteenth century have been used to show that they were similar to white families in structure and stability.[19] The majority of rural black families were nuclear, with a set of parents co-resident with children, and most black children were not the product of non-marital unions. According to these scholars, problems of family disruption and instability in the contemporary African American community are likely the result of the decades of discrimination and restricted economic opportunities that blacks have experienced since emancipation.[20]

So, what can we glean from this debate about the true nature of black family life during slavery? There can be no question that slave families were exposed to disruptive influences that were not shared by free families, black or white. Slave narratives and oral histories contain ample evidence that slave families were sometimes broken through the sale of family members and that young slave women were often forced to endure the unwanted sexual advances of males from the slave-owning family.[21] It would be surprising if these unique threats to slave families did not result in a higher level of non-marital childbearing, more female-headed families, and fewer children co-residing with both parents than would have been the case in the absence of such threats. The best available evidence, however, suggests that most slave families were patriarchal and stable, even if illegitimate childbearing and the disruption of unions were somewhat more common among slaves than in the southern white population.

In addition, other aspects of slave society were relevant to the way slave families were formed. Because of their nearly totally dependent status, slaves were not subject to the same economic-based constraints on certain important life transitions. For example, it was generally not necessary for slave couples anticipating marriage or stable cohabitation to accumulate sufficient resources to guarantee economic independence. As a result, they entered cohabiting unions at a relatively early age. Neither were slaves required to weigh the economic advantages and disadvantages in reaching childbearing decisions. Owners bore the bulk of expenses associated with the care, feeding, and clothing of children, even if they provided only a subsistence-level of support. In addition, slave parents had no need to restrict the sizes of their families and invest in fewer children as a strategy for increasing the children's opportunities. Rather, they had every reason to believe that their children would face a life of servitude much like their own. Therefore, slave women typically bore their first child at an early age and completed their reproductive careers with a very large family.[22] Owners generally stood to benefit from the acceleration of these demographic transitions.[23] Although deliberate slave breeding was likely an isolated phenomenon, it is unlikely that owners often intervened to delay a slave union or discourage early and frequent childbearing unless such behavior was perceived to be disadvantageous to the owner.

## Freedom: 1865 to 1900

The foundation of southern rural life was shaken profoundly when slaves gained their freedom. The reactions of emancipated slaves varied. Some remained loyal to former owners and stayed on the farm or plantation in much the same status they occupied before the war, although the number of freedpersons exhibiting such loyalty was almost certainly smaller than southern whites wanted northern critics to believe. Others quickly took advantage of their new freedom to move to southern cities or leave the region altogether. The loss of black population from southern rural areas through such mobility was not dramatic, however. By far the most common response to freedom was to remain in the southern countryside and maintain a connection with agricultural production.

For most who did remain in the rural South, and for their former owners, the primary challenge was to find a niche for black labor that was acceptable to both groups. As it turned out, it was impossible to satisfy both groups completely because of their extremely divergent expectations. White planters preferred an organization for agricultural labor that resembled as closely as possible the old slavery system and gave them absolute control over the black work force. The first choice of many whites was a gang labor system in which blacks worked the white-owned land under the watchful eyes of owners and overseers. The primary difference that distinguished the gang labor system from slavery was that white planters could no longer claim ownership rights over their workers (although in practice it sometimes seemed as though employers enjoyed such rights). In most other respects the two systems were very much alike, and both used corporal punishment to deal with recalcitrant workers or troublemakers. For southern whites, the gang labor system for harnessing black labor was nearly ideal. In addition to providing a substitute arrangement for maintaining control over workers, it also was unlikely to provide much opportunity for upward social or economic mobility for African Americans.

Most blacks expected more from freedom than the continuation of their social and economic subordination, only under a different name. Following the defeat of the Confederacy, hopes ran high among southern blacks that the federal government would undertake a massive program of land redistribution. Certainly, postwar conditions in the rural South seemed appropriate for such a revolutionary initiative. Many white planters had vast land holdings but no longer commanded a labor force to generate profits from that land. Yet rural blacks had no land (or little other capital for that matter) but enjoyed the newly acquired control of their labor. Furthermore, land redistribution would have punished the white aristocracy for their recent rebellion and compensated freedmen for two centuries of involuntary servitude. For southern whites the prospect of widespread land ownership among blacks was horrifying. Not only would it require some of them to give up large tracts of land, but it would also raise the former slave population to a social and economic plane equivalent to, or exceeding, that of many struggling whites—a prospect inconsistent with the common perception of African Americans as nearly subhuman.

The compromise that emerged from this dialectic was the sharecropping system, which would shape life in the rural South for decades to come.[24] Under this arrangement, white planters retained ownership of their land, and blacks obtained a degree of independence in controlling their own labor. Large land holdings were subdivided into several smaller plots or farms, usually fewer than fifty acres for black tenants. Each farm was occupied by a tenant family that took responsibility for raising the cash crop. In exchange for access to the land, the family compensated the owner in one of a variety of ways. Cash tenant families paid owners a specific annual rent in cash for a farm and then kept the profits from the sale of the crop. They were the elite of the non-owning farming class. Below cash tenants on the agricultural ladder were share tenants, who generally brought less capital (e.g., farm implements or draft animals) to the agreement and required greater support than cash tenants from a landowner. Share tenant families divided profits from the cash crop with the landowner after harvest, with the most common agreement calling for a 50-50 split. "Croppers," who offered only their labor to the agreement with owners, were at the bottom of the hierarchy of farm tenants. Although there was great variety in specific arrangements made between tenants and owners, the sharecropping system kept control of farmland securely in the hands of whites. For blacks, sharecropping was not as repulsive as gang labor because they were able to retain some degree of independent control over their labor and their lives.

The southern agricultural system, based so heavily on tenancy, was unique within the United States, and it was persistent. Of all farms occupied by southern blacks in 1900, more than three-quarters were operated by tenants. In contrast, only 27 percent of black farms in the North Atlantic region and 31 percent of black farms in north central states were operated by tenants. The same pattern existed among white farmers although in a less striking fashion. Thirty-six percent of southern white farmers were tenants, compared with 21 percent and 28 percent in the North Atlantic region and north central states. Southern tenancy remained disproportionately high well into the twentieth century.[25]

The long-term dominance of farm tenancy, especially sharecropping, among southern rural blacks had a substantial impact on demographic behavior and family patterns. In some respects that influence perpetuated demographic conditions that existed during slavery—for example, early marriage and large families. In general, prospective couples were not required to postpone marriage until they had accumulated adequate savings to establish economic independence. Indeed, farm ownership among blacks was a sufficiently remote possibility that many couples probably dismissed it in planning for the near future. White landowners, however, were eager to find young couples to operate their tenant farms, especially where labor was in short supply. Landlords typically provided sharecroppers with tools, animals, fertilizer, and seed with which to cultivate their land. Many also extended credit, usually at exorbitant rates of interest, so croppers could purchase food, clothing, and other supplies throughout the year. As a result of this system of production, which reduced the chances of land ownership and deemphasized the accumulation of capital as a prerequisite for independence, tenant farmers often married at a young age even though by doing so they were likely to become mired in perpetual debt to a landlord or local merchants.[26]

The tenancy system also presented few incentives for black sharecropping couples to limit the size of their families. In the agricultural economy of the South between 1870 and 1900, child labor was common and educational opportunities were limited, especially for blacks. Children began performing household chores at a very early age and working in the fields only slightly later. A white tenant farm mother, interviewed by Margaret Hagood in the 1930s, described quite well the contributions made by children, black and white, on tenant farms: "'They can begin toting in wood a stick at a time when they're two. Soon after I start 'em to drying knives and forks, because they can't break them, and when they're a little older, the other dishes. They can sweep by six and carry water in small buckets and tend the baby. By ten they can clean house, make beds, and straighten up, and by twelve or thirteen can cook a meal if they have to.'"[27] By helping in these ways, farm children also relieved their mothers of some household chores, thereby making it possible for them to join their husbands in the fields.[28]

Many landlords preferred to rent land to tenants with large families and were willing to give them access to more acres of farmland to work. The landlords' logic was sound: Families with several child workers produced larger crops, half of which belonged to the owner. In contrast to the slavery era, landlords did not absorb the costs of these large families because they were not responsible for food and clothing. Those expenses were taken from a cropper's share of the profit. In this system of domestic production, landlords and tenants alike seemed to benefit in some way from the high fertility rates of tenant women.[29] Only the tenant families were likely to suffer the consequences, however.

Yet there is some question about the economic rationality of large families, even within this system of agricultural production. Some sophisticated analyses of time allocation and the economic costs and contributions of children in agricultural societies suggest that children probably consume more than they produce, at least until they reach the teenage years.[30] One childless black farmer, Sam Bowers, interviewed during the Federal Writers' Project of the New Deal, also had doubts about the economic advantages of parenthood. He told the interviewer: "'My pa believed in big famblies, but I don't. No sir, I don't. No gang of chillun for me. I married Bessie Kelvin, a school teacher, in Febawary, 1911. She wuz teachin' den

an' she's still teachin'. We don't have no chillun. If we had a-had chillun
we couldn't a-got no-where.'"[31] Judging from the actual demographic
record, however, most black farm families either did not agree with Sam
Bowers's views on childbearing or were less effective at achieving their
family-size goals.

Other demographic consequences from the southern agricultural
economy arose following the Civil War. Because the system was relatively
effective at restricting the economic opportunities available to rural blacks,
their standard of living did not improve significantly between 1870 and
1900. As a result, mortality levels remained constant at a relatively high
level through the turn of the century.[32] High mortality, in turn, took a toll
on farm families—especially in the form of widows and orphans. In addition, the social and economic arrangements that developed to support the
sharecropping system tended to restrict the geographic mobility of black
farmers. Farm families were often forced to mortgage their crops for credit
with landlords or merchants in order to obtain food and other necessary
supplies. Often profits from the harvest were not sufficient to remove their
debt, and it was carried over to the next year. That type of debt peonage,
when supplemented by discriminatory legal restrictions against black
mobility, discouraged the migration of black farm families in search of
better opportunity. Furthermore, southern rural blacks did not enjoy an
abundance of competing opportunities. Occupational discrimination still
restricted African Americans' access to many jobs in southern cities and
to non-agricultural jobs in rural areas, for example, in textile mills.[33] Too,
waves of immigrants from southern and eastern Europe were filling many
jobs in the industrializing North.

It would be misleading to leave the impression that all black southern
farmers during this era were sharecroppers, tilling someone else's land.
Indeed, that was not the case. During the late-nineteenth century, between
20 and 25 percent of black southern farmers owned their land. The comparable figure for southern white farmers was about 60 percent.[34] When
compared with white-owned farms, however, an average black-owned farm
was smaller, had fewer farm implements and machinery, and was located
on poorer soil. Still, the level of ownership is impressive in view of the
obstacles that had been erected by the dominant white society.[35] There
existed, in many areas, a kind of gentlemen's agreement that whites would
not sell land to blacks, even to those who had the resources to buy. Blacks
who successfully circumvented these obstacles usually had a close relationship with an influential white benefactor willing to sponsor the black buyer

and vouch for his harmlessness. As Arthur Raper described the situation in *Preface to Peasantry,* his classic study of black farmers in Greene and Macon counties in Georgia during the 1930s:

> The typical Negro tenant hardly considers the ownership of land possible. Though the owner has a larger income, lives in a bigger house, eats better food, sends his children to school longer and more regularly, and controls his own time, he leaves the landless masses with little hope of achieving a similar status. They seem to realize that Negro landownership in these counties is still limited to those few whose exceptional contacts with some landed white man which lead him to violate the plantation system to the extent of doing for the particular Negro what he would least consider doing for them all.[36]

## Freedom: 1900 to 1940

In some respects the turn of the twentieth century is an arbitrary point at which to divide a description of the position of blacks in southern agriculture. The average black farmer certainly saw little change in status or the meaning of freedom throughout most of this period. Jim Crow still dictated the limits of behavior and achievement for most blacks in southern society. Restrictive voting legislation became even more firmly entrenched, virtually neutralizing the political influence of southern blacks. White lynch mobs continued to terrorize the southern black population, and 568 blacks were lynched during the century's first decade alone, primarily in rural areas.[37] Later events in this period, however, carried important implications for the future status of southern blacks—and for African Americans in general.

Until the eve of World War II, most southern farmers were tenants. Farm ownership remained as elusive as it had been during the late nineteenth century. Never, during this forty-year period, did the prevalence of black farm ownership rise above 20 percent. Even among that elite the average farm size hovered below fifty acres throughout the era. In contrast, white farm ownership held above 50 percent until late in the period, and the average white landholding was nearly twice that of blacks.[38]

A series of events during the first few decades of the twentieth century jeopardized even the meager stability and economic security enjoyed by black tenant farmers and some owners as well. The livelihoods of cotton farmers were seriously threatened as the boll weevil infestation continued its march from the Texas Gulf Coast to the southeastern Piedmont early in the century. Owners and tenants alike were forced from their land as the weevil destroyed their crops. Some were able to reestablish themselves in their former statuses after a relatively brief disruption, but others were either permanently reduced to wage-laboring status or abandoned the agricultural economy entirely.[39]

On the heels of the boll weevil disaster, during the 1920s, the rural South began to experience the initial symptoms of the economic downturn that was to become the Great Depression. With credit in short supply, markets faltering, and the southern soil suffering the consequences of too many years of intensive monoculture, many farmers could no longer scrape a living from the land, whether it was owned or rented. Although the depression saw some return movement from cities to the countryside by those seeking refuge in a more bucolic life-style, it was also a period of serious agricultural dislocation.

Even some of the New Deal programs that were introduced by Franklin Roosevelt's administration to restore a measure of stability and prosperity to southern agriculture worked to press tenant farmers further down the agricultural hierarchy. Among the programs was the Agricultural Adjustment Act of 1933, which encouraged southern farmers to give their exhausted soil a respite. The federal government paid them to keep fields out of cultivation. Although the program's designers intended to include tenant farmers in such payments, local county agents and white planters frequently conspired to prohibit that possibility. Land previously farmed by tenants was now withheld from cultivation by the owner for compensation from the federal government. Tenants were displaced and forced to either find a niche elsewhere in the agricultural economy or migrate. Because opportunities for black ownership were so circumscribed, wage labor was often the only alternative available to displaced black tenants. Increasing farm mechanization created the same kind of downward pressure as many owners chose to use wage workers in combination with improved machinery rather than tenants to farm their land.[40] Between 1910 and 1940 the proportion of agricultural blacks who were wage laborers rose sharply by 42 percent. During that same period black farm ownership declined by 50 percent, and the number of black tenants fell by 10 percent.[41]

Throughout this period of declining agricultural fortunes many southern black farmers struggled for survival. Battered by the economic decline and betrayed by the failing soil that had sustained them and the federal government in which they had often placed great hope, some sought to redress their grievances through more radical tactics. The Southern Tenant Farmers'

Union (STFU) attempted to organize landless farmers, including blacks, to improve their negotiating posture with white planters who controlled their financial destiny. The landowners' influence remained too powerful, however, for such a labor organization to go unchallenged. Organizers for the STFU frequently were threatened and sometimes killed. Howard Kester, one of the more well known, was nearly lynched as he met with union members in a church in Arkansas. Only the intervention of a large group of sympathetic farmers saved him.[42] Strikes orchestrated by the STFU were often met with violent repression, as happened in Arkansas in 1935.[43]

Partially as a result of these shocks to southern agriculture, the rural black population experienced profound demographic transitions between 1900 and 1940. The massive exodus of blacks from rural areas that occurred after 1910 is linked to the changing fortunes of black farmers during the era. The first wave of this exodus began around World War I as a series of circumstances coincided to create the conditions appropriate for black migration.

This Arkansas sharecropper, an active member of the Southern Tenant Farmers' Union, was evicted from his farm because of his involvement in the union. (Photo by Dorothea Lange, Library of Congress, LC-USF34-9549-C)

The timing of the migration was due largely to a strengthening of pull factors that drew southern rural blacks to northern states as well as to southern cities. Northern industrial activity was gaining momentum as the nation geared up for the war effort. At the same time, the war in Europe had slowed the flow of immigrants arriving in America. Desperate for workers to fill the positions that previously had been occupied by cheap labor from southern and eastern Europe, northern capitalists cast their eyes southward. In the past, race prejudice had caused them to overlook the southern black population as a potential labor pool—even though they shared the same nationality and language. With concern for profits finally overriding concern over race, northern industrialists sent labor agents into the South to round up black workers for factory work. Although influential southern whites often greeted the agents with great hostility and sometimes violence, they were successful in convincing large numbers of rural blacks to sever their southern roots and head north.

Northern industry was aided in its effort to attract southern rural blacks by powerful push factors. In addition to the declining fortunes of many black farmers, there were also a number of other economic and non-economic incentives for migration. The rural South offered inferior schools for blacks and relatively few attractive opportunities even for those successful enough to acquire extended educations.[44] Jim Crow restrictions assured that blacks would lead second-class lives and have access only to second-class services. Racial violence also continued to claim large numbers of black victims through 1920.[45] Political disenfranchisement assured that southern blacks would be powerless to change these distressing conditions through the voting booth. As a result, more and more came to agree with the Methodist Episcopal minister from Alabama who wrote to the *Chicago Defender*:

> Doubtless you have learned of the great exodus of our people to the north and west from this and other southern states. I wish to say that we are forced to go when one things of a grown man wages is only fifty to seventy five cents per day for all grades of work. He is compelled to go where there is better wages and sociable conditions, believe me. When I say that many places here in this state the only thing that the black man gets is a peck of meal and from three to four lbs. of bacon per week, and he is treated as a slave. As leaders we are powerless for we dare not resent such or to show even the slightest disapproval.[46]

The *Chicago Defender* was not only aware of the northward exodus but it also, after initial efforts to discourage black migration, promoted it. It ran powerful stories and illustrations that enumerated the many ways in which southern blacks were downtrodden and offered glowing descriptions of life in the North.

The scale of black out-migration from the South was reduced somewhat during the depression as employment opportunities in the North withered. Still, the 1930s saw a net loss of more than four hundred thousand blacks from the South as formidable push factors continued to operate. A second surge of migration began in the early 1940s when northern industries once again expanded production for the war effort. Still lacking sufficient numbers of immigrants from southern and eastern Europe, partially because of restrictive immigration legislation passed during the 1920s, the companies again relied on the labor of southern migrants. Once completed some years after 1940, the second diaspora had significantly changed the demographic profile of African Americans. A previously southern and rural population became significantly more northern and urban.[47]

Those southern black farmers who stayed behind experienced their own demographic transitions as fertility and mortality rates fell sharply between 1900 and 1940. At the turn of the century, the average black woman in the rural South bore roughly seven children and could expect to live to be about forty. The grandchild of that average woman in 1940 would have about five children and could expect to live to be fifty-eight.[48]

Fertility rates in the South, particularly among farm families, remained at traditionally high levels considerably longer than in other parts of the nation.[49] Indeed, at the turn of the century the childbearing patterns of black farmers were characteristic of what demographers refer to as "natural fertility" populations.[50] Put simply, this means that couples did not take steps to avoid having a child in response to the family size they had already achieved. The availability of only relatively crude contraceptive techniques can not account completely for that phenomena; other groups, including northern farmers, had already reduced the sizes of their families substantially by the turn of the century.[51] Rather, the explanation lies in the fact that incentives for large families were built into the social and economic environment of southern black farmers. Theirs was a society in which child labor represented an important contribution to a household's economy, and educational opportunities were poor. It was also a society in which children could offer at least some measure of security in old age.

Given the significant economic (and non-economic) contributions of children, it is understandable that couples were also concerned by relatively high levels of infant and child mortality early in the century. In order to guarantee that they had enough surviving children to perform these important functions, couples were likely to replace lost children, or insure against potential losses, by having surplus children. Of course, it is naive to think that couples engaged in this type of rational calculation and carefully constructed lists of the advantages and disadvantages of a larger family to arrive at childbearing decisions. Rather, acting in concert, these pronatalistic influences created an atmosphere in which deliberate intervention in the family-building process was relatively uncommon and, to many, unacceptable. Also contributing to the persistently high fertility rates among black farm couples was their isolation from other segments of society that thought differently about fertility and family life.[52]

During the first decades of the century, certain transformations occurred that began to undermine the pronatalistic foundation. More and more blacks in agriculture either toiled as wage laborers rather than tenant farmers or they combined the two activities. A wage-laboring household is less likely to function as a unit of domestic production. The labor of family members is sold on the market rather than applied directly to household production efforts. Although children in such families can still be economically active, they tend to do so at a later age and away from the home. Likewise, a wife's labor is typically less compatible with a large family because her work also is more likely to occur away from home. In addition, many of the goods and services produced within farm households must be purchased for cash or credit by wage-laboring families. The growth of a wage-labor family economy eroded the incentives for high fertility.[53]

Educational opportunities expanded during these decades, largely from the efforts of local black communities and with investments from northern philanthropists. Since the early years of freedom (and even before) rural blacks had placed high value on education and saw it is a potential route to success. Many farm families made great sacrifices to take advantage of the meager educational opportunities that did exist.[54] When those opportunities improved, it became even easier to educate the children of farm families. Still, there was a price for this decision. As the length of the school year increased it became more and more likely that children would be in classrooms when there was also work to be done in the fields. Too, basic expenses for clothing and school supplies were a significant burden for struggling farm families. Incentives to have large families began to evaporate as education reduced the labor contributions of children and increased their cost to farm households.

The rural South also grew less isolated from the rest of the nation during this period. Radio and the print media (e.g., the *Chicago Defender*) penetrated the region and opened farm households to ideas that had already taken hold among the urban middle class of the Northeast about family life, contraception, and sexuality. Northbound migrants also represented another vector for the flow of new ideas and information. Through letters and visits home they were able to introduce the more sedentary farm population to alien ideas and norms that, when coupled with the declining motivation for large families, likely had a significant effect on fertility rates.

Black mortality also remained extremely high through the beginning of the twentieth century. In fact, remarkably little progress had been made at increasing black life expectancy during the closing decades of the nineteenth century. That was not the case for whites, for whom mortality fell considerably during the same period. The persistently high mortality of southern blacks can no doubt be attributed to their disadvantaged economic position in society, which contributed to poor diets, unhealthful living conditions, and inadequate access to whatever health care system existed at the time. Yet mortality for rural blacks was lower than it was in cities because farmers could supplement their diets with home-grown vegetables, fruits, and meat. Too, the probability of disease transmission was lower because of less densely populated rural settlements.[55]

Because of reasons that are still not well understood, mortality among southern black farmers dropped between 1900 and 1940. Improved medical technology during the early twentieth century probably accounts for a significant part of this improvement. Blacks almost certainly benefited less than whites from such technology, however, given their economic status and restricted access to hospitals and clinics. Whatever the causes of the rural mortality decline, by 1940 black farmers were living significantly longer than had been the case, and their children were much more likely to survive infancy.

The demographic transitions that occurred during the first part of the century were potentially important for southern black farm families. That potential is easy to appreciate when it is realized that the structure of families is shaped by the reproductive behavior of parents as well as the mobility or death of its members. As the exodus to the North accelerated, it became more common for families to be separated. Husbands and fathers sometimes pioneered the way north and later sent for wives and children to join them after they were established. For other families the separation was permanent. The results of such separations, temporary or permanent, were more female-headed households and more children who were not residing with both parents.

Reductions in mortality had a much different effect on family structure. As life expectancies improved, fewer wives and husbands became widows or widowers prematurely. Also, fewer children were orphaned or left with only one surviving parent. Lower adult mortality, therefore, increased the amount of time that families were eligible to be headed by couples as well as the number of years of childhood spent in such families. Moreover, as infant survival became more assured, potentially more children were exposed to the influences of lengthened life expectancy for adults and the increased likelihood of parental migration.

Declining fertility during the era meant that falling mortality did not have the inflationary effect on surviving family sizes it might have had. Even though a higher proportion of newborns survived into their childhood years, parents were producing fewer newborns. The decline in fertility was substantial enough to outpace the improvement in infant survival and assure that average surviving family sizes declined between 1900 and 1940. Falling fertility rates also meant that children would have fewer siblings and that parents in old age would have fewer children with whom they could co-reside or draw upon for other types of support.

These southern farm families and the era in which they lived were buffeted by strong social and economic forces largely outside of their control. Beyond that, African Americans occupied a unique status in a culture that doubted their humanity, imposed limits to their freedom, and erected obstacles to restrict their opportunities. Furthermore, those social, economic, and cultural forces had an important influence on demographic behavior, which in turn determined the structure of families. It was that demographic and family heritage that black migrants carried with them as they abandoned the southern countryside in huge numbers during and after World War II.

## To the North

After describing family life on southern farms between 1910 and 1940, I will consider family life in northern cities. There are two reasons for that significant change in focus. First, the organization of southern agriculture changed dramatically after 1940, altering the fabric of rural life and affecting both the class structure and the racial caste system. Second, the exploding black population in northern cities shifted the nation's attention to a plethora of perceived problems plaguing urban families, including divorce, desertion, and illegitimacy. During the second half of the twentieth century black farmers grew increasingly irrelevant. Their dwindling numbers meant that black city-dwellers would dominate discussions of African Americans and their problems. Further, social scientists have taken it for granted that there was an important connection between the two populations. It is the exact nature of that connection which interests me.

Although there continued to be black farmers in the southern agricultural economy after World War II, their numbers plummeted as a result of many of the social forces mentioned earlier in this chapter. Agricultural reforms, especially farm mechanization, made it more efficient for landowners to consolidate a tenant's land into larger plots. Fewer wage laborers could use the new machinery to prepare and harvest the cash crops and do so more productively than could the tenant families they replaced. Owners of small farms found it increasingly difficult to compete with the larger agricultural enterprises in the production of cash crops. Many displaced tenants and owners moved to southern cities in search of opportunity. Others moved north and west as the nation's factories once again increased production to prepare for war—this time in Europe and the Pacific. As a result of these pressures and others the black farm population dropped sharply after 1940. As Jack Kirby has noted, "By 1970 a black southern farmer of any sort was almost as rare as a black middle western farmer."[56]

The number of southern farm households headed by blacks declined sharply after 1940 (fig. 1). In 1940 nearly 40 percent of all households headed by blacks were located on farms; in only ten years that figure had dropped to about 25 percent. By 1970 farms accounted for fewer than 5 percent of all black households in the South, documenting Kirby's observation. By the time the U.S. Census was taken in 1980 and 1990, black farm households had virtually disappeared from southern society.

Although additional insights might be gained by extending the examination of southern farm families into the decades after 1940, Figure 1 suggests the strongly diminishing returns to doing so. First, only in 1950 would there be sufficient farm households to support the types of statistical analyses that are conducted in the following chapters. For 1960 and later it would be virtually impossible. Perhaps more important than the lack of adequate data is the declining demographic importance of that population. As the

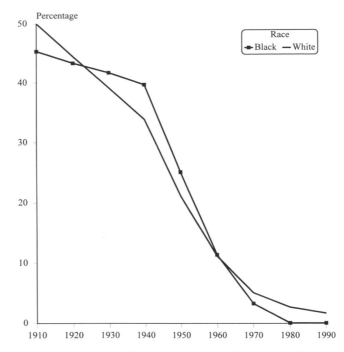

Figure 1. Percentage of Southern Households That Are Farms, by Race, 1910–90. (*Sources:* 1910 and 1940–90 Integrated Public Use Microdata Series, Social History Research Laboratory, University of Minnesota. Percentages for 1920 and 1930 are interpolated.)

trend in Figure 1 implies, black southern farmers represented a sizable proportion of the African American population during the first half of the twentieth century. That changed quickly after 1940. The transformation is even more substantial than indicated in Figure 1, which describes only the proportion of southern black households located on farms. With increasing interregional migration after 1920, a larger and larger share of American blacks lived in the West and North—and most resided in cities. Although farm families represented only 10 percent of all southern black households in 1960, they accounted for an even smaller proportion of all black households nationally. As the demographic dominance of black farm families declined so too did the extent to which they directly shaped the social, economic, and cultural experience of African Americans in general.

In 1910, 89 percent of all African Americans lived in the South, and only 27 percent resided in urban areas. By 1970 only 53 percent were southerners and more than 80 percent were urbanites.[57] The demographic redistribution produced by the Great Migration was that dramatic. As a result of these residential shifts, the average black family of the last half of the twentieth century has been exposed to a much different social and economic milieu than was the average black family during the first half of the century. That transformation has also been reflected in the shifting emphasis of social science research concerned with the African American population. The rural-agrarian emphasis that characterized the North Carolina School of the early decades of the century has given way to a preoccupation with African Americans in northern inner cities.[58] As social scientists studying the black population have shifted their focus to northern cities, concerns with sharecropping, debt peonage, and disenfranchisement have given way to discussions of residential segregation, joblessness, and public assistance. A strong interest in African American families has persisted, however, with a continuing focus on marital behavior, childbearing, family structure, and family stability.

Since World War II black families have experienced disturbing changes that have attracted the attention of social scientists and policymakers alike. First, marriage has become less common. In 1940, 74 percent of black women had ever been married; by 1990 only 63 percent reported that they had ever been married. Second, divorce has increased. In 1960 the divorce rate for black women was 78 divorces per 1,000 married women. By 1990 there were more than 350 divorced black women for every 1,000 married women. Third, non-marital childbearing has risen significantly. In 1940 there were 35.6 births for every 1,000 unmarried black women between 15 and 44 years of age; the comparable rate in 1990 was 88.9. Fourth, fewer children live with two parents. Roughly 80 percent of black children lived with two parents in 1960; by 1990 fewer than half lived with a mother and father.[59] A variety of explanations for these trends have been offered, including declining job opportunities for black men in inner cities, increasing economic status of black women relative to men, expanding availability of public assistance payments, and the rise of an oppositional inner-city culture in response to persistent segregation and discrimination in the North.[60]

Yet even before the postwar period, especially during the 1930s and early 1940s, social scientists also sounded alarms about the well-being of northern black families.[61] They pointed with concern to levels of desertion, divorce, and illegitimacy that they already considered to be too high—even at that early date. Although they did not totally ignore the possibility that structural forces (e.g., unemployment, residential crowding, and racial discrimination) affected the stability of urban black families, they tended to blame the newly arrived southern migrants for many family-related problems. They based this blame on two key assumptions: first, that the families of southern farmers were generally unstable and disorganized, and, second, that southern migrants transplanted their family patterns to northern cities. As supporting evidence they pointed to what they argued were significant differences between the families of migrants and non-migrants in northern cities.[62]

Although that connection has been accepted relatively uncritically by subsequent generations of social scientists and has been perpetuated by more recent researchers, it has not been tested rigorously.[63] There can be no doubt that the social and cultural heritage of the southern farm population lived on in new communities of the migrants. Indeed, the influence of the southern farm experience still survives in the predominantly urban African American community. Still, the questions remain. Did the influx of migrants from the rural South destabilize northern black families? Have the deleterious changes experienced by black families since the 1940s been the culmination of the continuing introduction of a dysfunctional family culture from the South? Only by carefully examining the family lives of African Americans in both settings can those questions be answered.

# 2

# Making a Living

Before the massive mechanization of agricultural production, life for most American farmers was a constant struggle for economic security. That was probably more true of southern farmers than it was of their counterparts above the Mason-Dixon Line. Nature had a rich repertoire of aggravations with which to challenge the resilience of southern farmers. In addition to weather-related disasters such as droughts and floods, there was a variety of pests such as the boll weevil that devastated cotton crops and the horn-worm that threatened tobacco plants.

Nature was not the only threat to the survival of southern farmers. Some rapacious landlords and merchants exploited them through uncharitable arrangements for dividing the cash crop and by charging usurious rates of interest on loans that tenants were forced to take out in order to get through the year. As a result, many farmers ended the year even further in debt than they were when it started. Tied to the same plot of land by the yoke of debt, their prospects for the following year were no brighter.

The farmers themselves, especially tenants, unwittingly collaborated in their own economic misfortune by using agricultural practices that made long-term profitability doubtful. They devoted the bulk of available acre-age to a cash crop and only rarely gave the land a chance to lay fallow. Against that discouraging backdrop southern farmers in the early twenti-eth century attempted to scratch a living from the soil—much as their parents and grandparents had done.

There was great continuity in the working lives of southern farmers across generations. The day-to-day routines of agricultural production were not all that different for farmers at the turn of the twentieth century than they had been shortly after the Civil War. It is only a slight exaggeration to say the same for the routines of most southern farmers during the Great Depression. Noting the long-term continuity in the lives of tenant farmers, Jacqueline Jones observed, "Tenant farm wives of the Great Depression lived lives similar to those of their grandmothers in the 1880s. . . . The sharecropper's cabin remained a permanent fixture on the southern landscape, and the succession of families who inhabited it continued to organize themselves and their work in a manner that defied the passage of time."[1]

An important part of the material basis for this continuity that "defied the passage of time" was the persistence of farm tenancy, cheap wages and the relatively slow modernization of agricultural production. Average monthly earnings for farm laborers (including board) were under $20 only in the South; elsewhere, people earned nearly $30 monthly and in some cases considerably more. The low price of farm labor and the dominance of tenancy discouraged most landowners from making large investments in farm machinery. As a result, southern states lagged far behind the rest of the nation in shifting to more mechanized forms of production. In 1940, for example, only 3.6 percent of the farmers in the east south central region owned tractors; those in the South Atlantic were not much better off at 5.6 percent (table 1). There was an even greater delay in the adoption of mechanized harvesting. It was not until after World War II, for example, that the use of mechanized cotton pickers became widespread. Mechanized harvesting of tobacco was delayed until the 1960s. Only rice production departed from this pattern of delayed modernization. Rice farmers were

*Table 1.* Farm Wages, Percentage of Farms with Tractors, and Percentage of Farms Operated by Tenants, by Region, 1940

| | Farm Laborers Monthly Earnings | Percentage of Farms with Tractors | Percentage of Farms Operated by Tenant |
|---|---|---|---|
| New England | $33.54 | 19.2 | 7.4 |
| Mid-Atlantic | 30.00 | 33.0 | 14.6 |
| East North Central | 29.40 | 39.9 | 27.9 |
| West North Central | 28.12 | 44.7 | 42.4 |
| South Atlantic | 17.46 | 5.6 | 42.2 |
| East South Central | 16.34 | 3.6 | 50.1 |
| West South Central | 19.61 | 14.9 | 52.6 |
| Mountain | 36.11 | 28.3 | 24.6 |
| Pacific | 42.84 | 27.6 | 18.5 |
| United States | 28.05 | 23.1 | 38.7 |

*Sources:* U.S. Bureau of the Census, 1975: 705–14, 1943a: 91–93, 46–48.

relatively early in adopting the types of farm mechanization that were more common in the North.

Once southern landowners made the transition to tractors and, eventually, to mechanized harvesting, their dependence on human labor was reduced dramatically, and the lives of most southern farmers changed permanently.[2] Until that time, however, making a living on a southern farm changed little from year to year—or even from decade to decade. With the exception of the west north central region of the country, southern farmers were substantially more likely than their counterparts in the rest of the nation to make a living as landless tenants tilling someone else's soil.

For the vast majority of southern farm families, economic survival centered around production of a cash crop. Exactly what was required to plant, cultivate, and harvest that crop varied. Pete Daniel has provided a thorough description of the work cycles demanded by three key cash crops in southern agriculture: cotton, tobacco, and rice. The first two dominated most of the states from which samples of farm families analyzed in this book have been drawn.[3] Rice cultivation was heavily concentrated in the Gulf Coast region of Texas and Louisiana and along the Mississippi Delta northward through Louisiana and Arkansas.

Cotton was king in much of the South during the late nineteenth and early twentieth centuries, and the rhythms of cotton production exerted a strong influence on local social structure and organization. The seasonal cycle began in the winter, when the land was broken and seeds planted. Planting was followed by the thinning of the seedlings and repeated chopping out of weeds. Toward the middle of summer the crop was laid by. The lay-by period offered a short respite from the intense demands of the growing cotton plants and gave farmers an opportunity to tend to other chores, work for wages on nearby farms, or enjoy more relaxing activities such as fishing and revivals. By late September or October the mature cotton bolls were ready to be picked, a task that continued throughout much of the fall. Once picked, the cotton was taken to be ginned, baled, and sold. Daniel notes, "This annual work cycle persisted from the late eighteenth century well into the twentieth."[4]

Each point of intensive activity in the cultivation cycle required the entire family. If that meant that farm wives needed to perform double duty in their homes and their fields—so be it. If it also meant that children were taken out of school or prevented from attending altogether in order to pitch in, that, too, was part of the "natural order of things." There was an especially heavy demand for family labor when cotton bolls were ready for picking. It is critical to harvest cotton before heavy fall rains are able to damage it and jeopardize the hard work that has been invested in the crop. The appearance of the soft, fluffy, white cotton bolls is deceptive, and picking them can be arduous and painful. "Did you ever pick cotton?" John Easton, a white tenant farmer, asked an interviewer for the Federal Writers' Project. "Well, let me tell you. The burrs sticks your fingers, scratches you hands and legs all over, and it ain't impossible to get stung by a stinging worm. When it turns cold, which it's apt to do before the last picking, your hands pretty near freeze off."[5] Easton's complaint, common among those who worked in the fields at harvest time, was expressed regularly in the songs of cotton pickers from the slavery era through the Great Depression.

Although less dominant than cotton throughout the southern region, tobacco production was also widespread and an important part of the rural economy. Like cotton farming, the cultivation of tobacco changed relatively little from the end of the nineteenth century through the middle of the twentieth.[6] Also like the cotton culture, the cultivation of tobacco was a family enterprise, and virtually all age groups contributed. Yet, Daniel notes, "The work was harder, dirtier, and in many ways more exacting than in any other commodity culture."[7]

Tobacco farmers began work in the winter as they prepared the plantbed in which the seeds would germinate. Tobacco seed was mixed with sand or ashes, spread and packed over the ground, and then covered with cloth. While the seeds were left to germinate, tobacco-raising families turned their attention to cutting wood that would be burned in curing barns after the tobacco leaves were picked and left to dry. When spring arrived, mules were used to break the land in preparation for transplanting the tobacco seedlings. After the plants established their roots, the ground was periodically plowed or hoed to loosen the soil. As the plants matured, families would break off terminal blossoms and suckers that, if left on plants, could slow the growth of tobacco leaves. They would also monitor plants for pests such as hornworms, which they would pick off and kill. By July some leaves would begin to turn yellow, and the harvest was ready to begin. Daniel describes this process of "barning" the tobacco, which included contributions from the entire family:

> Men primed three or four ripe leaves from each stalk and put armloads of leaves into a mule-drawn sled. The trucker, usually a young boy, drove the mule to the scaffold, where women and young boys and girls handed the tobacco bundle by bundle to the stringer. The stringer took each bundle of three or four leaves and tied it securely to the stick. . . . The stringer, who was usually a woman, set

a four-foot-long tobacco stick on a horse . . . and took the bundles and tied them to the stick. When each stick was filled, a stick boy put it in a rack or piled it on the ground. . . . It took about a dozen people—four primers, a trucker, four handers, and two stringers, and a stick boy—to fill a barn in a day.[8]

After harvest, as the tobacco cured, families would grade their crop and prepare it for market.

In contrast to cotton and tobacco, which were widespread throughout the South, rice farming occurred within a restricted geographic area and was also unlike other southern cash crops in that rice farmers were early in adopting mechanization. Originally dominated by Cajun farmers, the pre-mechanization era of rice growing had a labor-intensive cycle of production. The land was broken using plows pulled by oxen. After the rice was sown by hand over the tilled soil, farmers hoped for enough rain to saturate the planted areas. Some supplemented nature's supply of moisture by constructing small ponds to capture rain water that would be used to flood planted fields. If everything went well, the mature rice was cut by hand with sickles and then bundled into shocks that were left to dry. Finally, using mules to power the separator, the rice was threshed from the dried plants. The process could last from October through the new year.

Migrants to the Gulf Coast from the Midwest in the late nineteenth century soon changed the nature of rice production that had been practiced by the Cajuns. They adapted technology that had been used for growing wheat and quickly revolutionized the rice culture. By drilling wells and constructing levees they created irrigation systems that reduced their dependence on nature's supply of rain. By introducing gang plows and mechanical binders, reapers, and threshers they increased the productivity of farm labor and the size of family farms. The impact of these changes was dramatic. "In the space of ten years the prairies of Louisiana had been transformed from barren land sparsely populated with Cajuns, their cattle, and Providence stands of rice into a booming and highly mechanized rice-growing area. The new culture contrasted sharply with the technologically backwards methods in other commodity areas of the South."[9]

Dependence on different cash crops created different cultures within the rural South. In general, however, financial survival required a "family economy." Generating enough cash income was a perpetual challenge that often required contributions from all family members. Husbands and wives sold their labor to nearby farmers or worked for wages in local businesses, and children were sometimes employed as unskilled laborers by farmers who needed more workers than their own families could provide. Other families earned additional cash by raising and selling produce or doing laundry, sewing, tool repair, or furniture construction. The loss of a family worker through illness, death, or desertion could have a devastating impact on financial security.

The precarious economic status of southern farm families was perhaps most obvious in the conditions of their housing. The southern sharecropper shack (which can still be seen in many parts of the South) is well known in literature and film as a small, unpainted, ramshackle structure, usually

This sharecropper's cabin in Washington County, Mississippi, is typical of those that dotted the southern landscape for decades. (Photo by Dorothea Lange, Library of Congress, LC-USF34-17183-E)

with a dilapidated front porch perched uncertainly on short brick or stone pillars. Families live and sleep in two or three rooms heated by a wood stove, which is also used for cooking. For decoration and insulation, interior walls are often covered with newspapers, which are dirty from the smoke of the stove. Plumbing facilities are typically absent, as is electricity.

That grim picture was confirmed by Charles S. Johnson's survey of 916 rural families living in eight counties—six "cotton counties" and two "diversified farming counties." Although the survey was conducted during the depression, it likely provided a reasonably accurate portrait of housing in the rural South—at least after the turn of the century. Johnson, an African American sociologist, found that the majority of the houses were more than twenty-five years old and had major physical defects, including leaking roofs, broken porches, and defective floors. Fewer than half had adequate screening, and only 5.7 percent of rural families had access to an indoor water supply.[10] The dwellings of most southern farm families were neither inviting nor healthful environments.[11]

The diets of an average southern farm family posed an additional health risk, especially for children. As part of his intensive study of farm families in Greene County and Macon County, Georgia, during the mid-1930s, Arthur Raper gathered information about diets. Most consisted of "the three M's [meat, meal, and molasses], and baked 'taters'." Despite their easy access to land, surprisingly few farm families grew enough vegetables to supplement these staples adequately. As a result, farm diets were often deficient in essential vitamins and nutrients. "Their diet, rich in fats and low in vitamin content," Raper concluded, "is one of the main factors accounting for the low vitality, frequent ill health, high susceptibility to diseases, and high death rate among farm tenant families."[12] Naturally, the quality of diets varied markedly across social divisions within the rural South. Wealthier families (primarily owners) were able to buy food to supplement their diets or devote more land to raising food crops rather than cash crops. Because the majority of families struggled financially, however, Raper's description applied to a disturbingly large percentage of the southern farm population.

As part of their continual struggle for survival, many farm families also engaged in hunting and gathering activities. Being chronically short of cash, it was difficult to purchase the essential ingredients for a healthful diet. Therefore, fish, game, and wild plants were welcome additions to the dinner tables of many families. While telling of growing up in the rural South, Ned Cobb recounted the proficiency of his father as a hunter and fisherman:

"My daddy would catch fish, great God almighty. Catch 'em in baskets, two or three baskets; sometimes he'd catch more fish than the settlement could eat. And he'd get him some steel traps and go down to the creek—trap eels. Fish, eels, wild turkeys, wild ducks, possums, coons, beavers, squirrels, all such as that."[13]

Harvesting from nature was such an important part of a rural southern family's survival that government attempts to protect wildlife from depletion through restrictions on hunting and fishing spawned intense controversy and opposition. Some even viewed conservation efforts as a type of class warfare, arguing that wealthy planters, landowners, and merchants sought to increase the dependence of tenant farmers and agricultural wage laborers by removing a source of free food. Without access to wild flora and fauna, poor people would have to buy more foodstuffs from local merchants and borrow more money to do so. It is also true, however, that rapid population growth in the rural South, widespread destruction of natural habitats, and overhunting seriously threatened many indigenous species.[14]

Making a living on a southern farm was truly a family enterprise. Virtually every resource, on and off the farm, was exploited in the struggle for financial security—often against discouragingly long odds. That security was never achieved for many is illustrated by the poor and unhealthful conditions of housing and diets. Long odds, however, were an insufficient reason not to continue the struggle, and that is what southern farm families—husbands, wives, and children—did. I turn now to a more thorough description of the productive roles of family members as recorded in the 1910 and 1940 U.S. censuses.[15] To do so, I shall examine the occupations reported for husbands, wives, and children living in farm households at the time of enumeration.[16] It is also important to consider school attendance by children when describing their contributions to the family economy. The more time children spent in the classroom, the less time they had available to work in the fields or to do chores. That inverse relationship between schooling and child labor was widely recognized by parents and local governments alike. The former considered it when reaching decisions about their children's schooling; the latter considered it when faced with decisions about school financing or compulsory attendance laws.

## A Man Works from Sun to Sun

The rural South between 1900 and 1940 was a strongly patriarchal society with traditional gender roles.[17] Despite the collective nature of the family economy, husbands were considered the primary breadwinners. For the most part, they were responsible for organizing the activities of farm production, especially the cultivation and sale of the cash crop. If that income was insufficient to support a family, farmers would sell their labor for wages in the local market. As described by Ned Cobb, it was usually fathers and husbands who harvested additional food through hunting and fishing. When the cotton crop was laid by in mid-summer or a respite occurred in the work routine, men also served as their families' ambassadors to the outside world and would assemble at country stores with other ambassadors—around outside benches in the summer or pot-bellied stoves during the winter.

As one might expect, in 1910, regardless of the race or class of their family, at least nine out of every ten husbands identified themselves as farmers.[18] Thus, near the turn of the century family farms were the central locus of male productive activity. Between 1910 and 1940 the situation changed dramatically, and the percentage of husbands reporting occupations of "farmer" dropped to about three-quarters among owners and roughly two-thirds among renters, for black and white couples alike.[19] That shift suggests that it became much more difficult to make a living on southern farms between 1910 and 1940. It is no doubt safe to assume that most males, regardless of their reported occupation, continued working the land on their property. Increasingly, however, they found themselves working away from their farms to supplement the family income. That trend was significant enough to lead them to report occupations different from "farmer" as their primary productive activity in 1940.

Perhaps it should not be surprising that more families were required to combine farm and off-farm employment in 1940 than in 1910. The Great Depression hit southern farmers earlier than it did those in many other parts of the country. It was particularly difficult for tenants who had small plots of land and were perennially in debt to a landlord or merchant. Many farmers were forced to leave their land as markets shrank from the lack of cash and credit and prices fell. Among those who remained, it was common to scramble for any type of work to maintain a minimally adequate income for the family. Arthur Raper describes the desperation of southern farmers in Greene County, Georgia: "Now that cotton yields were low and the price down, the farmers who remained in Greene tried to find a substitute crop. Money was badly needed, and efforts of all kinds were made to get it. The town folks encouraged and cooperated, for they knew their only chance to stay in business was for the farmers to find new sources of income."[20] Some did receive support, however, including cash payments, from the Farm Security Administration, a New Deal program, designed to help the struggling farmers make it through the Depression.

Oral histories collected from those who struggled on southern farms during the Great Depression contain many references to the need to combine farm and off-farm employment in order to survive. As a white male from North Carolina recalled his childhood, "My daddy had seven children. We owned our own farm but we couldn't make a living on it and we couldn't make a living in the mill, so we worked at both. Many's the day I've worked on the farm until four o'clock in the afternoon and then gone on to the mill."[21] A black male, who had owned a farm in the South during the depression and eventually made his way to Newark, New Jersey, described the need to work away from the farm in order to make it through the lean years, "I worked at the church there in Chamberlain. . . . Every Friday and every Saturday I went and made my money then to support my wife and my daughter. That's what we'd eat off that first year. They paid me five dollars a day to work at the church."[22]

The magnitude of this transition in the reported occupations of farmers between 1910 and 1940 can be illustrated by considering the percentage who reported off-farm work as a primary occupation in both periods. Although I consider most reported occupations other than "farmer" as an off-farm occupation, there is no way to know whether a particular activity (e.g., blacksmithing) was performed on, or away from, the family farm. What is most important about these off-farm occupations, however, is that they indicate greater separation of a farmer's primary productive activity from the family farm and cash crop. Whether the actual work performed for such occupations occurred off the farm is of secondary importance. There was significant growth in the percentage of husbands reporting an off-farm occupation during this period (fig. 2). Although the increase occurred for both owners and tenants, it was especially sharp for the latter. Among black farm owners, for example, off-farm employment jumped from only 10 percent in 1910 to more than 20 percent in 1940. That increase was far more dramatic among black tenant families, rising sharply from only about 4 percent in 1910 to more than 30 percent in 1940. In general, similar increases in off-farm employment were experienced by white married men. African American husbands and fathers who reported off-farm employment in 1940 were involved in a wide variety of occupations. The majority, however, were engaged in such relatively unskilled work as laborer, farm laborer, and driver. Far fewer held more skilled jobs

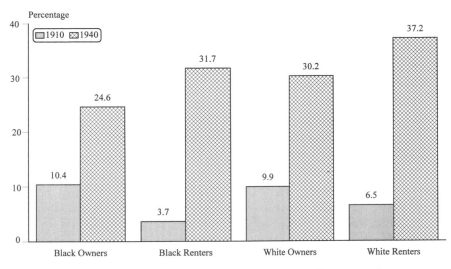

Figure 2. Percentage of Southern Farm Husbands Reporting Off-Farm Employment, by Race and Class, 1910 and 1940. (*Sources:* 1910 and 1940 Integrated Public Use Microdata Series, Social History Research Laboratory, University of Minnesota. Black oversample included for 1910.)

such as carpenter, cabinet maker, or brick mason. And only a handful were teachers, clergy, or other professionals.

Fortunately for many men who worked so hard for the security of their families and against such daunting odds, women worked just as hard toward the same objective.

## A Woman's Work Is Never Done

In 1939 Margaret Hagood's revealing study of the lives of southern farm women, *Mothers of the South: Portraiture of the White Tenant Farm Woman,* was published. Like her counterparts and fellow social scientists at the University of North Carolina—Charles S. Johnson, Howard Odum, Arthur Raper, and Rupert Vance—Hagood used ethnographic techniques to provide a richly detailed description of individuals in their natural habitats. The book was even more ambitious than its title suggests, however, because her portrait is accurate for most black women as well as for many farm owners. Like the North Carolina School of social scientists in general, Hagood recognized that the lives of southern farm women were shaped by forces that transcended the individual and were far beyond their control. "They suffer the direct consequences of a long-continued cash crop economy; they undergo extreme social impoverishment from the lack and unequal distribution of institutional services; and they bear the brunt of a regional tradition—compounded of elements from religion, patriarchy, and aristocracy—which subjects them to class and sex discrimination."[23]

The home and the field both placed great demands on women's time, and between them there was more than enough to fill the hours of her day. For the most part, women who lived on farms could expect relatively little help from their husbands as they performed the routine housekeeping tasks and domestic duties that consumed most of their time—cooking, cleaning, washing, and sewing. Where there were children (and usually there were children), they, too, were primarily the woman's responsibility.

While the sexual division of labor effectively excused males from chores in the home, it did little to protect women from grinding toil in the fields. Arthur Raper's description captures well a typical workday for a woman on a southern farm:

> She prepares the breakfast for the entire family, and, often leaving a small baby at the house with a young child, works until the middle of the day when she returns to the kitchen and prepares a hasty meal for her family. She goes back into the field in early afternoon and works until almost dark, returning to prepare supper and put tired children to bed. When the crop is poor she takes in additional washing or finds some neighbor who will give her a day's work now and then; when there is no work which she must do in the field or away from home, she gets out the family wash and attends to her housework, which usually includes the cultivating of whatever garden the family has and often the chopping of the wood for the stove.[24]

Because of the nature of their role in the family economy, occupations reported by farm women to census enumerators are somewhat less useful than for males in describing economic contributions. Unlike the work done by husbands, many tasks performed by wives—often unpaid work on family farms—were not recorded as occupations For example, although some women who worked exclusively on family farms were reported as "family farm laborers," others were not. Still, even if the absolute level of productive economic activity is undoubtedly underreported by the occupational information from the census, it is possible to sketch the broad contours of the more formal economic roles of farm women, especially variation across races, classes, and time periods.

Many observers have noted the historically higher levels of employment

A team of women uses hoes to work the cotton fields in the Mississippi Delta. The labor of African American farm women was often necessary for their family's economic survival. (Photo by Dorothea Lange, Library of Congress, LC-USF34-9397-E)

among married black women than among white women.[25] Although much evidence for this conclusion has been based on urban populations, census data reveal a similar pattern on southern farms (fig. 3). African American women more commonly reported gainful employment in 1910 than did white women. Among black married women, nearly 40 percent of farm owners and fully 60 percent of farm renters reported an occupation. Although a similar class differential existed among white married women, they were much less likely to report an occupation—7 percent of owners and 11 percent of renters.

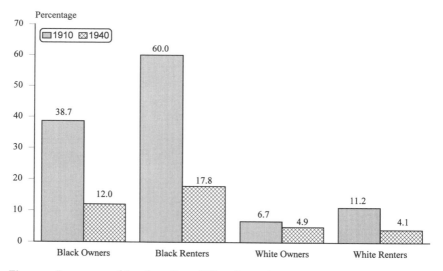

Figure 3. Percentage of Southern Farm Wives Reporting an Occupation, by Race and Class, 1910 and 1940. (*Sources:* 1910 and 1940 Integrated Public Use Microdata Series, Social History Research Laboratory, University of Minnesota. Black oversample included for 1910.)

Between 1910 and 1940 the percentage of married women reporting an occupation fell substantially for all race and class groups. The reduction was especially sharp for African American women, with the percentage among owners dropping from 39 to 12 and among renters from 60 to 17.8. That steep decline also produced a shrinking race differential. Whereas black owners were six times as likely as white owners to report an occupation in 1910, for example, they were only two and one-half times as likely to do so in 1940. Similarly, the race differential among farm renters fell from nearly five to one in 1910 to only four to one in 1940. Still, African American women remained considerably more likely than white women to report an occupation—even at the generally lower levels of labor force involvement observed in 1940.

Consistent with their higher levels of reported occupations, African American married women were also more likely than whites to have jobs that took them away from farms. For example, in 1910 nearly 10 percent of all black farm women, owners and renters alike, reported off-farm occupations; fewer than 2 percent of white farm women of both classes did so. Most black married women reporting off-farm employment worked as farm laborers, laundresses, cooks, and dressmakers.[26] Most white married women reporting off-farm occupations in 1910 worked as farm laborers and dressmakers. Black women continued to be more likely to work off farms in 1940, although the race differential fell significantly. Although black owners were roughly eight times more likely than white owners to report an off-farm occupation in 1910, by 1940 they were less than twice as likely to do so. Among farm renters the corresponding race differential was cut in half, from roughly five to one in 1910 to only 2.5 to one in 1940. In 1940 most black women working away from farms were employed as farm laborers, domestic servants, or laundresses; most white women with off-farm jobs were teachers or operatives of unspecified type.

The race differentials in occupations reported to census enumerators in 1910 and 1940 ring true when compared with previous evidence of historically higher levels of labor force participation by African American women. Still, because they describe only a very small part of their economic contributions to the household economy, caution must be exercised when interpreting census-based occupational data for married women who lived on farms in the South. Furthermore, the propensity for the women to report an occupation, or for the census enumerator to record one, may have been shaped by local racial customs and etiquette. Although census data provide interesting insights into the economic activity of southern farm women, this is one case in which it is no doubt prudent to rely more on the ethnographic evidence compiled by investigators such as Arthur Raper and Margaret Hagood or on the oral histories recorded by the Federal Writers' Project. A black farm laborer in South Carolina, for example, reported that "his wife, when she was not giving suck to an infant, or washing clothes or cooking or scrubbing floors—she scrubbed every floor twice a week—worked by his side with a hoe."[27]

It is safe to conclude that southern farm women assumed at least an equal share of the heavy burden required to keep the farms running. They and their husbands were perpetually engaged in some type of productive activity—sometimes complementary, sometimes overlapping. They were assisted in these efforts by their children, a third and significant source of labor for farm households.

## Children's Roles on Southern Farms

As in most traditional agrarian societies, farm families in the South depended on the labor of children to make the family economy work. The contribution could have been as simple as carrying water from the well or a nearby stream into the house, gathering firewood, or watching after a baby while the mother worked in the fields. The contribution could have been more directly productive, too. Older children worked alongside adults to chop and pick cotton, harvest tobacco, and tend livestock. In some cases children earned wages by hiring on as laborers on nearby farms. Although social scientists disagree over the precise age at which children turned from net consumers to net producers within families, there is little question that children of all ages were able to contribute something to the domestic enterprise. That is quite clear from the stories told to the interviewers for the Federal Writ-

African American farm children were generally required to begin working at an early age, like this young girl in Mississippi and (facing page) this thirteen-year-old boy in Georgia. (Photos by Dorothea Lange, Library of Congress, LC-USF34-9399-E and LC-USF34-17915-C).

ers' Project, many of which mention the hard work performed by children on southern farms. A white farmer, for example, recalled his childhood: "As soon as I was big enough to work, I had to do all sorts of jobs on the farm. I hoed corn when I was eight. I cut wood when I was ten. When I was thirteen I begun to plow. I worked in the tobacco field and tobacco barn as far back as I can remember. I don't know how young I was when I begun to help my mother by toting water from the spring. I couldn't have been over five."[28]

Although it was likely not impossible for a southern farm family to survive without the labor of children, doing so was a risk that relatively few parents chose to take. Like many aspects of southern farm life, the reliance on child labor persisted across the generations. Partially as a result of that reliance, southern states were relatively tardy in passing legislation to restrict child labor. When such legislation was adopted, it routinely exempted agricultural work because of the important contributions of children in rural areas.[29] Only with the introduction of mechanized farming techniques during the 1930s and 1940s did southern agriculture's dependence on child labor begin to wane.

As school systems expanded in the rural South during the early twentieth century, tension developed over the extent to which farm children would devote effort to their educations. Should they attend school regularly, thereby investing in their future human capital? Or should families exploit children's current labor value by placing higher priority on their productive role on farms? Certainly there was no unanimity in how families resolved this tension. Many perceived great value in educating their children and allowed them to spend as much time as possible in classrooms—removing them only when their labor contribution was absolutely necessary, such as during the harvesting season. A white farmer in South Carolina represents one extreme on the continuum of parental attitudes about education: "I coulda had a lot more expensive equipment on my place here, but I spent most of mine on the children. I wanted them to have a good education. I never held 'em outa school a day to work on the farm. I hired somebody to help. But they worked in the afternoon, and on Saturdays, and during vacation. They know how to work alright, and they're willing and ready."[30]

Not all parents were so generous in making personal sacrifices to allow their children to attend school. Some were skeptical of the returns to schooling in a society that was so dependent on a system of agricultural production that required relatively little training of its workers. Perhaps the cycle of the seasons and the demands of the cash crop were all that prospective farmers really needed to learn. Following an interview with one tenant farm woman, Margaret Hagood summarized the woman's skepticism about the value of schooling: "It's not the lack of clothes that keeps most people from sending their children to school. They just can't see the importance of it and they seem to think there shouldn't be any question about their staying at home until the cotton is picked, the corn shucked, the sweet potatoes dug, and everything else done the children can help with. [She] called attention to the fact that these are her own people she is talking about—they just can't see the value of an education."[31]

For some African American parents, the considerable obstacles of race in southern society provided further reason to question the importance of schooling. As one black tenant farmer volunteered, "Niggers has got to l'arn that they ain't like white folks, and never will be, and no amount of eddycation can make 'em be, and that when they gits outen their place they is gonna be trouble."[32] Yet the impressive increases in literacy and educational attainment for southern blacks during the late nineteenth and early twentieth centuries suggest that such beliefs put the farmer within a minority.

One-room schoolhouses like this one in the Mississippi Delta were often the only educational facilities available to African American children in the rural South. (Photo by Dorothea Lange, Library of Congress, LC-USF34-17520-E)

More than the rational decision making of individual parents determined the educational opportunities for southern farm children in this era. Southern governments invested considerably less in education than their northern counterparts. The situation was particularly egregious in rural areas and for blacks. Many schools were open for only a few months of the year and acquiesced to the requirements of the agricultural economy by closing their doors when the demand for labor was especially intense. Schools for African Americans were far inferior to those for whites. Buildings were often in poor repair, furnishings and supplies were sparse, and black teach-

ers were more poorly trained and paid than their white counterparts. Many
black students were forced to travel long distances to take advantage of
the meager facilities that the southern states did provide. High schools for
black students were especially scarce in the rural South. James Anderson
has noted that Georgia, Mississippi, South Carolina, Louisiana, and North
Carolina had no four-year public high schools for black children in 1916;
there were only fifty-eight public high schools for black children among
all sixteen states of the former Confederacy.[33] Yet blacks in the rural South
made great strides in educational attainment between 1900 and 1940 despite such obstacles. Although unable to compensate totally for the states'
abrogation of educational responsibility, the rural black population was
able to fill the void in part through financial contributions, volunteered
labor, and the creation of private schools.[34]

Evidence from the 1910 and 1940 U.S. censuses demonstrates how
southern farm households reconciled the competing issues of schooling and
work. A better perspective of the schooling patterns for southern farm
children is gained by comparing them with those for children living elsewhere.[35] Early in the century, southern children in general, especially black
children, were less likely to attend school than were their northern counterparts. In 1910 roughly three-quarters of all southern black children
between ten and fourteen attended school at some time during the year,
with a somewhat lower level of attendance for children living on farms.[36]
In contrast, schooling for black children living in the North was nearly
universal; 95 percent attended class (table 2). The "southern deficit" in
schooling was far smaller for white children; nine out of every ten attended
school at least part of the year in 1910. Attendance among southern black
children increased significantly between 1910 and 1940, erasing much of
the earlier regional variation. Black children living on southern farms continued to lag somewhat behind those living elsewhere, however. By 1940,
85 percent of ten-to-fourteen-year-old black farm children were enrolled
in school—only slightly below the percentage for white farm children in
the South (86 percent). That significant expansion was also accompanied
by a sharp decline in the percentage reporting an occupation to the census enumerator. In 1910, occupations were recorded for nearly 80 percent
of all southern black farm children between fifteen and eighteen, substantially higher than the percentages for those living elsewhere.[37] Thirty years
later, however, only 43 percent of black farm children reported an occupation. As a result of these striking changes, black children on southern

*Table 2.* Percentage of Children Ages 10–14 Enrolled in
School and Percentage of Children Ages 15–18 Reporting
an Occupation, by Race and Residence, 1910 and 1940

| | Percentage Enrolled in School | | Percentage Reporting Occupation | |
|---|---|---|---|---|
| | 1910 | 1940 | 1910 | 1940 |
| Black | | | | |
| Southern farm | 73.3 | 84.6 | 79.7 | 42.9 |
| Southern non-farm | 77.0 | 91.1 | 64.0 | 30.6 |
| Northern | 94.9 | 95.1 | 47.2 | 15.8 |
| White | | | | |
| Southern farm | 89.6 | 86.0 | 52.2 | 27.4 |
| Southern non-farm | 90.2 | 93.2 | 39.9 | 19.8 |
| Northern farm | 97.8 | 95.4 | 40.3 | 24.8 |
| Northern non-farm | 96.8 | 96.2 | 51.6 | 17.0 |

*Sources:* 1910 and 1940 Integrated Public Use Microdata Series, Social History Research Laboratory, University of Minnesota.
*Note:* Black oversample included for 1910.

farms were far more likely to attend school and much less likely to be gainfully employed in 1940 than they had been in 1910.

Within southern farm society itself, children's roles were not uniform across all sectors of the population. In addition to the temporal and racial variation summarized in table 2, children's schooling also varied by their families' tenure status as well as by the age and gender of the children. The children of farm owners were more likely than the children of tenant farmers to attend school at some point during the year of 1909 (table 3). Within classes, girls reported generally higher levels of school attendance than boys, although gender differences were quite small. Within African American farm-owning families, for example, 83.8 percent of daughters between ten and fourteen attended school, as did 83 percent of the sons of the same age. Comparable figures for the daughters and sons of farm tenants in 1910 were 72.2 percent and 70.2 percent, respectively.[38] Attendance within both classes and for males and females alike reached its highest level among those between ten and fourteen.

To a large extent, the percentage of children who reported an occupation in 1910 mirrors the variation in school attendance by class, gender, and age. Within age and sex categories the children of farm tenants were more likely to report an occupation than were the children of owners.

*Table 3.* Percentage of Children Enrolled in School and Percentage Reporting an Occupation, by Race, Sex, Age, and Class, 1910 and 1940

| | Percentage Attending School | | | | Percentage Reporting an Occupation | | | |
|---|---|---|---|---|---|---|---|---|
| | Black | | White | | Black | | White | |
| | Male | Female | Male | Female | Male | Female | Male | Female |
| **1910** | | | | | | | | |
| Owners | | | | | | | | |
| 5–9 years | 61.6 | 60.5 | 71.0 | 71.6 | 8.5 | 5.4 | 6.6 | 2.1 |
| 10–14 years | 83.0 | 83.8 | 92.4 | 93.4 | 63.6 | 43.4 | 49.1 | 18.7 |
| 15–18 years | 59.9 | 73.0 | 74.4 | 77.8 | 84.0 | 60.7 | 76.7 | 22.2 |
| Renters | | | | | | | | |
| 5–9 years | 46.1 | 48.3 | 58.8 | 59.8 | 10.2 | 7.0 | 7.6 | 4.2 |
| 10–14 years | 70.2 | 72.2 | 84.7 | 86.5 | 66.5 | 55.4 | 50.2 | 24.8 |
| 15–18 years | 41.1 | 56.1 | 62.1 | 67.9 | 88.5 | 74.0 | 81.5 | 32.0 |
| **1940** | | | | | | | | |
| Owners | | | | | | | | |
| 5–9 years | 64.6 | 71.0 | 63.1 | 62.2 | — | — | — | — |
| 10–14 years | 90.9 | 93.4 | 85.5 | 86.6 | — | — | — | — |
| 15–18 years | 55.6 | 66.1 | 57.4 | 66.0 | 49.5 | 15.0 | 38.7 | 7.0 |
| Renters | | | | | | | | |
| 5–9 years | 60.1 | 58.1 | 58.9 | 60.8 | — | — | — | — |
| 10–14 years | 83.1 | 86.3 | 86.7 | 87.0 | — | — | — | — |
| 15–18 years | 44.8 | 58.6 | 46.5 | 61.5 | 58.2 | 26.1 | 47.7 | 10.3 |

*Sources:* 1910 and 1940 Integrated Public Use Microdata Series, Social History Research Laboratory, University of Minnesota.
*Note:* Black oversample included for 1910.

Within classes, boys were substantially more likely than girls of the same age to report an occupation. Among black farm-owning families, for example, 43.4 percent of daughters between ten and fourteen reported an occupation compared with 63.6 percent of sons. An equally large gender difference existed within tenant families, although with somewhat higher absolute levels of reported occupations—55.4 percent for girls and 66.5 percent for boys. The relatively large percentage of older children (between fifteen and eighteen) reporting occupations partially accounts for the corresponding drop in school attendance at those ages and reflects the relatively early entrance of farm children into the rural labor force.[39]

What emerges from the evidence presented in table 3 is that for children over ten, especially for males, the percentage attending school plus the percentage reporting an occupation generally totals more than 100 percent. Among black males between ten and fourteen in farm-owning families, for example, the percentage reporting any school attendance (83 percent) and the percentage reporting an occupation (63.6 percent) total 146.6 percent. Clearly, it was common for these children to combine schooling and work throughout the year—a recollection verified in many personal accounts reported in oral histories recorded during the Federal Writers' Project. Although some children worked after school during the academic year, it was likely more typical for the school year to be delayed or cut short in order to accommodate the labor demands of farm households.

Roughly the same class, gender, and age variation in children's roles persisted through 1940, however there was a general increase in schooling and a decline in reported occupations for those between fifteen and eighteen. With some exceptions, school attendance remained higher among the children of farm owners than among tenants and higher for daughters than for sons. Conversely, the children of farm tenants were more likely than the children of owners to report an occupation in 1940, and sons were more likely to do so than daughters.

The census data, even in light of their limitations, paint an informative picture of children's roles on southern farms during this era. Clearly, children made important contributions to the productive function of the farm economy; large numbers of them began to work at a very early age. Even in 1910, however, the lives of most farm children included some schooling, although the extent varied considerably by race, class, and age. The thirty years between 1910 and 1940 were ones of both persistence and change. Although the basic differentials in schooling observed in 1910 survived through 1940, attendance rose sharply among southern farm children—for blacks and whites, owners and tenants, and sons and daughters. Although many children, especially males, continued to report occupations to census enumerators in 1940, it appears that far fewer children were gainfully employed then than in 1910. Those trends in children's roles were certain to have important implications for other dimensions of family life on southern farms.

## Conclusion

Making a living on the southern farm during the first decades of the twentieth century was a collective effort. Husbands, wives, and children all made important contributions to the family economy through their labor. But even the most strenuous efforts by all family members were not enough to guarantee a comfortable life for southern farmers. Nature, landlords, merchants, and external markets had a way of conspiring to keep a depressingly large percentage of these families struggling to stay on the right side of subsistence. The heavy toll that residing in ramshackle houses and consuming less than nutritious diets took on the health of these families was reflected in relatively high levels of morbidity and mortality.

Perhaps I am guilty in this chapter of having painted too bleak of a picture of the existence of these southern farm families. What about those families living in ornate mansions on large plantations who sent their children to exclusive private schools in the North? To be sure, such families were also part of the southern farm society. They represented, however, such a minuscule part of the entire population of southern farmers that to give them more prominence would seriously distort the truth. The truth, I believe, lies closer to the portraits of southern farm society sketched by Arthur Raper in *Preface to Peasantry, Sharecroppers All,* and *Tenants of the Almighty,* or by Margaret Hagood in *Mothers of the South,* or by Hortense Powdermaker in *After Freedom,* or by Charles Johnson in *Growing up in the Black Belt.*

As I proceed in the following chapters to describe the important demographic events that transpired in the lives of these southern farmers—marriage, childbearing, family disruption, and migration—I will return frequently to the points raised in this chapter. That is natural because those demographic events were shaped profoundly by the conditions under which these families made a living.

# 3

# The Married Life

Marriage was a crucial transition in southern farm society, as it is in all societies. It was an important step on the road to economic independence for the younger generation and usually the beginning of family formation. Marriage was also a prerequisite for building the family labor force that was the backbone of southern agriculture. Too poor to hire laborers, most southern farm households were required to rely on the labor contributions of family members, including wives, children, and sometimes non-nuclear relatives. Because there were so many productive chores that could be performed by all, from young children to grandparents, few family members enjoyed the privilege of idleness. But perhaps the heaviest burden of all fell on the farm wife and mother. Not only were they primarily responsible for the smooth functioning of households, but they also worked alongside their husbands and children in the fields.[1] When time permitted and economic necessity required they also scrambled to supplement family income by taking in laundry and sewing or selling their labor to nearby farms.

Farmers without wives were in serious jeopardy for a number of reasons. They were forced to perform the many household duties that were traditionally a wife's job while also bearing sole responsibility for preparing and tending the fields and harvesting a mature crop. Moreover, in an economy that was extremely dependent upon child labor, a wife was an important prerequisite for the conjugal creation of a family labor force. Indeed, landlords were keenly aware of the importance of family members to farm productivity and expressed a preference for tenants with wives and children.[2] In an arrangement that generally called for a 50-50 division in the profits from a cash crop it was obviously in a landlord's financial interest to have the tenant family produce the largest possible crop.

Women without husbands also faced daunting hardships. Like single males who headed farm families, single women were forced to absorb the entire burden of duties required to keep a household running while also generating income from crops and livestock. Moreover, female heads of southern farms were a relative cultural oddity in view of that patriarchal society's assumptions about gender roles in the family and economy.

Given the challenges faced by single family heads of either gender, it is not surprising that a large majority of southern farm households were headed by married couples. In 1910, for example, married couples headed 87 percent of southern white farm households and 84 percent of southern black farm households. Although the dominance of couple-headed farm households had declined somewhat by 1940, they still accounted for a clear majority: 85 percent for whites and 78 percent for blacks.[3] Most excep-

This elderly couple in Greene County, Georgia, were both born during slavery. Still marrried in 1937, they could recall when federal troops had marched through Georgia. (Photo by Dorothea Lange, Library of Congress, LC-USF34-17944-C)

A married sharecropping couple sit on the porch of their cabin in Mississippi. Such couples and their children were the backbone of the plantation system of agriculture that dominated the cotton South. (Photo by Dorothea Lange, Library of Congress, LC-USF34-17490-E)

tions to that pattern were due to the death of a spouse, which left a widow or widower to head farm households that most likely included children.[4] Understandably in this agrarian society, remarriage often occurred relatively quickly.

Generally, when social scientists compare and contrast the marriage patterns of different societies or trace changes in marriage over time within the same society they distinguish between the timing and universality of marriage. "Marital timing" refers to whether individuals are relatively young or old when they marry for the first time. The timing of first marriages provides a good indication of the speed with which new generations of adults establish independent households and begin building families. "Universality of marriage" refers to the proportion of people who will ever marry sometime during their lifetimes. These two dimensions of societal marriage patterns are often related. Many societies with relatively early marriage also have only a small proportion of members who remain single throughout their lives. Conversely, where marriage occurs relatively late in life, more individuals tend to remain single permanently. The general correspondence between the timing and universality of marriage is due largely to their joint dependence on the social, economic, and cultural forces that determine the utility and necessity of married life within a particular society. There are certainly exceptions to these patterns, however, and they remind us to resist the temptation to equate marital timing and universality in examining society's marriage patterns.

In their attempts to understand why societies differ in their marriage behavior (timing or universality), social scientists have identified a few ideal types that are believed to summarize the alternatives available to populations. The most well known are the marriage patterns described by John Hajnal, who was primarily concerned with the history of marriage patterns in European societies.[5] According to Hajnal, there were three distinct marriage patterns exhibited by societies around the world. The Western European Marriage Pattern, which is also found in many northern European countries, is characterized by first marriages that occur relatively late in life (e.g., $\geq 26$ years for males and $\geq 24$ years for females) and high levels of nonmarriage (e.g., $\geq 15$–$17$ percent for males and females). In the Non-European Marriage Pattern, exhibited by most of the developing world outside of Europe and its overseas settlements, people marry at considerably younger ages (e.g., $\leq 22$ years for males and $\leq 20$ years for females), and only a relatively tiny fraction of individuals remain single throughout their lives (e.g., $\leq 5$ percent for males and females). Largely by default, the Southern and Eastern European Marriage Pattern falls between the other two extremes.

According to Hajnal, the most powerful social forces shaping a society's marriage patterns are the cultural tradition of residence for newly married couples and the economic requirements for establishing independent households. Put simply, marriage should be delayed and less ubiquitous where couples are not expected to reside with parents (meaning that couples would need to marshal the resources to establish an independent household before marrying) and where economic obstacles to independence are more formidable.

The historical evidence with which to describe overall American nuptiality and situate American marriage within Hajnal's typology is relatively thin. The U.S. Census did not publish detailed tabulations of marital status (e.g., by age, sex, and race) until 1890. Information about the duration of marriages was not collected until 1900, and the order of marriage (e.g., first or second) was not distinguished until 1910. Yet we do know something about the broader contours of American nuptiality earlier in the nineteenth century. It is clear from scattered evidence, for example, that the United States in general never exhibited the Western European Marriage Pattern. Michael Haines has compiled evidence from the turn of the twentieth century that shows that 54.7 percent of African Americans were married between the ages of twenty and twenty-four—a much more rapid transition to marriage than was found, for instance, in Sweden, where only 19.4 percent were married at such an early age. Evidence from the other end of the life course shows that African Americans were also much more likely than Swedes to marry at some time during their lifetimes. Only 5.1 percent of American blacks between forty-five and fifty-four had never married in contrast to 18.8 percent in Sweden.[6] The timing and universality of marriage for African Americans at the turn of the twentieth century was similar to Hajnal's Non-European Marriage Pattern. Corresponding evidence for whites (through the turn of the twentieth century) suggests that marriage for them also was more nearly universal and occurred much earlier in life than expected by the Western European Marriage Pattern.

Although the paucity of good evidence on historical marriage patterns for specific sub-populations within the United States is a handicap, it is safe to conclude that marriage was even more common and occurred more rapidly in rural society, especially within the farm sector. The sharp deviation of American nuptiality from the Western European Marriage Pattern generally has been attributed to the weaker economic constraints facing prospective brides and grooms in the United States. Within agricultural populations, opportunity is largely determined by the availability of fertile but unclaimed and uncultivated land to which rural Americans enjoyed access throughout most of the nineteenth century. Even as the American frontier came to a close, there were still areas within the country in which potential farmland was widely available and relatively cheap. Young married couples were therefore able to establish independent farm households without waiting a long time to accumulate needed capital.[7]

## Marriage Patterns among Southern Farmers, 1910 and 1940

Scattered evidence is available regarding the historical marriage behavior of southern farmers.[8] No systematic effort has been made to describe the basic contours of nuptiality within this population, however. Given the critical function of marriage as the foundation on which the southern farm family (and therefore the southern farm labor force) was built, it is useful to know more about how that population formed marital unions. In examining the marital behavior of southern farmers in 1910 and 1940 I will focus on the two critical dimensions—timing and universality. At what age did most couples marry for the first time, and what proportion of individuals married at some point in their lives? Differences between African Americans and whites and changes experienced by both races between 1910 and 1940 help provide the answers.

In societies where marriage occurs relatively early in life, the percentage of the population that is still single drops swiftly with age. The rapidity of the disappearance of the single population therefore represents a good gauge of the timing of marriage in a population. By that measure, it is clear that marriage occurred early within the southern farm population near the turn of the century. Among African American women living on farms in 1910, about half (52.1 percent) were still single between the ages of eighteen and twenty-two, which implies that roughly half were married by their twentieth birthday (table 4). These women also married relatively young men. The typical black male farmer was in his early twenties (median = 22.8 years) when he married, leaving only slightly more than half (56.4 percent) of all farmers between twenty and twenty-four as bachelors.[9] Although variation certainly existed, an average African American couple that established an independent farm household consisted of a twenty-two-year-old man and a twenty-year-old woman. The average white female who lived on a farm married at about the same age as her black counterpart (20.8 years), whereas males were roughly two years older than black males when they first married (24.5 years).[10] It is possible that white males postponed their first marriages longer than black males in order to accumulate the resources necessary for farm ownership. Social and economic obstacles to ownership for blacks made such marital delay less likely.

Marriages are not distributed evenly across ages but are heavily concentrated in the earlier years. In societies where marriage is nearly universal, therefore, only a small percentage of individuals remains single into middle age and beyond. By considering the other end of the age continuum it is

*Table 4.* Selected Information on Marriage Patterns of Southern Farmers and Other Populations, by Race and Sex, 1910 and 1940

|  | 1910 | | | 1940 | | |
|---|---|---|---|---|---|---|
|  | Percentage Single[a] | Median Age at Marriage | Percentage Single (ages 45–54 years) | Percentage Single[a] | Median Age at Marriage | Percentage Single (ages 45–54 years) |
| Black females |  |  |  |  |  |  |
| Southern farm | 52.1 | 20.5 | 2.5 | 46.1 | 19.7 | 3.4 |
| Southern non-farm | 48.7 | 20.0 | 5.5 | 50.6 | 21.1 | 4.8 |
| Northern | 64.4 | 22.0 | 10.1 | 59.6 | 20.6 | 6.6 |
| Black males |  |  |  |  |  |  |
| Southern farm | 56.2 | 22.8 | 3.4 | 54.2 | 22.4 | 5.9 |
| Southern non-farm | 56.9 | 22.6 | 9.1 | 56.9 | 22.1 | 10.7 |
| Northern | 73.4 | 24.7 | 18.8 | 66.6 | 23.7 | 14.5 |
| White females |  |  |  |  |  |  |
| Southern farm | 56.4 | 20.8 | 4.3 | 53.6 | 20.3 | 4.6 |
| Southern non-farm | 55.1 | 20.3 | 11.2 | 54.3 | 20.3 | 9.0 |
| Northern farm | 71.1 | 22.7 | 4.7 | 65.7 | 21.7 | 4.7 |
| Northern non-farm | 70.8 | 22.4 | 11.0 | 70.6 | 22.3 | 9.9 |
| White males |  |  |  |  |  |  |
| Southern farm | 68.8 | 24.5 | 5.4 | 66.7 | 24.0 | 6.7 |
| Southern non-farm | 68.3 | 27.2 | 11.3 | 62.0 | 23.4 | 7.9 |
| Northern farm | 83.8 | 26.2 | 11.8 | 79.4 | 25.4 | 12.9 |
| Northern non-farm | 79.0 | 25.8 | 13.0 | 75.9 | 24.8 | 12.0 |

*Sources:* 1910 and 1940 Integrated Public Use Microdata Series, Social History Research Laboratory, University of Minnesota.

*Note:* Black oversample included for 1910.

a. Women ages 18–22 and men ages 20–24 are used in this column for percentage single.

possible to draw some conclusions about the universality of marriage within the southern farm population. In 1910, only a very small percentage of African Americans failed to marry at some time during their lives. Between forty-five and fifty-four, for example, only 3.4 percent of black males and 2.5 percent of black females were still unmarried. When one allows for illness, physical or mental disabilities, and alternative sexual orientations, these minuscule percentages suggest virtually universal marriage within the eligible population.[11] Although the percentages remaining single through ages forty-five to fifty-four were somewhat larger for the white farm population (4.3 percent and 5.4 percent for females and males, respectively), they are still small enough to suggest nearly universal marriage among whites.

Early in the century, then, southern farmers married when they were quite young, and only a small percentage remained single throughout their lifetimes. African Americans in particular exhibited marriage patterns consistent with the Non-European Pattern identified by Hajnal. Yet how does the marriage behavior of southern farmers compare with that found within other segments of the U.S. population in 1910? Farmers were not especially distinctive within the South for marrying early in their lives; indeed, there was little difference between farm and non-farm southern populations, both black and white, in the timing of marriage (table 4).[12] In contrast, large regional differences prevailed at the turn of the century for both races. Although roughly half of southern black women (farm and non-farm) had married by the time they were between eighteen and twenty-two, for example, only a third (35.6 percent) of northern African Americans did so.

To be sure, the majority of northern blacks lived in cities, and a basic urban-rural difference in marriage patterns may be responsible for such large regional variation. Marriage did occur substantially later among black residents of southern metropolitan areas, although still earlier than among northerners. Large regional differences also existed among African Americans in the proportions still single between forty-five and fifty-four, dwarfing the more modest differences between farm and non-farm southerners. A large percentage of northern black males never married—18.8 percent versus 3.4 percent for southern farm males. The corresponding difference for black females was smaller although still impressive—10.1 percent versus 2.5 percent.

Despite significant and sometimes dramatic changes in southern rural society during the first three decades of the twentieth century, the nuptiality patterns of farmers in 1940 were very much like those in 1910 (table 4).[13] Among farm males, black and white, the timing of marriage changed only slightly across the period. The average age at marriage for black men dropped from 22.8 to 22.4, for example, while white males experienced a similarly modest decline from 24.5 to 24.0. Marriage also occurred slightly earlier for farm women in 1940 than it had in 1910. The average age at first marriage for black women dropped to 19.7 (from 20.5), while among white women the average age at marriage fell from 20.8 to 20.3. In addition, by 1940 the majority of the southern farm population still married, whether early or late in life. Although non-marriage did become somewhat more common by 1940, the percent single between forty-five and fifty-four remained well below 10 percent for all races and genders.

Comparing the marriage patterns of black southern farmers with their northern counterparts indicates some regional convergence between 1910 and 1940. For example, the average age of marriage for northern females dropped from 22.0 to only 20.6 during the thirty-year period. The percent single at ages forty-five to fifty-four among northern women also fell substantially—from 10.1 to 6.7 percent. Black men who lived in the North experienced roughly similar trends. Their average age at marriage fell from 24.7 to 23.7, and the percent who never married among those forty-five to fifty-four slid from 18.8 to 14.5 percent.

Although marriage among southern black farmers remained earlier and more ubiquitous than it was in the North, the regional contrast changed markedly between 1910 and 1940, with the North growing more similar to the South. It is possible that this shift was partially due to interregional migration among African Americans between 1910 and 1940. Two pieces of evidence are consistent with such an interpretation. First, black southerners married earlier in 1910 and were much more likely to marry at some time during their lives than were black northerners. Second, 49.2 percent of all blacks living in the North in 1910 had been born in the South. By 1940 the comparable percentage had jumped to 67.3 percent.[14] Perhaps black southerners who married early in life migrated northward and thereby reduced the average age at marriage among northern blacks, raising the percent who had married by ages forty-five to fifty-four. The possibility that southern migrants influenced the marriage patterns and family structure of native northerners is explored further in chapter 7.

It is possible that the description of the marital status for southern farmers, like that presented in table 4, also could be influenced by selective off-farm migration. Those who were unsuccessful in locating an acceptable marriage partner could have moved to another rural area or even into the city to expand their search for a mate or pursue a single life-style. That possibility is greater for the older population because they had ample opportunity to relocate in response to their marital status. Although it is impossible to determine its magnitude, the selective migration of the unmarried likely results in an understatement of permanent non-marriage in this population. Such migration would need to be quite common, however, in order to change the inference of relatively low levels of non-marriage among southern farmers based on the evidence from 1910 and 1940. Nonetheless, it is possible that the changes in permanent singleness that occurred between 1910 and 1940 were more substantial than I have described. The economic distress caused by the Great Depression, which took a terrible toll on the southern agricultural economy, could have undermined the marriage chances of some individuals who subsequently left farms and therefore were no longer enumerated by the census as residents of the farm South.

## Explaining Marriage Patterns in the Farm South

To completely understand the foundation for any society's nuptiality patterns it is necessary to go beyond a consideration of the economic constraints emphasized by Hajnal, although the economic prerequisites for establishing independent households are certainly central to an understanding of marriage formation. In pursuit of a more comprehensive picture of the social and economic forces that shaped the marriage behavior of southern farm families I rely upon a conceptual framework proposed by Ruth Dixon and applied subsequently by other social scientists.[15] According to Dixon's framework, the timing and universality of marriage are determined by three factors: the availability of marriage partners, the feasibility of marriage, and the desirability of marriage. If two societies differ in their patterns of nuptiality or if a given society experiences changes in nuptiality over time, then one or more of these three factors must be responsible. Furthermore, any exogenous societal characteristic (e.g., migration, economic trends, and cultural shifts) that influences a population's marriage patterns must operate through one of these intervening forces.

### Availability of Marriage Partners

Marriage opportunities are determined, to some extent, by the demographic balance of males and females in a locale—the supply side of the marriage market. Put simply, males will be more likely to marry—and marry earlier—where there is an abundant supply of potential female partners. Women are thought to respond similarly to the supply of prospective grooms. In an ideal situation, measurement of the availability of prospective marriage partners also takes into consideration a variety of other factors. First, what is the appropriate geographic scope of the marriage market? From how large of an area, that is, do individuals generally select spouses? Second, what is the typical age difference between spouses? If, as is generally the case, men marry somewhat younger women, then the availability of potential mates can be affected by shifts in the sizes of adjacent age cohorts, usually because of changing fertility rates and also because of migration patterns that are selective by age and/or gender. Third, to be considered an appropriate potential marriage partner an individual may need to fit a profile that includes more than just age. Marriage is a largely endogamous institution. Spouses usually share characteristics such as race, religion, political orientation, and educational attainment. Therefore, the "marriage search" occurs among a restricted pool of eligibles defined by the conventions of marital endogamy within a society.[16]

Sociologists have concluded that the supply of potential marriage partners can have a strong influence on nuptiality (as well as other demographic transitions). Scott South has shown that a dearth of appropriate male marriage partners (because of employment deficits or incarceration) helps to explain the relatively low probability of marriage among African American women in the 1990s.[17] Evidence also suggests that the supply of potential marriage partners affected the likelihood of marriage historically in the United States. Most relevant to this study is the work carried out by Nancy Landale, who has examined nuptiality in rural America near the turn of the twentieth century. Landale has shown that rural white males throughout the nation were more likely to marry when relatively more women lived nearby. In southern states, rural whites and blacks, both males and females, tended to marry earlier when a surfeit of potential marriage partners lived in the same county.[18]

How might the likelihood of marriage within the southern farm population have been constrained by a deficit of potential marriage partners or enhanced by a surplus? If we assume that the southern farm population was a closed population in 1910 and 1940, then we only need consider those factors that created imbalances in the sizes of adjacent cohorts of men and women.[19] Because farm fertility was declining throughout this period, for example, males looking to marry younger women would have found a shrinking supply of potential mates as the era progressed. Demographers term that process the "marriage squeeze." As a result, the likelihood (timing and universality) of marriage for males should have declined, which may partially account for the modest increase in the percentage single among males forty-five to fifty-four between 1910 and 1940. Female members of the smaller cohorts could be more sanguine about marriage chances. Perhaps the small drop in average age at marriage for white females between 1910 and 1940 was due to the more favorable sex ratio women enjoyed in later birth cohorts. Of course, the marital destiny of a birth cohort is not determined entirely by its size relative to older, or younger, cohorts. Other social forces (e.g., employment prospects or real estate prices) may blunt, or even erase, any marriage-related disadvantages of cohort size. Cohorts may also adjust to a restricted pool of potential marriage partners by broadening the definition of an acceptable spouse, perhaps in terms of age, race, religion, or social class. Of course, the potential to broaden one's pool of potential marriage partners in this way may be restricted by law or social custom. Prohibitions against miscegenation in the South, for example, would have prevented most individuals from considering interracial marriage as a possible response to a marriage squeeze.

In truth, the southern farm population was not really closed between 1910 and 1940. Some individuals did move to nearby cities or to "new" rural areas in search of opportunity. To the extent that such movement was concentrated among specific age groups or within one gender, it could have had a significant effect on the balance of males and females in a given locale. Like the decline in farm fertility, population redistribution within the South accelerated between 1910 and 1940. As a result, nuptiality within the southern farm population was likely affected more strongly by the supply of potential marriage partners in 1940 than in 1910. The exact nature of the effect is difficult to anticipate, however, because the characteristics of migration streams into and out of local areas were so variable. In some areas large numbers of males moved to northern cities. In other areas the migration stream was composed disproportionately of single females moving to nearby southern towns and cities or off farms in response to non-agricultural employment opportunities.

Overall nuptiality in the southern farm population probably was relatively unconstrained by sex ratio imbalances near the turn of the century. Farm fertility, although declining, had not changed dramatically enough to produce adjacent age cohorts of significantly different size. Migration and residential mobility were certainly occurring but not nearly on the same scale as would occur later in the century. Therefore, if one considers only the potential impact of mate availability, marriage should have been earlier and more nearly universal in 1910 than in 1940. Although the very minor changes in overall southern farm nuptiality that occurred between 1910 and 1940 (table 4) are generally consistent with that expectation, they do not suggest a dramatic shift in the availability of potential marriage partners. Yet it is possible that marriage patterns within specific areas were more sensitive to gender imbalances produced by declining fertility and increasing mobility during that period than were those for the farm South as a whole. To be sure, the timing and universality of marriage would not have been identical in all areas, nor would all areas have experienced the same changes in age composition as a result of falling fertility or increasing migration.

## The Feasibility of Marriage

The supply of potential marriage partners is only one force that shapes a society's nuptiality patterns. It is also necessary to consider how feasible it is for couples to marry—even where potential spouses are plentiful. In a culture where couples choose whom and when to marry and in which most newlyweds are expected to establish independent households rather than co-reside with parents, the feasibility of marriage is largely determined by economic factors.[20] Where the economic opportunities for prospective couples are relatively promising, marriages can occur earlier and a larger percentage of the population will be able to marry at some time. In an agrarian society, economic opportunity, and therefore the feasibility of marriage, is largely determined by the ease (or difficulty) with which young married couples can gain access to farmland. Within the rural South, two distinct avenues provided access to farmland: ownership and tenancy. The agrarian South was unique within the United States for its prolonged heavy reliance on tenancy rather than ownership, and African Americans faced especially daunting obstacles in attempts to acquire ownership of farmland. These characteristics of southern farming had important implications for the feasibility of marriage and created different incentives for early marriage among blacks and whites.

Southern agriculture was transformed following the Civil War by the widespread adoption of farm tenancy (chapter 1). Tenancy was a compromise between the massive redistribution of land preferred by southern African Americans and retention of a gang labor system of labor organization that was reminiscent of slavery but preferred by white landowners. At first, tenancy was an especially dominant status among southern black farmers and less common for whites. Gradually, however, as their economic fortunes declined during the waning years of the nineteenth century and early years of the twentieth, more and more white farmers sank into tenancy. By the time of the 1940 U.S. Census, the racial differential in farm tenancy had shrunk modestly.[21]

Yet tenancy meant somewhat different things for blacks and whites in the rural South. For blacks, farm tenancy generally was a terminal status, and many black tenants had little hope of ever climbing much higher on the agricultural ladder. Whites were more likely to consider tenancy a temporary status that might lead, ultimately, to ownership. Even if that transition never occurred, it was at least a possibility. The key difference in the prospects for white and black tenants was a racial caste system that severely restricted the economic mobility of southern blacks. Not only did it handicap rural blacks in their effort to accumulate the savings necessary to purchase their own farms but it also presented an obstacle with which few whites had to contend—the need to obtain the endorsement of local white landowners.[22]

The organization of southern agriculture carried important implications for marriage. Because tenancy, especially sharecropping, required little accumulation of capital, it was often feasible for couples to gain access to land at an early age. In many cases they brought only their family labor to the agreement with the landlord and had few, if any, other assets. Early marriage was not as feasible for prospective couples who intended to become farm owners, however. They were more likely to postpone marriage as they saved to purchase land and the necessary equipment to cultivate it. Overall, the rural South's dependence on farm tenancy created downward pressure on ages at first marriage and upward pressure on the proportions ever marrying. Considering the persistent racial barriers to ownership, these pressures were stronger for blacks than for whites. The information about the timing and universality of marriage among southern farmers reported in table 4 is consistent with these expectations. Blacks and whites married at relatively young ages, and the majority married at some time during their lifetimes. Furthermore, African Americans, especially males, were more likely than whites to marry, and they married at a younger age.

Scattered evidence from near the turn of the twentieth century suggests that tenancy, even within the rural South, was important in determining geographic variation in marital timing. Taking into account all southern rural residents, marriage occurred earlier in counties that had higher levels of farm tenancy.[23] Considering only southern black farmers, marriage occurred significantly earlier among those living in counties where tenancy rather than ownership was the rule.[24]

Even where farm ownership was possible, its likelihood was also affected by the cost of land. Other things being equal, early marriage was more feasible for prospective couples where land was less expensive. There was considerable geographic variation in the average cost of farms throughout the South between 1910 and 1940. In 1910, for example, the average southern farm had a value of $4,227, with the extremes running from an average of $571 in Jackson County, Kentucky, to $86,137 in Pecos County, Texas. By 1940 the real cost of farms had dropped slightly to an average of $3,997, with the most expensive farms found in Crockett County, Texas ($71,392) and the least expensive farms in Scott County, Tennessee ($455).[25]

The evidence regarding the impact of farm costs on southern marriage patterns is mixed. For all rural residents (farmers and non-farmers combined), whites who lived in areas where land was more expensive tended to delay marriage longer than those living where land was cheaper. In contrast, black nuptiality was not significantly related to areal variation in land cost.[26] When consideration is restricted to only black southern farmers, however, evidence suggests that the average age of marriage for males was positively affected by the cost of land. That is, men were able to marry earlier where land was cheaper.[27] It is difficult to reconcile these conflicting findings in view of the different samples used. Given the lower probability of farm ownership among blacks, it is not surprising to find that the cost of land was more salient for white marital behavior. Still, some southern blacks were able to buy land, and one would expect the likelihood of their doing so to respond to the affordability of farmland.

On the whole, the organization of southern agriculture, and its heavy reliance on tenancy, should have made marriage relatively feasible, especially for African Americans. Because tenancy remained relatively stable for southern blacks between 1910 and 1940 and a minority owned their farms, no dramatic change in marriage would be predicted on the basis of shifting ownership patterns alone. Indeed, only relatively minor changes in African American marriage patterns occurred (table 4). Yet tenancy grew among southern whites during the first half of the twentieth century. As a result, it is possible that marriage became more feasible between 1910 and 1940 within the agricultural economy. Again, the falling age at first marriage for white females (table 4) is consistent with this inference. Because tenancy was less likely to be the "terminal status" for white farmers, however, their ambitions to own a farm eventually may have led some white couples to postpone marriage despite the relatively easy availability of tenant farms.

As prospective couples considered whether marriage was feasible they also needed to think about the feasibility of early parenthood. That concern was especially salient where family limitation within marriage was not practiced widely—which was the case among southern farmers early in the twentieth century. Early parenthood is more feasible where and when children have net positive economic value or at least their net costs are modest. Children were able to make important economic contributions to many southern farm households, starting at a relatively early age (chapter 2).

Indeed, for some families and in some settings the economic contributions from children were critical in making the farming enterprise succeed, even if success meant only an ability to live at a subsistence level from year to year. As a result, it is unlikely that the anticipated cost of children played a significant role in delaying marriage within this population.

Two significant social changes between 1910 and 1940 may have had counterbalancing effects on the impact of prospective parenthood on marriage timing. First, the practice of family limitation within marriage became more common, which somewhat uncoupled marriage from early parenthood.[28] As a result, couples had even less reason to avoid early marriage out of concern over the cost of children. Second, children's roles changed substantially between 1910 and 1940. As educational opportunities expanded in the South more children attended school, and those who attended spent more time in the classroom. Although farm children continued to make important contributions to the family economy, the clear trend was toward greater expense and reduced economic benefits associated with children.[29] Whether that trend changed the feasibility of early marriage in the farm South is not apparent from the very modest changes in the timing or universality of marriage that occurred between 1910 and 1940 (table 4). Of course, it is possible that other social forces were operating (e.g., increasing tenancy, changing cost of farmland, or changing supply of potential marriage partners) to offset the effect of children's roles on nuptiality.

## The Desirability of Marriage

The final ingredient in Ruth Dixon's framework for understanding nuptiality is the desirability of marriage. According to Dixon, the strength of the motivation to marry may affect timing and universality, even where there is an ample supply of potential marriage partners and it is economically feasible to marry. That motivation will be inversely related to the "social and institutional alternatives to marriage and childbearing and by the extent to which these alternatives are considered rewarding."[30] Dixon argues that the marital behavior of women is especially sensitive to the social forces that determine the desirability of marriage.

Because the rural South remained a traditional society throughout the first decades of the twentieth century there can be little doubt that the motivation to marry was quite strong. This was a patriarchal society in which males held firmly onto the reins of power within the family and within the society at large. Women were valued primarily for their contributions as wives and mothers, and there were relatively few alternatives to marriage and motherhood for women.[31] The route to economic security generally led directly to married life and parenthood. As suggested earlier, the penalties for remaining single within this society were formidable. In order to pursue an alternative path to economic security, single women were often forced to migrate to nearby towns or cities or to rural areas that had non-agricultural employment opportunities such as textile mills. Even outside rural areas, non-traditional roles were relatively restricted for southern women.[32] The degree of patriarchy in southern society is also suggested by the overwhelming dominance of males in virtually all spheres of life, including politics, business, religion, and education.[33]

Once married, women were expected to bear children, sometimes several children. Within an economy that was partially dependent upon child labor, childlessness could be a serious hardship for a farm couple. In the short term it deprived them of needed family labor; in the longer term it might also deprive them of a source of security in their old age. For farm women, however, the penalties of childlessness transcended economic considerations. As in many patriarchal societies, the worth of a woman was partially determined by her reproductive performance and subsequent skill at motherhood.

The desirability of marriage may have grown somewhat weaker between 1910 and 1940 as the educational attainment of women improved, as more non-agricultural opportunities penetrated some areas of the rural South, as movement from the countryside to the city became more common, and as the practice of family limitation within marriage spread. Still, the pillars of this traditional and patriarchal society remained solid, and it is likely that a strong motivation persisted for women to marry and bear children.

In general, all three factors that Dixon emphasized (availability, feasibility, and desirability) likely encouraged early marriage and discouraged permanent non-marriage in the farm South, which is consistent with the earlier description of marriage patterns in 1910 and 1940. In addition, social and economic conditions, especially the dominance of farm tenancy and racial barriers to ownership, would have exaggerated their effect for blacks, resulting in even earlier marriage and lower proportions nevermarrying than for whites, also consistent with the earlier description.

Changes in southern farm society between 1910 and 1940 may have produced concomitant changes in marriage patterns by affecting the "proximate determinants" Dixon identified. Yet it is difficult to anticipate their precise influence, and they may have had counterbalancing effects. Increasing geographic mobility, expanding educational opportunities, and economic dislocation caused by the Great Depression would have reduced the opportunities and incentives for early marriage. Therefore, these same social forces may have resulted in a larger proportion of the farm population who remained single. It is possible, however, that increasing tenancy among all farmers between 1910 and 1940 worked in the opposite direction.

The ability to assess the applicability of Dixon's conceptual framework to marriage patterns within the entire farm South is hindered by these potentially conflicting influences. As a result, the ability to gain a fuller understanding of the important social forces affecting nuptiality within this population is also handicapped. One avenue of escape from this predicament is to turn to a consideration of how the marriage behavior of southern farmers differed across geographic areas where prospective couples encountered varying levels of the proximate determinants Dixon described: mate availability, feasibility, and desirability.

## Contextual Influences on Marital Timing

It is clear that marriage within the farm South occurred relatively early in life for males and females, blacks and whites. The population was not monolithic, however. The characteristics of individuals varied, as did the structural conditions of the areas in which they resided. Such individual and contextual differences may have created more (or fewer) opportunities for marriage and thereby have influenced the marital timing of southern farmers. To explore that possibility I focus more intensively on the younger members of the population—specifically, males between twenty and twenty-four and females between eighteen and twenty-two. Individuals within these age groups who were already married can be considered "early-marriers." By identifying the social and/or economic factors that distinguish early-marriers from all others, it may be possible to further illuminate the initiation of family formation among southern farmers.

In searching for the important determinants of marriage, especially the characteristics of communities that shaped the opportunities and motivations for early marriage, it is once again useful to use Dixon's theoretical framework as an organizational scheme. First, it is possible that early-marriers were more common in areas where potential mates were relatively more abundant. If so, there would likely be fewer early-marriers among males where the sex ratio was higher (i.e., proportionately more males). In contrast, early marriage would be more likely for females under the same conditions.[34] Second, more young people are expected to be married where marriage is more feasible. Drawing from the earlier discussion, the feasibility of early marriage should have been greater where farm tenancy was more common and land values were lower. Both factors are expected to have reduced the waiting period required of prospective couples as they positioned themselves economically to establish an independent household. Third, the transition to marriage should have occurred more rapidly where the desirability of marriage was greater. The desirability of marriage for the southern farm population, especially females, should have been greater where there was less competition to the traditional female roles of wife and mother. More educated women should have had greater access to opportunities (especially economic) that competed with traditional roles. Likewise, competing alternatives should have been more abundant for women living in closer proximity to urban areas that offered greater opportunity to non-agricultural employment.

In order to assess the importance of these social and economic factors on early marriage in the farm South, I have estimated logistic regression models, by race and sex, for 1910 and 1940. Logistic regression is an appropriate statistical technique when the dependent variable of interest is a dichotomy, which is true in this case where individuals at the time of the census were either still single (had never married) or had ever been married (currently or in the past). The logistic regression procedure can be used to determine whether independent variables are important in explaining why some individuals fall into the different categories on the dependent variable (ever versus never married). It does this by generating a coefficient for each independent variable, indicating the strength of its relationship with the dependent variable. A positive coefficient means that a higher value on the independent variable increases the likelihood of early marriage. A negative coefficient means that a higher value on the independent variable decreases the likelihood of early marriage. Of the independent variables discussed previously, only education (literacy in 1910 and years of schooling in 1940) pertains to individuals. All other independent variables are contextual, meaning that they describe the characteristics of the areas within which individuals lived.[35]

The coefficients obtained from the logistic regression are presented in table 5 for the analysis of early marriage in 1910. Considering first the evidence for African Americans, it appears that the availability of potential marriage partners played an important role only for females. Young black women living in areas that had a relative abundance of men were much more likely to be married than were women living in areas where men were in short supply. That finding reinforces evidence from other research that has indicated a similar relationship in both historical and modern settings.[36] Turning to the feasibility of marriage, black males and females were more likely to marry early if they lived in areas where farm tenancy was more extensive. The probability of marriage at different levels of farm tenancy can be estimated to put this relationship into better perspective. Where tenancy was more common among black farmers (one standard deviation above the mean), for example, the probability of being married was .55 for males and .57 for females. Where tenancy was much less prevalent (one standard deviation below the mean), the corresponding probabilities were substantially lower—.33 for males and .36 for females.[37] In contrast, land values apparently were unrelated to black marital timing, probably because of the relatively low probability of farm ownership among southern African Americans.[38] Likewise, neither literacy nor percent urban is significantly related to black marriage timing, suggesting that desirability played an insignificant role in shaping black marriage patterns during this earlier period—once the availability of potential spouses and the economic feasibility of early marriage are accounted for.

The corresponding evidence for white farmers offers similarities and contrasts to those for blacks. Mate availability behaved similarly as a pre-

*Table 5.* Coefficients from Logistic Regression Analysis of Marital Status for Males Ages 20–24 and Females Ages 18–22, by Race, 1910

|  | Blacks | | Whites | |
|---|---|---|---|---|
|  | Males | Females | Males | Females |
| Age | 0.553*** | 0.484*** | 0.389*** | 0.410*** |
| Mate availability |  |  |  |  |
| Sex ratio | 0.013 | 0.041*** | −0.014 | 0.021* |
| Feasibility measures |  |  |  |  |
| Tenancy | 0.021*** | 0.021*** | 0.012*** | 0.018*** |
| Farm value | −0.023 | 0.007 | −0.287*** | −0.316*** |
| Desirability measures |  |  |  |  |
| Literacy | −0.149 | −0.017 | −0.705*** | −0.412* |
| Percentage urban | 0.002 | 0.000 | −0.012** | −0.009* |
| Intercept | −14.956*** | −15.424*** | −5.484*** | −8.489*** |
| Number of cases | 952 | 1,298 | 1,816 | 1,951 |

* p ≤ .05; ** p ≤ .01; *** p ≤ .001

*Source:* 1910 Integrated Public Use Microdata Series, Social History Research Laboratory, University of Minnesota.

*Note:* Black oversample included.

dictor of white and black marriage in 1910. The availability of potential marriage partners had a significant effect on the likelihood of marriage for young women but not for young men. The role of farm tenancy in encouraging early marriage was also similar across races. Like blacks, whites were more likely to be married where tenancy was more common, although tenancy was somewhat less important for whites. The most notable racial contrasts in the determinants of early marriage concern the importance of land costs and the relevance of desirability. Among whites, higher land costs exerted a strong depressing effect on the likelihood of early marriage. Where land was relatively expensive (one standard deviation above the mean), for example, the probability of marriage was only .25 for white males and .38 for white females. Where land was considerably cheaper (one standard deviation below the mean), marriage was much more likely: .34 for white males and .48 for white females.[39]

That land costs were relevant for whites and not for blacks is not surprising. The greater likelihood of farm ownership for whites made the cost of buying a farm a more salient factor in their family-building strategies. The powerful effects of tenancy and land costs indicate that feasibility strongly affected marriage patterns for whites; specifically, the likelihood of early marriage was much greater where establishing independent farm households was economically feasible. Unlike blacks, the desirability of marriage was also important for whites. Literate whites were significantly less likely than illiterates to be married, and early marriage was rarer for whites who had easier access to urban areas. Among whites living in entirely rural counties (0 percent urban), the probability of marriage was .32 for males and .45 for females. In counties that were 20 percent urban, the probability of marriage was lower: .27 for males and .40 for females.

The determinants of early marriage changed relatively little for African Americans between 1910 and 1940 (table 6). Female marital timing continued to respond to the availability of male marriage partners, whereas male marriage was again insensitive to the supply of female partners. The feasibility of marriage, as represented by the dominance of farm tenancy, also continued to affect both male and female marriage. For both sexes, early marriage was more likely in areas where farm tenancy was more common. In areas of high tenancy in 1940 (one standard deviation above the mean), the probability of marriage was .53 for males and .58 for females. Where tenancy was less dominant (one standard deviation below the mean), the probability of marriage fell to .38 for males and .50 for females.[40]

*Table 6.* Coefficients from Logistic Regression Analysis of Marital Status for Males Ages 20–24 and Females Ages 18–22, by Race, 1940

| | Blacks | | Whites | |
| --- | --- | --- | --- | --- |
| | Males | Females | Males | Females |
| Age | 0.442*** | 0.437*** | 0.392*** | 0.418*** |
| Mate availability | | | | |
|   Sex ratio | 0.007 | 0.038*** | 0.006 | 0.011* |
| Feasibility measures | | | | |
|   Tenancy | 0.017*** | 0.009*** | 0.013*** | 0.015*** |
|   Farm value | −0.008 | −0.040 | 0.042* | 0.039* |
| Desirability measures | | | | |
|   Schooling | −0.067*** | −0.142*** | −0.072*** | -0.168*** |
|   Percentage urban | 0.367 | 0.332 | -0.507* | −0.164 |
| Intercept | −11.438*** | −11.096*** | −9.964*** | −8.776*** |
| Number of cases | 2,104 | 2,501 | 5,587 | 5,638 |

* p ≤ .05; ** p ≤ .01; *** p ≤ .001

Source: 1940 Integrated Public Use Microdata Series, Social History Research Laboratory, University of Minnesota.

In a departure from the evidence for the earlier period, one measure of the desirability of marriage—years of schooling—had a significant effect on the probability of early marriage for black men and women. Individuals who had more education, and presumably more alternatives to traditional roles, were less likely to marry. For those with more extensive schooling (one standard deviation above the mean, or 7.5 years for males and 8.7 for females), the probability of marriage was only .41 for males and .44 for females. Comparable probabilities for the less educated (one standard deviation below the mean, or 1.8 years for males and 2.9 for females) were .50 for males and .64 for females.

There was also considerable stability between 1910 and 1940 in the forces determining the timing of first marriages for whites. Early marriage was more likely for males and females who were less educated and lived in areas dominated by farm tenancy, and a surfeit of males continued to increase the proportion of women who married at a relatively early age. Some changes in the determinants of early marriage also occurred over time, however. In 1940 the likelihood of marriage for white females was no longer influenced by their exposure to a greater urban presence. In addition, the relationship between land costs and marriage (for both males and females) changed dramatically for whites. The findings for 1940 suggest that marriage was more likely where land was more expensive—

exactly opposite of the pattern observed for 1910. Perhaps that surprising change reflects greater migration of young unmarried individuals from such counties. That migration may have been prompted by increased economic dislocations caused by the Great Depression and the search for greater economic opportunity, either where farmland was cheaper or in a non-farm setting. Thus, although the findings for 1940 still provide support for a linkage between nuptiality and the desirability and feasibility of marriage for whites, it is somewhat less unanimous than was found for 1910.

In sum, evidence suggests that Dixon's theoretical framework has impressive utility for the study of marriage timing in the farm South. Of the three forces she identified, the availability of marriage partners receives perhaps the weakest support, apparently operating for females but not for males. Indicators of the feasibility of marriage were important for both races at both periods. The level of farm tenancy was a particularly powerful determinant of early marriage—suppressing marriage in areas where tenancy was lower and encouraging early marriage where it was higher. That relationship was universal, applying to both races and both sexes in 1910 and 1940. White marriage patterns also responded to the desirability of marriage in both periods, although somewhat more consistently in 1910. For blacks, however, only the significant effect of education in 1940 suggests the importance of desirability for the likelihood of early marriage. It is noteworthy that even in this population with quite early marriage variation in the timing of marriage existed and was related to such a variety of social and economic conditions.

It is not feasible to conduct an analysis of the contextual influences on permanent non-marriage within the older population like that done for early marriage. The most significant problem is that the marital status (ever married versus never married) for those forty-five to fifty-four was the result of a series of decisions made in the distant past. Assuming that the median age at first marriage described earlier in this chapter had remained constant for several years, the married members of this older cohort first made the nuptial transition roughly twenty to thirty years in the past. Furthermore, many had likely moved during that period. The characteristics of their places of residence in 1910 or 1940, therefore, were not necessarily the same as those for the areas in which they lived when they married or for the areas in which they lived when they chose not to marry.[41]

## Conclusion

A southern farm household was a joint enterprise requiring the coordinated labor of husband, wife, and children. The "farm man" needed a wife. The "farm woman" needed a husband. As a result, marriage occurred at an early age and was nearly universal. The organization of southern agriculture was especially facilitatory for early and nearly universal marriage. The strong dependence of southern agriculture on tenancy relaxed certain economic restraints on early marriage and allowed young couples to establish independent households without accumulating significant assets. In addition, the rural South during the first four decades of the twentieth century was a traditional and patriarchal society. Women did not have abundant alternatives to the traditional roles of wife and mother. In Ruth Dixon's terminology, marriage was both feasible and desirable, and in the absence of large changes in cohort size or migration selective for age and sex, potential marriage partners were generally available.[42]

# 4

# Building the Southern Farm Family

The family labor force was the backbone of southern farm households, most of which were too poor to hire outside workers on a regular basis. As much as farm households required the collaborative effort of husbands and wives, they also depended heavily on the contributions of children. Child labor was not considered a pernicious practice within the rural South. Indeed, it was taken for granted that children would pitch in at a tender age and continue working alongside their parents until leaving home to begin building their own families. Toddlers were able to gather firewood for the ubiquitous wood-burning stove. Older children could watch after their younger siblings, tend livestock, or fetch water from the outside well or stream. In her autobiography, Sarah Rice recalled that even when very young she was responsible for sweeping the sandy front yard around her Alabama house clear of leaves and other debris.[1] Recollections of chores performed during childhood, similar to Rice's, are common among the oral histories recorded in the farm South by the Federal Writers' Project during the New Deal. As they grew older, children labored in the fields with nearly the same proficiency as adult workers.[2]

In contrast, the costs of raising children could be modest. Food was an unavoidable expense, but part of the farm diet could be produced at home or gleaned from nature by hunting, fishing, and gathering. Other expenses were more optional. Children's wardrobes were usually limited, and individual clothing items had a long life expectancy that was often achieved through repeated mending. Toys and entertainment were a luxury—if they were available at all. The most significant entertainment for some children occurred during church revival season, when traveling shows brought some relief from an otherwise routine existence. Expenses associated with medical care and education were two items that had the potential to increase substantially the cost of raising children. Some farm families avoided the former by either letting nature take its course or relying primarily on traditional treatments, and it was relatively easy to elude the latter by simply keeping children out of school. Compulsory attendance laws were slow to take hold in the rural South.

Considering the important contributions of children to the family economy but their modest cost, it should not be surprising that southern farm households were well known for their large size. In many, family-building began quickly after marriage and ceased only when physiological changes associated with aging had severely reduced a woman's fecundity.[3] Especially early in the century it was commonplace for farm families to include more than ten children. A black retired farmer in North Carolina recalled, for example, "There were seven girls and three boys in my family. That's what I call a reasonably large family. I never taxed my mind about the number of children we would have. I just let what happened, happen. I do not think a large family keeps a man from making money, that is, if he teaches his children to work. I really like a large family."[4]

Not everyone was as enthusiastic about the virtues of large families. Financial circumstances varied from farmer to farmer, and there were some households in which too many children placed a severe burden on poor parents. Many families were engaged in a constant struggle to put enough food on the table. For them, a large family may have been more the result of ignorance of effective birth control techniques or reluctance to engage in that "deviant" practice than a deliberate economic strategy. Others hoped that life would promise more for their children than the perpetuation of the cycle of poverty that was so common within sharecropping families. Some of these parents were successful at keeping the sizes of their families small in pursuit of their ambition.

Just as the timing of first marriage varied for young men and women in the farm South, family-building strategies after marriage also were not uniform. Some families had ten children or more and the parents, like the black farmer from North Carolina, saw no reason to worry about family size. At the other extreme, some farm couples remained childless or had only one or two children. Likewise, the pace of childbearing within marriage did not remain constant over time. Estimates of age-specific marital fertility rates, for example, show that the total marital fertility rate for black

In many families, siblings were born within relatively short intervals, leading to a large number of children with only a few years separating the oldest and youngest. These children's father was a turpentine worker whose wages were a dollar a day. It is quite likely that they were displaced sharecroppers. (Photo by Dorothea Lange, Library of Congress, LC-USF34-9425-C)

farm women fell from 7.4 children in 1910 to 5.3 in 1940. Marital fertility also fell among white farm women—from 7.0 in 1910 to 4.4 in 1940.[5]

## The Fertility of Southern Farm Families

### Patterns of Completed Family Size

Most women have completed childbearing by the time they reach their mid- to late forties. Therefore, the childbearing histories (number of children ever born) for women over forty-five usually describe completed family sizes.[6] Completed family size is a convenient tool for summarizing the level of fertility within a population and for describing reproductive histories. Indeed, women who were forty-five to sixty-four in 1910 reached the peak of their childbearing years during the closing decades of the nineteenth century.[7] In 1910 the average black farm woman in the South reported that she had borne nearly nine children (table 7). To put that impressively high level of fertility into better perspective, it is nearly three more children than the average black woman of the same age living in the South but not on a farm and roughly four more children than the average black woman in the North. Clearly, many couples, to achieve an average level of completed fertility that high, must have had extremely large families. Nearly half reported having more than ten children (fig. 4). At the other extreme, small families were rare among black southern farmers early in the twentieth century. Only 2.4 percent remained childless, and 8.3 percent more reported one or two children ever born.

Completed family sizes that large suggest that childbearing among black farm couples followed what demographers refer to as a "natural fertility" regime.[8] Couples made little or no attempt to reduce the likelihood of an

*Table 7.* Children Ever Born (CEB) and Percentage Childless for Once-Married Black Couples, by Age of Wife and Residence, 1910 and 1940

|  | Residence | | |
|  | Southern Farm | Southern Non-Farm | Northern |
| --- | --- | --- | --- |
| 45–64 years |  |  |  |
| Mean CEB |  |  |  |
| 1910 | 8.9 | 6.0 | 4.8 |
| 1940 | 4.7 | 3.6 | 2.2 |
| Percentage childless |  |  |  |
| 1910 | 2.4 | 13.1 | 19.5 |
| 1940 | 12.0 | 25.0 | 32.4 |
| 20–44 years |  |  |  |
| Mean CEB |  |  |  |
| 1910 | 4.4 | 3.0 | 2.2 |
| 1940 | 3.0 | 1.9 | 1.8 |
| Percentage childless |  |  |  |
| 1910 | 10.6 | 22.0 | 33.8 |
| 1940 | 21.2 | 35.5 | 38.7 |

*Sources:* 1910 and 1940 Integrated Public Use Microdata Series, Social History Research Laboratory, University of Minnesota.

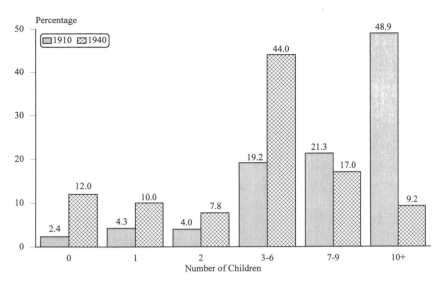

Figure 4. Number of Children Born to Once-Married, Spouse-Present, Black Farm Women 45–64 Years of Age, 1910 and 1940. (*Sources:* 1910 and 1940 Integrated Public Use Microdata Series, Social History Research Laboratory, University of Minnesota.)

additional birth in response to the number of children they already had. Rather, for most, one birth followed another until wives grew too old to bear any more children. Although some couples with relatively small families may have practiced abstinence, birth control, or abortion, it was probably more common for non-volitional factors to be responsible for those couples remaining at the lowest parities (e.g., 0–2 children ever born). For example, prolonged separation of spouses or diseases that impair fecundity (e.g., venereal disease, rickets, pellagra, and genital tuberculosis) can result in small families in a natural fertility population.[9]

Fertility among white farm couples was also high in 1910, averaging nearly seven children. Like the fertility histories of black couples, the average for whites is also substantially above those for other contemporary populations of whites, including farm couples in the North whose families averaged one and one-half fewer children (table 8). The two-child difference in completed family size between black and white southern farm couples is due almost entirely to the much smaller percentage of very large families among whites (fig. 5). Only one in four of all white couples had ten or more children, for example, compared with one out of every two black couples. The smaller average family size for white couples was not

*Table 8.* Children Ever Born (CEB) and Percentage Childless for Once-Married White Couples, by Age of Wife and Residence, 1910 and 1940

|  | Residence | | | |
|---|---|---|---|---|
|  | Southern Farm | Southern Non-Farm | Northern Farm | Northern Non-Farm |
| 45–64 years | | | | |
| Mean CEB | | | | |
| 1910 | 6.8 | 5.3 | 5.3 | 4.6 |
| 1940 | 4.6 | 3.2 | 3.7 | 2.8 |
| Percentage childless | | | | |
| 1910 | 4.7 | 8.2 | 6.1 | 11.0 |
| 1940 | 8.1 | 14.0 | 11.8 | 17.6 |
| 20–44 years | | | | |
| Mean CEB | | | | |
| 1910 | 4.0 | 2.9 | 3.3 | 2.6 |
| 1940 | 2.9 | 1.8 | 2.6 | 1.7 |
| Percentage childless | | | | |
| 1910 | 6.7 | 14.9 | 10.3 | 18.2 |
| 1940 | 13.0 | 24.8 | 16.2 | 25.6 |

*Sources:* 1910 and 1940 Integrated Public Use Microdata Series, Social History Research Laboratory, University of Minnesota.

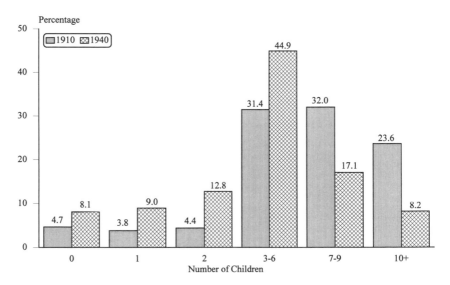

Figure 5. Number of Children Born to Once-Married, Spouse-Present, White Farm Women 45–64 Years of Age, 1910 and 1940. (*Sources:* 1910 and 1940 Integrated Public Use Microdata Series, Social History Research Laboratory, University of Minnesota.)

the result of more whites having very small families. Indeed, the percentages of black and white couples with fewer than three children were similar: 10.7 and 12.9, respectively. Rather, the difference is due to the much higher percentage of white couples who had between three and nine children: 40.5 and 63.4 for blacks and whites, respectively. What distinguished the completed fertility histories of black and white farm couples in 1910 was a significantly higher probability that black couples would proceed from high-parity births to very high-parity births (more than 10). Because it is unlikely that white couples experienced greater physiological difficulties than black couples at the higher parities, it must be assumed that they took deliberate steps to prevent additional births after they had five, six, seven, or more children.

In a span of only thirty years the completed family sizes of southern farmers changed dramatically. By 1940 the average black farm couple had fewer than five children, a reduction of more than four from 1910. Although the average family sizes of southern black farm couples in 1940 remained substantially higher than those observed for African American couples in other regions and residences, a sharp downward trend in fertility brought completed family sizes more in line with those of other populations. The striking decline was due largely to two noticeable changes in family-building patterns between 1910 and 1940. First, very large families became much less common. Only about 10 percent of couples had ten or more children in 1940, down from nearly half of all couples in 1910. Second, small families increased markedly. By 1940, for example, 22 percent of black couples reported having fewer than two children and fully 12 percent remained childless; in 1910 fewer than 7 percent had only one child or were childless. It is well known that childlessness among African American women rose sharply among those reaching childbearing age during the Great Depression.[10] These data suggest that the processes leading to childlessness, even among southern farmers, had begun to intensify well before the depression.

Family sizes for white couples also fell significantly between 1910 and 1940, although on a much more modest scale. Thus, by 1940 the completed family sizes of black and white farm couples were virtually identical: 4.7 and 4.6 children, respectively. White couples also shared in the two major shifts in family-building patterns that affected the completed family sizes of black farmers: a sharp drop in the number of families with ten or more children (from 23.6 percent in 1910 to only 8.2 percent in 1940) and a substantial increase in the number of families with fewer than two children (from 8.5 percent in 1910 to 17.1 percent in 1940). Some distinctiveness remained, however. Childlessness was considerably less common among whites, for example, and two-child families were more frequent.

Clearly, the family-building strategies of southern farm couples were transformed dramatically during the first part of the twentieth century. The decline of very large families was accompanied by a shift toward smaller families, which eventually became the norm in American society.

### Patterns of Cumulative Fertility in 1940

One limitation to using completed fertility to describe the family-building strategies of southern farmers is that the childbearing measured may have occurred far in the past. Indeed, the women in these couples, between forty-five and sixty-four in 1940, were at their peak childbearing years somewhere between 1905 and 1925. To bring the description of family-building behavior even closer to 1940 it is necessary to turn to the fertility histories of younger women (those between twenty and forty-four at the time of census enumeration).[11] For the younger members of the cohort in particular, childbearing subsequent to 1940 would alter significantly their ultimate family sizes. Therefore, it is inappropriate to refer to the fertility of these couples as "completed" family sizes. It was childbearing that was still in progress in 1940—what demographers often refer to as "cumulative fertility." Parallel evidence of cumulative fertility for women from twenty to forty-four in 1910 can be used to assess the degree of change over time.[12]

Although still somewhat higher than family sizes observed for their counterparts in other locations, it is clear that the fertility of black farm couples continued to decline through 1940. The average "young" black couple in 1940 had borne three children (table 7). Comparable black couples in 1910 had already borne more than four. As with the older couples, that drop in average family size was primarily due to sharp reductions in the prevalence of large families (more than seven children) and a simultaneous rise in childlessness (fig. 6). Indeed, in 1940 more than 21 percent of young black farm couples had yet to experience their first birth, although some would go on to have their first child after 1940. Even so, the level of childlessness had doubled since 1910, when it stood at 10.6 percent among couples in which women were between twenty and forty-four.

The average family size among young white farm couples was virtually identical to that for black couples, 2.9 and 3.0 children ever born, respectively (table 8). These similar averages, however, were the products of

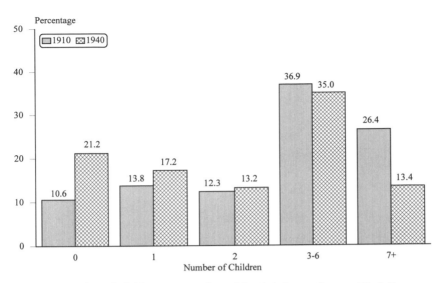

Figure 6. Number of Children Born to Once-Married, Spouse-Present, Black Farm Women 20–44 Years of Age, 1910 and 1940. (*Sources:* 1910 and 1940 Integrated Public Use Microdata Series, Social History Research Laboratory, University of Minnesota.)

somewhat different family-building patterns. Large families of seven or more children were considerably less common among white farmers (26.4 percent for blacks and 19.9. percent for whites), as was childlessness (10.6 percent for blacks and 6.7 percent for whites). Yet white couples were substantially more likely to have borne one or two children (fig. 7). These racial differences echo those observed for the completed family sizes of older couples. Especially intriguing is the much greater prevalence of childlessness among black farm couples, a difference that appears to have emerged during the first few decades of the twentieth century. That trend is particularly intriguing in light of the sizable corresponding percentage of black couples characterized by relatively high fertility when compared with whites. How can this impressive rise in childlessness among black farm couples be explained?

## Childlessness among Black Farm Couples

Traditionally, studies of childlessness have focused on women who have completed their reproductive careers—those forty-five and older. Despite the upturn in childlessness among southern farm women between forty-five and sixty-four, the absolute number of childless women included in

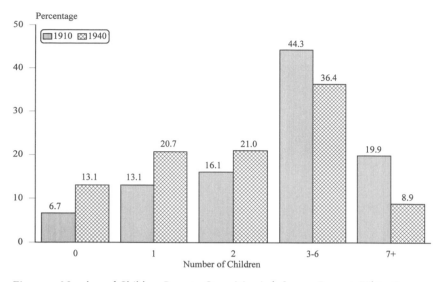

Figure 7. Number of Children Born to Once-Married, Spouse-Present, White Farm Women 20–44 Years of Age, 1910 and 1940. (*Sources:* 1910 and 1940 Integrated Public Use Microdata Series, Social History Research Laboratory, University of Minnesota.)

the IPUMS for 1940 was still quite small. There were only fifty-three childless older black couples in 1940, for example, too few to support an extensive investigation of differentials that might provide insights into the reasons for increasing childlessness. For that reason my focus remains on the same group of younger black farm couples in which the women were between twenty and forty-four.

The growth in childlessness within the younger group between 1910 and 1940 was substantial; it doubled from 10.6 to 21.2 percent. Some of these childless women became mothers when they bore their first child after the census enumeration. Therefore, increasing postponement of first births among young couples between 1910 and 1940 could create an impression of rising childlessness. Does that mean it is inappropriate to focus on the younger age group to examine patterns of childlessness? Probably not as long as it is recognized that childlessness among the younger couples does not necessarily imply permanent childlessness. I base that assertion partially on the important work on historical childlessness done by S. Philip Morgan.[13]

According to Morgan, childlessness, whether contemporary or historical, is primarily a process of the sequential postponement of births. That is, relatively few couples decide early in their marriages to completely forego parenthood and then practice perfect contraception for the rest of their lives. Rather, for a variety of reasons, they decide it is in their best interest to postpone a first birth, with most fully intending to have children later in marriage. As time passes, most couples do make the transition to parenthood. For some, however, that transition never occurs. Two reasons are common: First, the social and economic forces that originally motivated them to postpone childbearing continue or intensify, and, second, they delay too long and become incapable of conceiving or bearing live children, usually because of the wife's declining fecundity. Morgan has shown that the postponement of first births is highly correlated with fertility-control decisions at later parities. Therefore, examination of the factors related to the postponement (possibly temporary) of first births among younger women is a reasonable way to approach the questions of increasing childlessness and group differences in childlessness. Social characteristics associated with postponement of first births, even by those who eventually proceed to parenthood, are likely to also be associated with permanent childlessness.

There is an important distinction between voluntary and involuntary childlessness, and the logic just described applies only to the former. Even sequential postponement of first births, resulting in permanent childlessness, may be considered voluntary. Most were probably aware that the likelihood of parenthood declined with age and that they increased the risk of permanent childlessness by continuing to postpone a first birth. For other couples, however, their childless state was not the result of choice. A variety of factors can severely reduce the chances of conception and live birth, including diseases and permanent damage done by inexpert abortions.[14] To cause childlessness, however, these must occur early in life, especially in populations where the average age at first birth is relatively young, as among southern farm couples. In such cases, childlessness results from threats to the couples' physiological capacity to reproduce rather than from volition. Where childlessness is primarily involuntary, we should not necessarily expect to observe a strong correlation between the delay of first births and fertility control at higher parities. That distinction also carries important implications for the correlates of childlessness. Voluntary childlessness is expected to be more common among more privileged social groups, as is deliberate fertility control in general. In contrast, involuntary childlessness should appear more frequently among those who have poorer health and nutrition—among less privileged social groups.[15]

Historically, voluntary childlessness in the United States has been associated primarily with couples living in northeastern cities. For instance, demographers have estimated that more than half of all childlessness in the urban Northeast at the turn of the twentieth century was volitional. Estimates of voluntary childlessness in the rural South for the same time period suggest very little, if any, deliberate childlessness.[16] The description of southern farm fertility and childlessness in 1910 (tables 7 and 8) is certainly consistent with such a conclusion; only 2.4 percent of older black couples and 4.7 percent of older white couples remained childless. But what could have happened between 1910 and 1940 to raise so markedly the occurrence of childlessness (or at least postponed first births) among southern farm couples?

Previous research on historical childlessness has linked changes in women's roles to increases in childlessness. Did farm couples delay first births in order to accommodate the occupational or social aspirations of women? In light of my earlier description of southern farm society as traditional and patriarchal regarding gender roles it seems unlikely that competition between a farm woman's familial role and her work role could have created pressure for delayed first births and, potentially, childlessness. Indeed, there is little reason to believe that the familial and economic roles of southern farm women evolved significantly between 1910 and 1940. If they had, however, we would expect to witness larger increases in childlessness among higher-status women—those with access to occupational alternatives to early motherhood.

Did worsening economic conditions increase the hardships associated with family life and child-rearing within farm households and thereby encourage fertility delay? Certainly, social and economic dislocation caused by the Great Depression in the farm South may have exerted such an effect. As Morgan writes, "The Depression hit the turn-of-the-century cohort as their members moved into their late twenties and early thirties. This social and economic crisis was widely credited with disrupting and delaying patterns of family formation."[17]

The farm women who were twenty to forty-four in 1940 were born sometime between 1896 and 1920. Much of their childbearing (or lack of it) was experienced during the depression. Therefore, it is possible that the process Morgan identified partially reflects voluntary decisions by these couples to postpone childbearing until economic conditions improved. Although the economic distress caused by the Great Depression may have been felt more keenly by less privileged farmers, I again would expect to find voluntary birth delay to have been more heavily concentrated among the upper strata. That group likely was better acquainted with the more effective methods of birth control and able to use them efficiently. An explanation of childlessness based on the economic dislocations caused by the Great Depression, however, would predict higher levels of childlessness among poorer segments of southern farm society than would the explanation based on changing roles for farm women.

Most treatments of childlessness among African Americans between 1910 and 1940 have emphasized involuntary factors.[18] Could those forces have contributed to the rise in childlessness between 1910 and 1940? Increasing levels of venereal disease among the black population have been assigned primary responsibility for increasing involuntary childlessness, but other diseases have also been implicated. Evidence does suggest that venereal disease became a more serious problem among African Americans during this era and had a negative impact on fertility.[19] It is also possible that the depression worsened general health conditions for southern farm blacks (and whites), increasing the incidence of primary subfecundity and sterility. If those involuntary forces postponed first births and raised levels of childlessness, their effect should have been most salient for less privileged social groups. In sum, the voluntary and involuntary explanations for increasing childlessness in 1940 make conflicting predictions about the involvement of different socioeconomic groups. That fact will be helpful in examining the differentials in childlessness in 1910 and 1940.

I have estimated the effects of two "social status" characteristics on childlessness among the younger cohort of black farm couples in 1910 and 1940: education and farm ownership.[20] The 1910 information for education refers to wife's literacy, whereas the 1940 measure is for years of school completed. Farm ownership status distinguishes couples who owned from those who rented. Table 9 shows the predicted levels of childlessness by education and ownership.[21] In keeping with the lower levels of childlessness and high levels of overall fertility near the turn of the twentieth century, the differentials in expected childlessness are relatively minor. There is essentially no difference, by education or ownership, in levels of childlessness in 1910. Patterns for the earlier period are consistent with natural levels of childlessness that were not strongly affected by volitional or involuntary forces that varied significantly by social status.

By 1940 the absolute levels of childlessness increased (tables 7 and 8), and the status differentials grew larger. An especially sharp gradient in childlessness by farm ownership emerged between 1910 and 1940. By a factor of two to one, black farm owners were more likely than renters to report having no children. It is difficult to reconcile that class differential

*Table 9.* Predicted Proportions Childless among Black Farm Couples, by Class and Wife's Education, 1910 and 1940

|                            | 1910 | 1940  |
|----------------------------|------|-------|
| Wife's education[a]         |      |       |
| High                       | .071 | .147  |
| Low                        | .070 | .168  |
| Class[b]                    |      |       |
| Owner                      | .072 | .281* |
| Renter                     | .070 | .143  |

* statistically significant at p ≤ .05

*Sources:* 1910 and 1940 Integrated Public Use Microdata Series, Social History Research Laboratory, University of Minnesota.

a. Holding marital duration and tenure status constant at their means. For 1910, high education means literate (can read and write) and low education means illiterate. For 1940, high education is one standard deviation above the mean years of completed schooling, and low education is one standard deviation below the mean.

b. Holding marital duration and literacy or education constant at their means.

with the involuntary explanation for childlessness because the significantly higher social status of black farm owners likely meant that they enjoyed somewhat better health and diets than did tenants, although the difference may not have been dramatic. The differential by tenure status does not necessarily confirm a voluntary postponement of first births among farm owners, yet it is certainly consistent with such an interpretation. The very modest difference in childlessness by years of wife's schooling for black couples is not significant statistically.

The emergence of significantly higher levels of childlessness among the more privileged black farm couples in 1940 is consistent with explanations that emphasize voluntary forces. Farm owners were nearly twice as likely as tenants to postpone first births. The large majority of black farmers were tenants, however, and the relatively high levels of childlessness among them suggests that other influences were also at work—either involuntary forces or economic distress among lower-status couples. Although the complete story of childlessness among southern African Americans during this period must await further investigation, it does seem likely that the sizable increase in childlessness (or delay of first births) among southern black farm couples was at least partially due to voluntary choice. Perhaps, as Morgan hypothesized, the economic distress associated with the Great Depression led some to postpone first births within marriage. Some within this group would proceed to parenthood at a later time, but others would not.

## Theoretical Perspectives on Southern Farm Fertility

Social scientists have spent considerable time and energy attempting to explain why some societies (or groups) have higher fertility than others and why childbearing patterns change. In the process, a large literature has developed that identifies a variety of societal characteristics that might be responsible for differentials and trends in family size. Those characteristics may be lumped, crudely, into two categories: "structural" and "cultural." Structural forces refer to a wide variety of macro-level characteristics that describe a society's (or group's) level of modernization—for example, education, urbanization, children's economic activity, and children's survival. In turn, modernization determines the economic rationality, or irrationality, of a large family. In contrast, cultural explanations emphasize more heavily a society's (or group's) ideational system (beliefs, values, and norms) and that system's implications for reproductive preferences and behavior. Cultural preferences for male children or cultural proscriptions against the use of birth control in marriage, for example, can affect fertility behavior. Additional insights into the family-building strategies of southern farm couples may be gained by considering the structural and cultural forces that were at work during the early decades of the twentieth century.

### Traditional Demand Theories of Fertility and the Southern Farm Experience

Since the 1940s demand theories, especially traditional demographic transition theory, have provided the dominant theoretical paradigm for studying fertility and fertility change. According to transition theory, reproductive decision making is a rational process determined largely by the economic advantages or disadvantages of given family sizes. Most important, the balance of costs and benefits associated with children determine societal fertility levels. Where children make important contributions to the family economy, incentives for childbearing will be relatively powerful and families will be large. In contrast, the motivation to limit family sizes will be stronger where children's value is primarily emotional and they are more expensive to raise.

Although originally based on the experience of western European societies and their overseas settlements, transition theory predicts that all societies eventually will traverse three stages: pre-transition, transition, and post-transition.[22] In the pre-transition era, fertility is high because unlimited childbearing is economically rational. Fertility during this stage is often referred to as "natural," meaning that couples make no attempt to reduce the likelihood of an additional birth in response to the number of children they already have.[23] In the lingo of demographers, couples do not practice "parity-dependent" control over childbearing. During this pre-transition era, most women complete their reproductive careers in their late thirties or early forties after having borne an average of seven children or more. Not all of their offspring will survive to adulthood, however, because infant and child mortality is also high during this demographic stage. In fact, the possibility of losing children before they mature is thought to be an additional incentive for high fertility in the pre-transition era. Parents hedge against the possibility of losing children before they reach maturity or replace those who die.[24]

The earlier description of family sizes among southern farm couples, especially African Americans, provides some indication that the southern farm population was in the pre-transition stage (or not far past it) near the turn of the twentieth century. Average completed family sizes of 8.9 children for blacks and 6.8 children for whites and the relative frequency of very large families (e.g., more than ten children) suggest the rapid and prolonged childbearing within marriage that typically occurs during the pre-transition era. These very high levels of marital fertility and the implied infrequency of deliberate control over family size are consistent with the economically rational model of family-building articulated by demographic transition theory or other demand theories of fertility. Of course, they are incapable of proving the accuracy of transition theory's explanation of high fertility during the pre-transition era.

Between 1910 and 1940 the levels of marital fertility dropped by more than two children for both black and white farm couples (tables 7 and 8). Once again, it is possible to reconcile that transition with the expectations of traditional transition theory. Certainly, the survival chances of infants and children improved between 1910 and 1940.[25] As more children reached adulthood fewer births were required to assure the same number of surviving offspring. Couples that did not adjust their fertility accordingly faced the possibility of having more children than their economic circumstances warranted.

Major structural changes in southern society also occurred between 1910 and 1940 that could have altered the net economic value of children to farm parents, thereby making unrestricted fertility less economically rational. By 1940 farm production had become more mechanized. On some farms, tractors and other equipment were replacing unskilled farm labor, including children.[26] Opportunities for schooling also expanded, removing children from the fields for longer periods of time and increasing their cost to parents.[27] Schooling required sacrifices from some families in or-

This young child of a couple living on a plantation in Mississippi in 1937 would live to see profound changes in southern agriculture as the adoption of tractors and other farm equipment reduced the need for child labor and displaced many tenant farmers. (Photo by Dorothea Lange, Library of Congress, LC-USF34-17420-E)

der to provide children with the necessities. In some cases, those expenses forced children to forego schooling, as reported by the wife of a farm laborer in Bolivar County, Mississippi, in the later 1930s during an interview with Charles S. Johnson, "Last year I just didn't have money to send 'em at all [to school]. You know yourself if you ain't got no shoes to wear and can't dress like the other children, and all the other children making fun of you, you wouldn't go neither."[28] Finally, the Great Depression made life harsher for virtually all southern farm families and made it more difficult to support large numbers of children.

The confluence of these social forces may very well have changed the calculus of family-building decisions for southern farmers. Couples could have decided to adjust family-building strategies to fit better the altered social and economic climate that demanded such change.[29] Other stories may be told, however, that also account for their high fertility near the turn of the century and its subsequent decline.

### Alternative Theoretical Perspectives on Fertility and Fertility Decline in the Farm South

In recent years, demand theories of fertility, such as traditional transition theory, have come under attack. Some scholars argue that the same demographic history that demand theories claim to explain is more consistent with an alternative theoretical paradigm that offers a sharply different explanation for the levels and changes in southern farm fertility. Whereas demand theories emphasize the rational adjustment of human fertility to prevailing social and economic conditions, the diffusion-innovation paradigm focuses on the knowledge and acceptance of birth control and its spread through societies.[30]

How would the diffusion-innovation model explain the high levels of marital fertility among southern farmers in 1910? Rather than claiming that large families were economically rational, diffusion-innovationists would argue that much childbearing during the pre-transition era was unwanted. Some farm couples may have preferred smaller families but were unable (or unwilling) to put their preferences into practice. Either they did not know how to avoid pregnancies and childbirth or they were reluctant to do so because the practice of birth control within marriage was socially unacceptable, even when the requisite knowledge was in place. As partial evidence for the existence of unwanted births in the pre-transition era, the diffusion-innovation model turns a standard transition theory premise on its head. It claims that high infant and child mortality in the pre-transition stage was partially due to neglect, abuse, and infanticide. Thus, rather than viewing high mortality as an incentive for high fertility, perhaps it was high because parents had few alternatives to achieving their desired family sizes.[31] The comments of contemporaries perhaps allow determination of whether there is support for the assertions of the diffusion-innovation model.

One of the specific objectives of the interviews conducted during the Great Depression's Federal Writers' Project was to determine attitudes and beliefs regarding family size and contraception. As a result, many of the southerners interviewed provided revealing glimpses into this private part of their family lives. Many comments are consistent with the arguments made by diffusion-innovation theorists.

Several southern farm couples expressed concern over the sizes of their families. Typical of these expressions was the comment by the wife of a white tenant farmer. Referring to her husband, she reported, "He said the younguns was coming too fast and that with more mouths to feed and me not able to work half the time we'd soon find ourselves starving to death."[32] Others were similarly concerned over the number of children they had and lamented not knowing how to control fertility. The wife of a black farmer in North Carolina said:

> I've been tied down with babies ever since Roy and me was married. I have thought many times that I simply could not stand to have another baby, but when it gets here I love it just like I do the rest of the younguns and there is no sacrifice I would not make for it. Anyway, I don't think it is right for us to keep on bringing chillun into the world when we know we are not able to feed and clothe them that are already here. While we have tried to give our chillun enough to eat, I know they go hungry because we ain't got money enough to buy food for them.

Her husband (Roy) added, "While I loves my chillun, every one of them, I sure do wish we had known something about that birth control stuff you mentioned."[33]

In addition to a basic ignorance about birth control, the oral histories reveal a widespread disapproval of efforts to limit family sizes. There is a strong sentiment, often heard now among women in developing countries, that it is up to God to determine how many children a couple has and it is sinful to intervene in that divine process. Comments by a white farmer in Alabama are typical of that belief: "Hit's ag'inst the law set down in the book. God sent 'em, an' hit ain't for man to meddle with God's doin's."[34] Another farmer in North Carolina was even more emphatic: "No sir, I certainly don't believe in birth control. I think that everybody should have all the children God intended them to have. There's never been a child born or destroyed that God didn't intend. . . . I believe that abortion's the worst crime a person can commit. Where does these sexual maniacs come from?"[35] Some of these "sexual maniacs" were midwives who helped women abort by telling them of abortifacient concoctions that could be made from local flora.[36]

In describing the lot of women in the rural South, historian Jack Kirby suggests that domestic violence was not rare, "Marriage was a cruel trap, motherhood often a mortal burden; husbands were too often obtuse, unfaithful, drunken, and violent. The collective portrait is less of bliss than of pathos."[37] Indeed, domestic violence was frequently reported by southern farm wives during the interviews for the Federal Writers' Project. In at least one woman's experience, such violence was also a bizarre form of birth control. The wife of a white farmer in North Carolina recalled being beaten by her husband: "We'd been married four months and I found out that I was going to have a baby. He didn't like younguns and he was mad about it so when he got drunk the first time after he knowed it he beat me. I lost that one and I like to of died, but he was so sorry that he done it I had to forgive him. . . . The next time he beat me I was six months gone. He knocked me down and stomped on my stomach. I lost that one, too."[38] Although I found no references among the oral histories to deliberate abuse, neglect, or infanticide in reaction to unwanted births, the behavior of this farm husband certainly suggests the potential for such behavior, and more than one episode of domestic violence reported by southern farmers involved a pregnant wife.[39]

Because the oral histories were collected in the late 1930s, the stories refer to experiences during the transition period described earlier. Therefore, they probably underestimate the degree of ignorance and disapproval of birth control that existed closer to the turn of the century. By the late 1930s more farm couples were no doubt aware of ways to limit the number of children they had, and birth control had become more socially acceptable. For instance, the same wife of the white tenant farmer in North Carolina who was concerned about not being able to feed all his children reported having used cotton-root tea to abort a pregnancy. Later she had a tubal ligation while undergoing an appendectomy.[40]

How would the diffusion-innovation perspective account for the change in fertility during the transition stage? Although it acknowledges the role of social and economic changes like those identified by demand theories, the diffusion-innovation model emphasizes more heavily two non-structural forces. First, it claims that knowledge of birth control practices increases, giving couples the ability to limit births. Second, ideational shifts occur that make the practice of family limitation within marriage more socially acceptable. In other words, society begins to think differently— more approvingly—of married couples taking steps to avoid having children. Both processes are thought to occur through the diffusion of information, norms, and values from one segment of society to another.

Evidence for a diffusion process in the rural South between 1910 and 1940 is still quite limited, but certain patterns of differential fertility suggest such a process. First, fertility fell much earlier in southern cities than in rural areas. Within rural areas, family sizes dropped earlier in non-farm households than among farmers.[41] Although not definitive, and also consistent with structural explanations, that residential pattern of fertility decline may reflect the diffusion of anti-natalistic behavior from the city to the countryside. Second, there was considerable geographic clustering of fertility patterns near the end of the transition era. Even controlling for shared social and economic characteristics, counties tended to have fertility levels similar to those observed in adjacent or nearby counties.[42] Because this spatial clustering of fertility levels was independent of such fertility-related structural characteristics as education, urbanization, industrialization, and mortality, it suggests a cultural diffusion process. Third, also near the end of the transition era, fertility was lower in counties that had greater exposure to radios and national magazines—potentially important vectors for the spread of fertility-related information and ideas.[43] Finally, moral reformers within the South perceived, and bemoaned, exactly the kind of cultural transformation described by the diffusion-innovation perspective. Even early in the twentieth century they warned against "a rapid breakdown of family values, traditional sexual roles and sexuality, and the institutions and values that had upheld them."[44] They were especially con cerned with the increasing tendency for couples to postpone marriage and limit childbearing.

As is often the case in the social sciences, proponents for these competing theories of fertility behavior and fertility change have pitted them against each other as though it is possible for only one theoretical perspective to have scientific merit. Increasingly, however, complex social phenomena such as childbearing patterns are being viewed as the result of multiple causes—possibly reflecting the influence of social forces consistent with more than one theoretical perspective.[45] That is the conclusion that I prefer to draw from this discussion. On the one hand, the decline in southern farm fertility between 1910 and 1940 was the result of an altered social and economic environment—especially adjustments to childbearing patterns made by couples in reaction to the reduced potential for children to make significant economic contributions to household production. On the other hand, family-building strategies also may have been affected by ideational shifts resulting from the spread of new information about birth control and ideas about its acceptability within marriage.

## Conclusion

In both 1910 and 1940 southern farm families were larger than those found elsewhere in the country. Children played an important role in southern farm households, so perhaps it should not be too surprising to find that those households typically included many children. There was a widespread perception among southern farmers that children were a real asset to a family's economy. Still, not all farm couples were equally enthusiastic about the advantages of large families, and some did connect their financial struggles with the number of mouths they had to feed.

Between 1910 and 1940 the family-building patterns of southern farm couples changed dramatically. Average family sizes dropped sharply, more couples delayed childbearing, and some forewent parenthood altogether. The latter two trends were especially noticeable for African American farm couples, and some evidence suggests that the trends were at least partially volitional. My best guess about the causes for the increasing delay of first births and for rising childlessness is that the severe economic disruptions caused by the Great Depression encouraged couples to postpone childbearing—sometimes permanently. Of course, the role of involuntary forces (e.g., increasing subfecundity due to venereal infections) must also be acknowledged. These striking shifts in the family-building patterns of southern farmers took place despite the persistence of strong disapproval of birth control and efforts to limit family size within this population.

The most popular theoretical models of fertility and fertility change would offer conflicting explanations for the levels and trends in southern farm fertility. Demand theories emphasize important structural shifts that occurred in the rural South during this period, including declining infant and child mortality, increased farm mechanization, expanded schooling, and reduced dependence on child labor. In contrast, the diffusion-innovation perspective stresses explanations based on ideational shifts that increased the acceptability of birth control within marriage at the same time that improved knowledge of various family planning techniques diffused throughout southern society. Most likely, the social forces identified by both theoretical perspectives influenced the family-building strategies of southern farm couples and their change over time. The result of the confluence of those social forces was a dramatic drop in the size of southern farm families in the span of one generation.

# 5

# Keeping the Family Together

Spouses and children could not take for granted the perseverance of south-ern farm families. The longevity of marital unions was threatened by death, desertion, and divorce. The living arrangements of children were also vul-nerable to the same disruptive forces that broke apart married couples. Obviously, children could not live with parents who had died or no longer lived in the same household, but these are forces that affect the stability of family life everywhere. As with all social forces, however, they can vary over time and affect groups differently.

## Threats to Marital Unions in the Farm South

### Death

Historically in the United States, mortality has posed the greatest threat to marital unions.[1] Although death rates had fallen during the latter part of the nineteenth century, life expectancy in 1900 was still relatively short by modern standards. Samuel H. Preston and Michael R. Haines, for ex-ample, estimate that the average baby born in 1900 could expect to live about fifty-one years if white and roughly forty years if black. The life ex-pectancies of white and black babies born in 1990 were seventy-six and sixty-nine years, respectively.[2]

Information about mortality within the South is more difficult to come by because most southern states were late in joining the Death Registra-tion Area. Information about mortality by type of residence (e.g., farm or non-farm) within the South is nonexistent. Nonetheless, scattered evidence provides a rough idea of southern life expectancies. It appears that southern whites in the early part of the twentieth century could expect to live until their mid-fifties, compared to the mid-forties for blacks.[3] It was primarily the high risk of death for infants and children that kept these life expectancies so low. Still, adults were also exposed to higher probabilities of death than they now are, and those probabilities produced relatively large numbers of widows and widowers.

By 1940 things had improved considerably. In general, life expectancy at birth had increased by roughly ten years for blacks and whites alike, yet black children were exposed to an elevated probability of losing one or more parent. Whites born in the rural South in 1939 could expect to live about sixty-four years if they were male and more than sixty-seven years if they were female. African Americans remained at a distinct disadvantage, however. Black males born in 1939 could expect to live an average of fifty-six years, with black females enjoying only two more.[4] Even under these improved conditions, death was a reality for adult African Americans; nearly 18 percent of all twenty-year-old blacks (male or female), for example, could expect to die before turning forty-five. The comparable risk of death was substantially lower for southern whites—9 percent for males and 7 percent for females.

The impact of adult mortality on southern rural society is clearly evident in the oral histories recorded during the Federal Writers' Project. Many deaths the respondents described occurred during, or soon after, childbirth—an especially dangerous experience for women in settings where they had many children and health care was poor. Maternal mortality took its toll on white and black women alike. William Carter was a black farmer and merchant in North Carolina who experienced the tragedy of losing his wife during childbirth. The FWP interviewer wrote of him: "Carter thought he was blessed. He not only knew nothing of birth control but considered every child a gift the lord provided him as future labor for his land. But there was one child too many. Carter couldn't afford the doctor, who charged $39 to born a baby, and so he used a midwife at $5. All the other children had come through all right but Carter says the midwife must have forgotten something because with the fifth child his wife died."[5] Midwives were present at many successful southern births but, clearly, not all couples were so fortunate.

A white farmer in North Carolina told a similar story, although it concerned his mother and was more sinister: "My mother died before I was seven years old. . . . I never knew what was really the matter except that she had a baby before time. . . . After I got to thinking about it I remembered that Daddy beat her with the firepoker the night before she died the next morning. It was so real that I can close my eyes and still see her clutching at his side and screaming. He put me out of the room and the doctor came and Daddy looked worried. The next time I saw Mama she lay in the casket with the baby on her arm."[6]

## Divorce

Divorce was a much less serious threat to the longevity of marital unions during the first decades of the twentieth century. Statistics indicate that the annual incidence of divorce in the United States changed very little between 1910 and 1940. It hovered around thirty divorces per one thousand existing marriages. When looked at a different way—the probability that a marriage eventually ends in divorce—the frequency of divorce rose somewhat during this thirty-year period but remained far below modern levels.[7] Still some "moral crusaders" pointed to an increasing incidence of divorce as evidence of the breakdown of traditional family values in American society during the first part of the century.[8]

Although no published evidence is available with which to describe the frequency of divorce among southern farmers, the relative isolation of the population and the cost involved suggest it likely was relatively uncommon. Furthermore, in some areas divorce was not a legal option.[9] It was primarily the relatively high cost of legal divorce that prompted a justice of the peace in North Carolina to regret that he was unable to grant divorces more often:

> Now and then they come to ask me how to go about gettin' a divorce. I wish it was in my jurisdiction to give 'em divorces. I tell 'em they need fifty dollars to start it, and then the lawyer will tell 'em how much more it will take. That's where it stops in most cases that consult me, for fifty dollars is out of their reach, fifty dollars is between them and peace. . . . When I see a pore wife worked to death and imposed on by a sorry man, with her little children hungry and naked and neglected, I wish I could buy her a divorce. That's another thing the country needs . . . and that's needed worse'n anything in God's world, for the sake of the pore folks! More divorces is what the country needs![10]

Fifty dollars was a large sum for poor dirt farmers who often ended the year owing money to a landlord or merchant. As the justice of the peace mentioned, that amount was only the first installment in what could become a prolonged indebtedness. In addition to the financial sacrifice required by divorce, often it was not convenient for countryfolk to retain a lawyer to negotiate the legal obstacles involved. Some unhappy farm couples did invoke the legal system to end their marriages, although it was probably far more common for unions to dissolve informally through the departure of one of the spouses.

## Desertion and Separation

Although the statistical evidence is largely missing, oral histories, diaries, and firsthand accounts of family life in the rural South between 1910 and 1940 suggest that desertion and separation were common. Those interviewed during the Federal Writers' Project referred frequently to wives abandoned by husbands or children abandoned by parents. Some families were disrupted by a parent migrating in search of employment. It was common, especially during hard times, for struggling farmers to pursue opportunities in southern cities or to make the longer trek across state lines. In many cases these economically motivated separations were meant to be temporary, with spouses and children poised to follow as soon as "the migrant" was established financially. Sometimes things went according to plan. Often, however, families divided in this way were never reconstituted as intended.

Other cases of family disruption were not undertaken with such noble motives. Occasionally a spouse, usually the husband, decided to pursue extra-marital romantic interests or decided that the current marriage was not working out satisfactorily. A typical example is an abandoned wife who took up residence with a white sharecropping family in North Carolina. The wife of the sharecropper informed the interviewer that "Susie's husband run off and left her with this here girl, and that child was born four months after he left her. I'm tryin' to take care of them now; he ain't give one red cent to their support."[11]

It was not always necessary for a woman to be legally married in order to be deserted. In *Growing Up in the Black Belt*, Charles S. Johnson includes an interview with Stanley Byrd, a black man living in Coahoma County, Mississippi. Byrd told Johnson that he had a four-year-old son, although he was only nineteen himself and not married. He went on to describe his relationship with his son and the boy's mother: "I see him often, and his mother too, but I don't have nothing to do with her no more. She just told me about it, but didn't try to make me marry her. I didn't want to marry her because she was too dark. I wasn't thinking about marrying, and wuld of tried to get out of it if she had wanted me. Lots of people know its my kid. . . . People 'round don't make no difference, though some don't have too much to do with the girl. They never act like they think I ought to marry her though."[12] Regardless of the circumstances or motivation, however, the result was the same: a family headed by a female and children left without a co-resident father.

## African American Family Structure: The Continuing Debate

Few issues in the social sciences have been debated as fiercely as the history of African American families and family structure. Perhaps the best point of departure for summarizing that literature is by noting the status of black families in the United States at the end of the twentieth century.

To many social scientists, the black family in the 1990s constitutes an institution in distress. A few statistics reveal the cause for their concern. By the end of the 1990s, more than two-thirds of all African American babies were born to unmarried mothers. That very high level of non-marital fertility had two additional, and profound, effects on the structure of black families. First, fully 46 percent of all black family households in 1995 were headed by females, compared to 14 percent for whites.[13] Second, most black children begin life residing with only one parent and will spend much of their childhood in a female-headed household. For example, 58.3 percent of those under eighteen in 1995 lived with their mother only—three times the level observed in the white population (18.3 percent).[14] The socioeconomic implications of these family patterns can be summarized by the fact that nearly 70 percent of black children under six who were living in a family headed by their mother were also living in poverty. In contrast, only 19.3 percent of African American children living with both parents were below the poverty line.[15]

Although the family patterns of African Americans have changed considerably since the 1960s, these were generally the same conditions that prompted Daniel Patrick Moynihan to write *The Negro Family: The Case for National Action* (1965). In that provocative report, Moynihan characterized black families as being matrifocal and unstable. He also blamed many of the social problems in the black community on a "deviant" family structure and organization. Moynihan argued that the disorganized African American family of the mid-twentieth century was the legacy of a life under slavery during the nineteenth century. Slaves had been denied the right to establish meaningful marital unions, and even relatively stable cohabitations were subject to disruption at the whim of owners. As a result, slave mothers bore primary responsibility for raising children and naturally emerged as their families' center and strength.

In making his controversial argument Moynihan drew heavily from the work of E. Franklin Frazier, an African American sociologist who wrote extensively about black families of the 1930s. Frazier strove to discount explanations for black behavior and family patterns that emphasized an "African heritage." Such explanations were popular at the time among social scientists who claimed that behavioral differences between the races were primarily due to the inherent inferiority of African culture or genes. Frazier not only dismissed biological explanations for behavior but also argued that African cultures were too diverse, and the slavery experience too destructive, for an ancestral heritage to exert a strong, uniform effect on twentieth-century black society. Rather, if black family structure had assumed a unique form, then it had to be the result of experiences on the American continent. According to Frazier, two events were especially critical in shaping black families: slavery and migration.

The institution of slavery could be destructive; whatever family forms had been imported from Africa were soon obliterated by the random mixing of different African ethnicities and the callousness of slave owners. It was difficult to perpetuate cultural patterns of any kind when the co-resident slaves on a plantation did not share the same ethnic ancestry. It was equally difficult to emulate the European family pattern of white society when some owners felt little remorse over breaking up nuclear slave families for profit. The legacy of the slavery experience carried over into freedom. "It is not surprising, therefore," Frazier writes, "that the Negro family, which was at best an accommodation to the slave order, went to pieces in the general break-up of the plantation system."[16] He was referring to elevated levels of illegitimacy and female-headed families among African Americans in the rural South. But Frazier did not claim that all slave families were exposed to such destructive forces. A more stable, patriarchal family organization emerged among the most privileged slaves—those who interacted most closely with the dominant white culture of the owners.

Despite the problems that most African Americans inherited from slavery, Frazier perceived considerable stability of family life within the rural South. As changing social conditions began to drive rural blacks to cities, however, even those sources of stability were threatened. Migration sometimes split families apart as one spouse, more often the husband, pioneered the way to a new location in search of better economic opportunities. New attractions, diversions, and temptations in the city were not conducive to family stability. Like slavery before it, the black migration stood accused by Frazier of creating elevated levels of illegitimacy, marital disruption, and female-headed households, but this time in the urban North rather than the rural South.

Frazier was not the only social scientist who held such views. Charles S. Johnson was also in general agreement. He, like Frazier, had been educated at the University of Chicago and studied with Robert Park. Later, along with the North Carolina School of rural sociologists, he wrote extensively about the lives of rural southerners during the Great Depression. In an innovative research project for his time, Johnson interviewed 2,250 black children in the late 1930s to gather the evidence on which he based *Growing Up in the Black Belt: Negro Youth in the Rural South*. His profiles revealed the frequency with which children were exposed to family disruption. Other contemporary observers echoed the concerns expressed by Frazier and Johnson, including Gunnar Myrdal, Arthur Raper, and Carter Woodson.[17]

The intellectual tradition that had such a powerful influence on Moynihan's argument was not the work of racists nor of scholars insensitive to the inhospitable social environment facing blacks in the United States. All were respected social scientists deeply concerned about racial prejudice and discrimination. All were strong proponents for environmental rather than biological explanations for racial differences in behavior and achievement. Both Frazier and Johnson played key roles in counteracting the largely racist perspectives of the previous generation of social scientists, including the work of eugenicists who had been so influential in shaping scientific thought about racial differences as well as public policy. As a group, the scholars were also accomplished and socially engaged. E. Franklin Frazier was on the faculty of Morehouse College in Atlanta until 1927, when he was virtually driven from town after publishing a controversial and unpopular article, "The Pathology of Prejudice." He later taught at Fisk University and then became chair of the sociology department of Howard University in Washington, D.C. Charles S. Johnson also taught at Fisk University and later became its president. Earlier in his career he had served as director of research for the Urban League and editor of its periodical, *Opportunity*. Arthur Raper was one of the founding members of the Commission on Interracial Cooperation, a group promoting better treatment for blacks and increased interracial harmony, as well as author of *The Tragedy of Lynching*, a powerful indictment of that brutal southern ritual. Although it is possible that their descriptions of black families were not entirely accurate or that their inferences about underlying causes were in error, there is no reason to suspect the motives behind their scholarship.

Moynihan's conclusions about African American families generated a maelstrom of controversy and a flood of research critical of his work as well as that of his predecessors. Two arguments were essential to the critical response. First, a group of scholars led by Herbert Gutman, claimed that slavery was not as disruptive to black families as Moynihan and others had claimed. Through careful analysis of plantation records Gutman showed in *The Black Family in Slavery and Freedom* that a typical slave family was patriarchal and relatively stable. Furthermore, Gutman's and others' comparisons between the family forms of blacks and whites following emancipation revealed that only relatively small racial differences existed. Like their white counterparts, black families were typically headed by couples rather than females. That included the families of rural blacks living in Louisa County, Virginia, that were studied by Crandall Shifflett and those in the rural areas of Edgefield County, South Carolina, studied by Orville Vernon Burton.[18] If the legacy of slavery was really to blame for the relatively disorganized black families Moynihan observed in the 1960s, then should not the same—or possibly even more exaggerated—disorganization have been present in earlier decades?

The second argument sought to counteract the implication drawn from Moynihan's work that something pathological about African American culture led to matrifocal and unstable families. That argument claims that if African American families were basically nuclear and stable shortly after emancipation, but matrifocal and disrupted by 1960, then something must have happened during the intervening period to account for the change. Rather than the persistence of a cultural pattern established during slavery, proponents of this argument blamed a lack of economic opportunities in America's cities, especially for African American males. In the face of job discrimination and a changing urban economy, black males were unable to offer the kind of financial security required to head stable families. Economic obstacles rather than cultural deficiencies accounted for the current status of black families in the United States.[19] Burton's description of the early emergence of differences in black family structure between rural areas and towns in Edgefield County is consistent with that explanation.[20]

Other contributions to the debate have shown that racial differences in family structure are not new, as some have inferred from the work of

Gutman and others. Using census data, S. Philip Morgan and his colleagues have documented significant racial differences near the turn of the twentieth century. For example, black women were more likely than white women to be living apart from their husbands, and black children were less likely to live with both parents. These differences were only partially due to the higher mortality of African American adults and were geographically pervasive. Because they existed in the North and South, in town and countryside, Morgan et al. concluded that the racial differences in family structure early in the century could not have been due to African American migration to the North and to cities.[21] Furthermore, Steven Ruggles used a series of decennial censuses to show that the patterns described by Morgan and his colleagues were long-standing, extending from 1880 through 1980, although the magnitude of racial differences changed over time.[22]

How do Ruggles and Morgan et al. explain the persistent racial difference in family structure? They acknowledge that social and economic forces are certain to play an important role. Both groups of scholars express a strong preference for cultural explanations, however. Using oral histories collected by the Federal Writers' Program, Deanna Pagnini and S. Philip Morgan infer greater tolerance among southern blacks for marital disruption and non-marital childbearing. They do not speculate, however, about the possible origins of this cultural difference.[23] In contrast, Antonio McDaniel, a sociologist, asserts that racial differences in the living arrangements of children as identified by Ruggles, Morgan et al., and others reflect the inheritance of a "child fosterage" tradition that is common among African societies and that was carried to the New World by the enslaved population.[24] Thus, we have come full circle. Contemporary discourse on the history of African American families is headed in the very direction that E. Franklin Frazier tried so vigorously to discredit. Of course, modern proponents are pursuing an Afrocentric orientation sympathetic to cultural and ethnic diversity rather than a racist ideology grounded in the belief that Africans and African Americans are inherently inferior to whites.[25]

It is possible to extract from this debate over African American family patterns information that is useful for an examination of marital and family stability among southern farmers. Perhaps it is best to approach the topic by considering the primary social forces hypothesized in this literature to affect black family structure: (1) the legacy of slavery; (2) cultural traditions inherited from Africa; and (3) the effects of migration.

Geography alone would suggest that southern black farmers should have been strongly influenced by the legacy of slavery. After all, slavery was concentrated in rural areas of the South and organized primarily around an agricultural economy. That influence should have been especially strong early in the twentieth century. Although only the older individuals in 1910 (say, sixty and over) would have lived during the slavery era, virtually all the others were separated from the Peculiar Institution by only one generation. If slavery had produced an unstable and matrifocal black family—as Frazier, Moynihan, and others have claimed—then it should be especially apparent in the evidence for southern farmers in 1910. When compared with whites, there should be elevated levels of marital instability and more children living apart from parents. By 1940 the legacy of the slavery experience should have weakened because most southern farmers were separated by at least two generations from their slave ancestors. At the very least, the "slavery explanation" would not predict a strengthened impact on black farm families as time passed.

Roughly the same expectations surround the hypothesized effect of an African cultural heritage on black family patterns. To the extent that such a linkage existed it should have been strongest within the rural South, given the greater concentration of African Americans to sustain such a cultural lineage—much as the cultural heritage of European immigrants was more persistent in communities and neighborhoods whose populations consisted largely of fellow countrymen. Furthermore, the impact of African heritage on black family structure (i.e., marital stability and living arrangements of children) should have been more powerful in 1910 than 1940, or at least not stronger in 1940. Most research on the experience of immigrant groups shows that the influence of cultural patterns from the country of origin is strongest among the first generation and weakens considerably by the third generation.[26] By 1940 the importation of slaves into the United States had been illegal for more than 130 years.[27] That is a very long time for ethnic ancestry to remain viable and for such ancestry to exert a significant impact on marital and family behavior.

The impact of migration on southern rural society during the first half of the twentieth century was nothing short of profound. Movement to southern and northern cities accelerated sharply when World War I accelerated the economy and the flow of immigrants from Europe slowed to a trickle. The southern agricultural economy could not offer the opportunities available (or perceived to be available) in the industrial North. In addition, cities, north and south, offered attractions not available in the rural South, such as better schools, hospitals, paved roads, and a greater variety of entertainment. For blacks, migration also offered an opportunity to escape the threat of violence that had taken so many lives during the late nineteenth and early twentieth centuries. The migration had a disruptive effect on southern farm families, at least temporarily and sometimes permanently. In contrast to the effects of the legacy of slavery and the inheritance of African customs, the impact of migration on the stability of southern farm families should have intensified between 1910 and 1940. Rural-to-urban and interregional migration, especially among African Americans, was relatively light before 1910. Between 1910 and 1940 the pace of migration quickened, and the impact on southern rural society intensified.[28]

## Marital Stability of Southern Farm Couples

In chapter 3 the marriage patterns of southern farmers were analyzed by distinguishing those who had ever married from those who had never married. That distinction, especially its variation by age, was useful for describing both the timing and universality of marriage. By focusing only on farm residents who had ever been married it is possible to determine the fate of their most recent marriage and thereby gain a better understanding of marital stability. Marital unions were vulnerable to three types of instability: widowhood, divorce, or separation. Clearly, the probability of a marriage falling victim to these forms of instability was somewhat dependent upon age. Most important, older couples faced a higher risk of their marriage ending through the death of a spouse than did younger couples. In addition, marriages of shorter durations (more common among younger people) were more likely to dissolve through separation.[29] Likewise, gender may have played a role in the specific type of marital disruption that farm couples experienced. A higher rate of mortality among males would, for example, produce more widows than widowers, or husbands may have been more inclined to abandon wives than vice versa.[30]

### Widowhood

Early in the twentieth century the death of a spouse was the greatest threat to the stability of marriages among southern farm couples, as it was for the general population of the United States. Roughly two out of every three disrupted marriages for black farm couples in 1910 ended because of the death of the husband or wife. Even marriages among the youngest couples were more likely to end because of the death of a spouse than from divorce or separation (table 10). As might be expected, given the generally higher

*Table 10.* Current Marital Status of Ever-Married Black Men and Women on Southern Farms, by Age, 1910 and 1940

| | 1910 | | 1940 | |
|---|---|---|---|---|
| Age | Female | Male | Female | Male |
| 20–34 years | | | | |
| Married | | | | |
|   Spouse present | 88.4% (96.2) | 92.0% (97.0) | 87.6% (93.0) | 91.5% (93.7) |
|   Spouse absent | 3.5   (3.8) | 2.9   (3.0) | 6.6   (7.0) | 6.2   (6.3) |
|   Divorced | 1.6 | 0.7 | 1.6 | 0.8 |
|   Widowed | 6.6 | 4.5 | 4.2 | 1.5 |
| 35–49 years | | | | |
| Married | | | | |
|   Spouse present | 85.6% (97.2) | 91.8% (97.5) | 81.8% (94.7) | 90.4% (95.1) |
|   Spouse absent | 2.0   (2.3) | 2.4   (2.5) | 4.6   (5.3) | 4.7   (4.6) |
|   Divorced | 0.8 | 0.8 | 1.4 | 0.9 |
|   Widowed | 11.5 | 5.1 | 12.2 | 4.1 |
| 50–64 Years | | | | |
| Married | | | | |
|   Spouse present | 69.3% (96.5) | 87.4% (96.5) | 68.6% (94.7) | 83.1% (93.9) |
|   Spouse absent | 2.5   (3.5) | 3.6   (4.0) | 3.8   (5.3) | 5.4   (6.1) |
|   Divorced | 0.5 | 0.3 | 0.7 | 1.3 |
|   Widowed | 27.6 | 8.6 | 26.8 | 10.3 |

*Sources:* 1910 and 1940 Integrated Public Use Microdata Series, Social History Research Laboratory, University of Minnesota.

*Note:* Percentages in parentheses for married spouse-present and married spouse-absent categories are based only on the currently married population.

levels of mortality among black males, widowhood resulted in more women than men heading families following the death of a spouse. Because there were more widows than widowers, children were more likely to live without a father than without a mother. Even the relatively modest levels of widowhood among younger women could have deprived a meaningful number of young black children of their fathers.[31]

Adult mortality also represented a threat to marriages among white farm couples (table 11). Among whites, the death of a spouse accounted for the largest share of disrupted marriages—nearly three out of four. Among younger couples (twenty to thirty-four), the prevalence of widowhood was about two and one-half times greater for black women than for white and roughly one and one-half times greater for black men. The racial differential at older ages was much smaller because mortality took an increasing toll on black and white marriages alike. The impact of mortality, however, was considerably weaker among white families than for blacks.

By 1940 widowhood had become somewhat less common for African

*Table 11.* Current Marital Status of Ever-Married White Men and Women on Southern Farms, by Age, 1910 and 1940

| | 1910 | | 1940 | |
|---|---|---|---|---|
| Age | Female | Male | Female | Male |
| 20–34 years | | | | |
| Married | | | | |
|   Spouse present | 96.0% (98.9) | 95.6% (98.7) | 94.6% (97.2) | 95.4% (97.2) |
|   Spouse absent | 1.1　(1.1) | 1.2　(1.3) | 2.7　(2.8) | 2.7　(2.8) |
| Divorced | 0.4 | 0.5 | 1.1 | 0.9 |
| Widowed | 2.5 | 2.6 | 1.7 | 1.0 |
| 35–49 years | | | | |
| Married | | | | |
|   Spouse present | 92.0% (99.3) | 94.0% (99.3) | 92.3% (98.1) | 94.8% (98.2) |
|   Spouse absent | 0.6　(0.7) | 0.7　(0.7) | 1.4　(1.9) | 1.8　(1.8) |
| Divorced | 0.4 | 0.4 | 0.7 | 0.9 |
| Widowed | 7.0 | 5.0 | 5.6 | 2.5 |
| 50–64 years | | | | |
| Married | | | | |
|   Spouse present | 77.2% (98.2) | 88.5% (98.4) | 80.3% (98.1) | 89.6% (97.3) |
|   Spouse absent | 1.4　(1.8) | 1.4　(1.6) | 1.6　1.9) | 2.5　(2.7) |
| Divorced | 0.6 | 0.6 | 0.7 | 0.8 |
| Widowed | 20.8 | 9.5 | 17.4 | 7.2 |

*Sources:* 1910 and 1940 Integrated Public Use Microdata Series, Social History Research Laboratory, University of Minnesota.

a. Percentages in parentheses for married spouse-present and married spouse-absent categories are based only on the currently married population.

American farmers, however the change was less than dramatic (table 10). Only among the younger couples (twenty to thirty-four) can the decline be described as substantial—36 percent for females and 67 percent for males. The prevalence of widowhood among older black couples remained stable between 1910 and 1940. As a result, mortality, especially after middle age, remained a potent threat to the longevity of black marriages during the 1930s. The relative toll of widowhood on the marriages of black farm couples did decline over time, however, primarily because of the increase in spousal separations. Although mortality accounted for roughly two-thirds of all marital disruption in 1910, it was responsible for less than half (47.4 percent) by 1940.

White farmers enjoyed a more significant decline in widowhood between 1910 and 1940 (table 11). By 1940 white farm couples were approaching the modern situation in which mortality is a serious threat to family stability only at the older ages. That decline produced an even sharper race differential in widowhood in 1940, especially at younger ages. In 1910, for example, black women thirty-five to forty-nine were roughly one and one-half times more likely to be widowed than white women; by 1940 they were more than twice as likely. For whites, however, widowhood remained the dominant cause of marital disruption in 1940 (50.7 percent), primarily because spousal separations did not increase as sharply for whites.

## Separation

In contrast to the generally declining threat from mortality during this period, the marriages of black farm couples were exposed to an increasing risk of disruption through spousal separation.[32] Early in the century, relatively few current marriages for African Americans were disrupted through spousal separation (table 10). The vast majority of currently married black couples were living together, and at no age were more than 5 percent of spouses absent from their current marriage. In 1910 separations accounted for only about one-quarter of all marital disruptions experienced by black farm couples, although that percentage had increased substantially by 1940. The percentage of currently married women with an absent husband, for example, increased by 84 percent for those twenty to thirty-four and by 130 percent for those between thirty-five and forty-nine. As a result of this trend, by 1940 spousal separations and mortality accounted for roughly equal shares of the marital disruptions experienced by black farm couples of all ages (43.8 percent and 47.4 percent, respectively).

White farm couples also experienced a rise in the proportion of current marriages with spouses living apart (table 11). Spousal separations accounted for a larger percentage of all marital disruption for white couples in 1940 than in 1910 (35 percent versus 17 percent, respectively). Despite the growing frequency of absent spouses among white couples, however, their absolute level of marital separation in 1940 remained substantially below the levels observed for blacks in 1910. That considerable race differential is consistent with Pagnini's and Morgan's conclusion that southern black couples were less likely to value marital stability "at all costs" than were whites.[33]

## Divorce

Divorce was extremely unlikely to terminate the marriages of southern farm couples, either black or white (tables 10 and 11). In contrast to the trends for widowhood and separation, divorce remained relatively stable as a cause of marital disruption among black farm couples between 1910 and 1940. Less than 10 percent of all marital disruption among black farm couples was the result of divorce in both periods. Divorce among white farm couples increased somewhat more than it did for blacks between 1910 and 1940 but continued to account for a far smaller percentage of all marital disruptions than did widowhood or spousal separations.

In sum, mortality was the most significant threat to the stability of black and white southern farm marriages between 1910 and 1940. Compared with mortality, divorce was a relatively rare event for this population and never posed a significant threat to marital stability. Although most current marriages, for both races, were intact, a meaningful minority was disrupted through the absence of a spouse—especially for African American couples— and the likelihood of spousal separation rose substantially between 1910 and 1940. From the perspective of married farm couples, the proximate causes of marital disruption were in flux. From the perspective of children, however, both mortality and parental separation resulted in the same outcome. They removed at least one parent from farm households and altered the living arrangements of children.

## The Living Arrangements of Children on Southern Farms

Contemporary accounts of life in the rural South early in the twentieth century suggest that the children of African American farmers were exposed to significant risks of family disruption, which often meant that they lived in households in which only one or neither parent was present.[34] The oral histories collected during the Federal Writers' Project contain many references to children living with only one parent or to those who had been taken in by kin or friends of the family. The causes for such fosterage were varied—parental death, absence, or indifference. A black man in Louisiana, for example, reported, "I ain't had no children by this wife but I been raisin' Lucien. He ain't no blood kin to me, he's my wife's nephew. His mother an' father is dead an' they willed him to her so I been takin' care of him."[35] A white male sharecropper in North Carolina also told of raising several children who were not his own: "I call Robert my son, though we never had no children of our own. We took Robert, some o' Mary's kinfolks, when he was six months old aster [after] we found out his mother didn't want to keep him, and I reckon he's close to us as a own son would be. We're raisin', or tryin' to, three more children o' somebody else's. This little boy and two of his sisers was Mary's brother's children, and when he died we tuk 'em here with us to do the best by 'em we could."[36]

Census data from 1910 attest to the substantial proportion of black farm children who did not live with both parents (table 12 and fig. 8).[37] One out of every five who were fourteen or younger lived in disrupted families. The likelihood of living with both parents was especially low among older children (74.9 percent), largely because of a higher probability of older parents dying. Even the youngest farm children (zero to four), however, had nearly a one-in-seven chance of living in a household where at least one parent was absent. In contrast, even the oldest white child had a greater probability of living in an intact family than did the youngest black child (86.6 percent versus 85.3 percent, respectively). As might be expected from previous references to the matrifocal black family that emerged in the rural South after emancipation, it was more common for black children to live with only their mothers (9.2 percent). Equally influential in

*Table 12.* Living Arrangements of Southern Farm
Children, by Race and Age, 1910 and 1940

|  | 1910 | | 1940 | |
|---|---|---|---|---|
|  | Blacks | Whites | Blacks | Whites |
| **0–14 years** |  |  |  |  |
| Both parents | 79.9% | 91.3% | 76.6% | 91.4% |
| Mother only | 9.2 | 3.7 | 9.4 | 4.2 |
| Father only | 2.6 | 2.6 | 2.9 | 1.8 |
| Neither parent | 8.3 | 2.4 | 11.1 | 2.6 |
| **0–1 years** |  |  |  |  |
| Both parents | 88.1 | 96.7 | 82.9 | 95.2 |
| Mother only | 7.3 | 2.1 | 7.4 | 2.8 |
| Father only | 0.8 | 0.5 | 1.2 | 0.7 |
| Neither parent | 3.8 | 0.6 | 8.6 | 1.3 |
| **0–4 years** |  |  |  |  |
| Both parents | 85.3 | 95.6 | 81.0 | 94.4 |
| Mother only | 8.5 | 2.5 | 8.2 | 3.2 |
| Father only | 1.3 | 0.9 | 1.6 | 0.7 |
| Neither parent | 4.9 | 1.0 | 9.2 | 1.7 |
| **5–9 years** |  |  |  |  |
| Both parents | 79.1 | 90.9 | 76.6 | 92.1 |
| Mother only | 9.0 | 3.7 | 8.9 | 3.8 |
| Father only | 2.9 | 2.9 | 3.0 | 1.8 |
| Neither parent | 9.0 | 2.5 | 11.5 | 2.3 |
| **10–14 years** |  |  |  |  |
| Both parents | 74.9 | 86.6 | 72.3 | 88.2 |
| Mother only | 10.3 | 5.3 | 11.1 | 5.6 |
| Father only | 3.5 | 4.1 | 4.1 | 2.6 |
| Neither parent | 11.3 | 4.0 | 12.4 | 3.6 |

*Sources:* 1910 and 1940 Integrated Public Use Microdata Series,
Social History Research Laboratory, University of Minnesota.

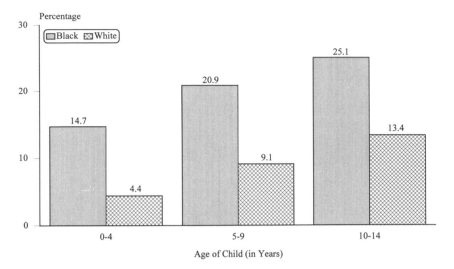

Figure 8. Percentage of Southern Farm Children Not Living with Both Parents, by Age and Race, 1910. (*Source:* 1910 Integrated Public Use Microdata Series, Social History Research Laboratory, University of Minnesota.)

shaping their living arrangements, however, was the sizable percentage who were living with neither parent (8.3 percent).

How do these patterns of residence for southern farm children in 1910 compare with those for children living elsewhere? Among African Americans, southern farm children zero to fourteen were more likely to live with two parents (79.9 percent) than were their southern counterparts not living on farms (65.8 percent) or black children living in the North (77.3 percent). Place of residence had relatively little bearing on the living arrangements of white children, however. White southern non-farm children were somewhat less likely to live with both parents (87.5 percent) than were those on farms (91.3 percent). Similar patterns by type of residence existed in the North: 92.2 percent for farm children and 89.3 percent for non-farm children. Thus, neither the evidence for blacks nor that for whites suggests that southern farm children were exposed to higher rates of family disruption near the turn of the century than were children who lived in other areas.

Between 1910 and 1940 the situation worsened for black farm children as the likelihood of living in a disrupted family rose by 16 percent. The increase was especially sharp at the youngest ages. Children under four experienced a 29 percent jump in the probability of living in a disrupted family, whereas the increase for older children (ten to fourteen) was a more modest 10 percent. Contributing to those deteriorating living arrangements were relatively large increases in the proportions of African American farm children, especially younger ones, who lived with neither parent. The living arrangements of white children changed relatively little over the years, however. Those over five enjoyed small improvements in their chances of living with both parents (figs. 8 and 9). Those divergent trends led to a growing racial gap among southern farm families in the proportion of children who lived with one, or neither, parent.

By 1940 African American children on southern farms enjoyed a substantially higher probability of living with two parents than did southern children not living on farms (67.2 percent) or black children living in the North (67.6 percent). The 16 percent increase in the prevalence of disrupted families among black southern farm children between 1910 and 1940 was dwarfed by the corresponding 43 percent increase in the North. Among whites, the residential variation in living arrangements of children in 1940 remained virtually identical to those observed in 1910.

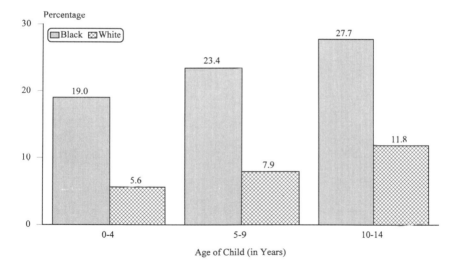

Figure 9. Percentage of Southern Farm Children Not Living with Both Parents, by Age and Race, 1940. (*Source:* 1940 Integrated Public Use Microdata Series, Social History Research Laboratory, University of Minnesota.)

A substantial group of African American farm children in both 1910 and 1940 lived apart from both parents (8.3 percent in 1910 and 11.1 percent in 1940). Who were these children? And with whom were they living? In 1910 the majority lived with other relatives, although the pattern of co-residence varied somewhat by age and time period. Younger children were more likely to live with grandparents—58 percent of zero to four-year-olds and 48 percent of those five to nine. Although most older children also lived with relatives (82 percent), they were less likely than younger children to reside with grandparents and more likely to live with other relatives, especially aunts and uncles. In 1940 most "parentless" children lived with relatives, and even more lived with their grandparents. Among the youngest age group, those residing with grandparents grew to 75 percent; 58 percent of the older children did so. Most of the remaining children lived with other relatives, especially aunts and uncles.

It appears then that southern black farmers had a broad network of kinfolk who were willing (or at least able) to take care of children when neither parent could. Others have referred to the existence of such a network for African Americans and have concluded that it represents a cultural characteristic, perhaps even an inheritance from African family traditions in which child fosterage was relatively common.[38] Of course, it is also possible that such residence patterns simply reflect the black community's adaptation to a relatively serious level of marital disruption. Children from disrupted families had to live somewhere, and the best option available was to live with nearby relatives.

Without additional information it is impossible to adjudicate definitively between these conflicting interpretations. The oral histories collected during the Federal Writers' Project may prove to be helpful, however. In most cases, when interviewees mentioned the reason that they were supporting a child of relatives (or non-relatives) it was because of some crisis that affected the parents—usually death, desertion, or illness. Despite such anecdotal evidence, McDaniel and Morgan claim that child fosterage was not the result of crises facing black families. Although intriguing, their empirical analysis of child fosterage in 1910 is only suggestive of the underlying causes of the larger proportion of African American children living away from both parents. Until more definitive evidence becomes available, it seems most reasonable to assume that most cases in which children did not live with parents were the result of necessity rather then cultural preference. That does not mean, however, that African American family patterns were not affected by cultural influences.[39]

## The Role of Non-Marital Childbearing

The considerable threat of marital disruption experienced by black farm couples clearly influenced the living arrangements of children in the affected families (figs. 8 and 9). In some cases, however, children lived with only their mothers because their parents were not married and not cohabiting. The living arrangements of these children were the result of non-marital childbearing rather than marital disruption. There is ample anecdotal evidence of illegitimacy in the southern farm population, such as Johnson's account of nineteen-year-old Stanley Byrd, who had fathered a child with a woman he would not marry because "she was too dark." The oral histories gathered during the Federal Writers' Project also contain descriptions of non-marital childbearing. Perhaps it was such evidence that led Nicholas Lemann to describe the rural South as "the national center of illegitimate childbearing."[40]

It is difficult to obtain empirical evidence of non-marital childbearing during the early decades of this century. Some insights may be gained, however, by examining the marital status of mothers as reported in the 1910 and 1940 censuses. Although admittedly crude, I will assume that the percent of mothers who reported themselves as "never married" at the time of the census provides a reasonable indication of the level of non-marital childbearing.[41] Only a minuscule percentage of black mothers on southern farms had never been married—less than 1 percent in 1910 and 1940 (table 13). If taken at face value, that evidence suggests that non-marital childbearing did not play a significant role in determining the living arrangements of African American children in 1910 or 1940. Furthermore, the drop in percentage of never-married mothers between 1910 and

Table 13. Percentage Never Married among Mothers of Children Ages 0–14, by Residence and Race, 1910 and 1940

| Residence | Black | | White | |
|---|---|---|---|---|
| | 1910 | 1940 | 1910 | 1940 |
| Southern farm | 0.89 | 0.45 | 0.02 | 0.07 |
| Southern non-farm | 2.89 | 1.07 | 0.23 | 0.09 |
| Northern | 0.81 | 0.81 | | |
| Northern farm | | | 0.02 | 0.03 |
| Northern non-farm | | | 0.04 | 0.09 |

Sources: 1910 and 1940 Integrated Public Use Microdata Series, Social History Research Laboratory, University of Minnesota.

1940 suggests that the declining proportion of children living with two parents was not the result of increasing non-marital childbearing. Residential contrasts in the percentage of mothers who were never married do not support Lemann's characterization.

Using the reported marital status of mothers as the only indication of the level of non-marital childbearing is somewhat risky. Many women undoubtedly married after experiencing a birth out of wedlock and therefore would be considered "ever-married" at the time of census enumeration rather than "never married." To partially circumvent that problem we can examine the living arrangements of infants—children less than one year old (table 12). I shall assume that the majority of those infants living with their mother only were born out of wedlock. In addition, some large (although unknown) percentage living with neither parent were also likely born to unmarried women and then turned over to kinfolk to raise. Non-marriage is not the only possible reason for why these infants did not live with both parents. One or both parents may have died during the year (or less) since the child's birth, or they could have been away from the home at the time of census enumeration. Despite these alternative explanations, the living arrangements of infants provide additional evidence of non-marital childbearing not available from the marital status of mothers.

The living arrangements of southern farm infants suggest a somewhat higher incidence of non-marital childbearing. In 1910 about one in nine (12 percent) African American infants was not living with both parents. Most lived with their mothers only, but many lived with neither parent. Only about 3 percent of white infants did not have both parents present in the household, which suggests a much lower level of non-marital fertility. Between 1910 and 1940 the likelihood of African American infants not residing with both parents rose sharply to one in six. Although the proportion of infants living only with their mothers remained relatively constant, the proportion residing with neither parent jumped sharply (by 126 percent). The proportion of white infants living with both parents also fell during this period, but the change was much more modest and left more than 95 percent residing with their mothers and fathers.

In view of the sharp rise between 1910 and 1940 in the proportion of African American infants living apart from both parents it may be useful to once again examine more carefully the specific living arrangements of this group. That is, with whom were they living? Like their older counterparts, African American infants not living with either parent were most likely to be residing with grandparents—68 percent in 1910 and 74 percent in 1940. Those who were not living with grandparents were most likely to reside with other relatives, primarily aunts and uncles.

The "truth" about the level of non-marital childbearing in the farm South probably lies somewhere between the evidence based on the marital status of mothers and that for the living arrangements of infants. The former tends to underestimate the level, and the latter tends to overestimate it. It is likely safe to conclude that non-marital childbearing was more common within the African American farm population than among whites and that its incidence rose between 1910 and 1940. As a result, it did contribute to the relatively high, and growing, proportion of black children who did not live with both parents. In contrast, neither type of evidence suggests extraordinarily high levels of non-marital childbearing among black southern farmers. Those levels were dramatically lower than is observed within the African American population at the close of the twentieth century.

## Conclusion

The emphasis throughout this chapter has been on the sources of marital disruption and their deleterious effects on the living arrangements of children. However, most married couples—indeed, large majorities— still lived together at the time of the census. Further, most farm children lived with two parents. These general observations are true of both races in both periods. Concern with family disruption should not obscure the fact that southern farm families were quite stable during the first half of the century.[42]

Nevertheless, the southern farm environment was not entirely benign for family life. There were significant threats to the durability of marriages and therefore to the living arrangements of children. In general, African American marriages were at greater risk of dissolution than were the marriages of whites, and black children were less likely than white children to live with both of their parents. These patterns are consistent with the findings of previous investigators who have suggested greater family instability, historically, among the African American population.[43] It also appears, based on the imperfect empirical evidence at our disposal, that higher levels of non-marital childbearing among blacks contributed to the decreased likelihood that African American farm children would live with both parents (or even one parent). Between 1910 and 1940 family instability grew for both blacks and whites, although the change was more substantial for African Americans.

Can these patterns and trends for southern farmers be reconciled with previous work on African American family structure? Truly definitive conclusions would require a much more sophisticated investigation of the causes of the trends and differentials that have only been described here. Still, some tentative observations are in order. The greater vulnerability of African American marriages and the concomitant implications for the living arrangements of children might be interpreted as support for explanations that emphasize the effects of the legacy of slavery on black family structure. That is, an unstable (and somewhat more matrifocal) family institution, which evolved during the years of slavery, extended into the twentieth century. Likewise, the living arrangements of black farm children—especially the higher proportion who lived with neither parent—could be viewed as support for the existence of the inheritance of an African ancestral heritage that included extensive child fosterage. Thus, the static racial differentials described in this chapter are generally consistent with cultural interpretations of black family structure during this era.

It is much more difficult, however, to reconcile the trends in African American family stability between 1910 and 1940 with such cultural explanations. It seems likely that any legacy of slavery or African heritage should have had a weakening influence on African American family patterns over time. More conservatively, there is little reason to expect such cultural influences to have intensified. Yet that is exactly what is observed. Between 1910 and 1940 the characteristics of black family structure generally associated with these cultural influences grew more exaggerated. African American marriages became more vulnerable, and more black children were living apart from one or both of their parents. Therefore, it seems that the shifting fortunes of black farm families must be attributed to other social forces that operated during this era. Foremost among them were the Great Depression and the massive migration of rural blacks.

The economic distress caused by the depression and the disruptive effects of migration on family life in the South could have produced the trends in African American family stability described in this chapter. Why were the trends more dramatic for blacks than for whites, who were also exposed to these same social forces? Undoubtedly, that question requires a more complex answer than can be provided here. I suspect, however, that an adequate answer must be based on the more marginal social and economic position of African Americans in southern society. Economic and social discrimination assured that most southern blacks enjoyed less opportunity, and suffered more serious financial hardship, than most southern whites—even in the best of times. In the worst of times those chronic disadvantages were likely translated into even more intense social disorganization, including increased family instability.

As things grew more difficult for blacks in the rural South, or as better opportunities became available elsewhere, more and more individuals and families made the difficult decision to leave their farms. Some moved to nearby southern cities. Others bet their futures on the promise of greater freedom and opportunity in the North. Inevitably, increased geographic mobility posed an additional threat to family stability. Spouses were separated, and children were left with relatives. Because of its potentially profound impact on southern farm families, the migration of this population deserves careful examination. That topic is taken up in the following chapter.

# 6

# The Mobility of
# Southern Farm Families

The image of southern sharecroppers abandoning their run-down cabin in a truck piled high with personal belongings remains fresh in the American memory. John Steinbeck's description of the exodus to California in *The Grapes of Wrath* captured the public's attention during the Great Depression, and the Joad family became a prototype for the thousands of families forced onto the road by the economic havoc, agricultural change in the South, and failing southern soil. There was much fact in Steinbeck's fiction, and the serious dislocation and hardships he described in *The Grapes of Wrath* and other books reflect the true experiences of many southern farm families—black and white—during the 1920s and 1930s. Many can still recall family struggles to find new opportunity during that time of so little opportunity. The experiences of some of these families were also captured by the 1940 U.S. Census, which was conducted before the country had emerged from the Great Depression and which devoted much more attention than any previous census to the migration histories of the American population.

## Migration before World War I

When social scientists study migration, they often focus, implicitly or explicitly, on push and pull factors. In order to determine the potential for migration within a given population, at a particular time, they ask two key questions: What incentives are operating to motivate people to leave the place they live (push factors), and what attractions exist elsewhere to draw people away from their current residence (pull factors)? Although somewhat simplistic, push and pull factors provide a convenient framework around which to organize a discussion of the historically specific motivations for geographic mobility. A more complete picture is gained when one also considers obstacles that may have discouraged potential migrants from following through on their migratory desires. In some situations even the strongest push and pull forces are inadequate to overcome financial, social, logistical, or legal impediments to migration.[1]

Before World War I, southern farmers were exposed to a variety of push factors, many of which varied by race and social class. Poor farmers, black and white alike, especially tenants, had ample reason to want to escape, or at least to improve upon, current situations—whether that meant exchanging a current landlord for a better one nearby or moving much greater distances. They suffered many hardships that may have motivated them to move: perennial debt, poor health, inadequate access to education, and limited potential for upward social mobility.

Some push factors were colorblind, but others were not. Black farm families had additional incentives to relocate, perhaps even to leave the South entirely. By the early twentieth century they had been politically disenfranchised through the passage of restrictive voting legislation in virtually all southern states.[2] Formal and informal mechanisms were in place to deny them the ability to compete economically on an equal footing with whites.[3] State and county governments allocated outrageously unequal financial support for black and white schools, resulting in vastly inferior educational opportunities for African American children.[4] Between 1900 and 1915 alone, southern mobs lynched 845 blacks.[5] As a result of these and other push factors, pressures were building among southern farmers for migration during the pre-war era, especially for blacks. Yet were there equally strong opportunities attracting them elsewhere?

Early in the century the forces pulling southern farmers to alternative locations were likely somewhat weaker than the push factors creating an incentive for them to leave. Pull factors also varied by race and class. Farm-to-farm migration had long been a tradition. The availability of cheap and fertile land lured owners and renters alike to relocate—especially toward the Southwest and West as new agricultural territory opened. An alternative landlord offering better or more land, more generous credit, or a more pleasant personality could entice tenant families to abandon one situation for another. It was such circulation within the southern plantation economy that led to the adoption of "anti-enticement" laws and other strategies in an effort to restrict the mobility of farmers.

In general, however, non-farm opportunities within the South did result in some movement to urban areas but were not strong enough to lure most families away from their agrarian roots. Non-agricultural opportunities were limited before World War I, especially for African Americans. Modest industrial development in the South had created some non-agricultural employment opportunities early in the century, and textile mills attracted many white families into company textile towns.[6] Blacks were not especially welcomed in textile mills, however, or in most other manufacturing establishments except for the most menial of jobs.[7] In cities, black males were employed primarily as unskilled laborers, and females were most likely to toil as domestic servants.

Those potential migrants who turned their eyes to the North or West also saw relatively few attractive opportunities. Those areas had experienced much more industrial expansion and urban growth than the South by the early twentieth century, developments that created a plethora of non-farm employment opportunities. Unfortunately for prospective migrants from the South, however, immigration to the United States had also reached unprecedented levels during the first decade of the century. Between 1901 and 1910 nearly nine million people entered the country, roughly one new immigrant for every one hundred residents.[8] While previous waves of immigrants often made their ways to the nation's agricultural heartland, the new immigrants, mainly from southern and eastern Europe, settled primarily in large urban centers of the northeast and north central regions.[9] With such a large supply of cheap workers, which replenished itself each year, northern industrialists and employers had little reason to recruit from below the Mason-Dixon Line, especially among an African American population they judged to be inferior to immigrants.

There were also a variety of obstacles to overcome for those southern farmers who had decided that it was in their best interest to relocate. Distance was a serious problem, because travel was difficult and expensive before World War I. The costs and inconvenience of resettlement could also be serious impediments to mobility. That was especially true of the pioneering cohort of migrants who could not rely on support and assistance from a group of friends and relatives that had migrated before them. Add to these obstacles the cultural adjustments that came from abandoning agrarian pasts for city life, and the challenges facing potential migrants appear overwhelming indeed.

According to Jay Mandle, African American southern farmers faced an additional set of constraints that restricted their geographic mobility in the late nineteenth and early twentieth centuries. They had always enjoyed some freedom of mobility within the plantation economy, but opportunities for mobility outside of the plantation economy, or outside of the southern region itself, were extremely sparse. Influential southern whites were able to erect obstacles to black migration, partially by restricting the potential for the development of pull forces that would have encouraged mobility among black farmers. Mandle identifies a set of obstacles they erected in an effort to protect an abundant supply of black farm tenants and laborers: restrictions on land ownership, lack of non-plantation employment opportunities in the South, employment discrimination in the North, impediments to labor recruitment within the South, and debt peonage.[10]

Although not included in Mandle's list, even violence was sometimes used to limit the ability of tenant farmers to sell their labor. It was common for them and other black laborers to accumulate debt throughout the year as they borrowed from employers to buy food, clothing, or other necessities. Often that debt continued from year to year, leading to a form of peonage that tied workers to their current landlord or employer. White planters and employers enjoyed nearly unrestricted freedom in enforcing the conditions of their employees' indebtedness, including the right to engage in armed pursuit of "escaped" workers and force them to return to work. Laborers who resisted ran the very real risk of injury or death at the hands of employers or employers' hired thugs.[11]

What was the result of these disparate forces on the migratory behavior of southern farmers? Clearly, they moved during the pre-war era as they had for decades. The limited available evidence suggests that most moves were over a relatively short distance, generally from one farm to another. Rural-to-urban and south-to-north relocations were considerably less common. Although many farmers were exposed to strong push forces, the attractiveness of destinations outside the southern agricultural economy were comparatively anemic—if they were known at all. In addition, African Americans were exposed to a unique set of constraints on their freedom to move. Important changes were on the horizon, however, as the effects of World War I began to be felt.

## Migration and World War I

During the second decade of the century the balance of push and pull factors operating on southern farmers changed significantly. Although many of the same pressures (e.g., landlessness, debt, and penury) continued to make some look elsewhere for opportunity, important new events increased the intensity of those pressures even more. Perhaps the most important of these was the arrival of the boll weevil and its disastrous effects on cotton production.

The weevil is a relatively innocuous-looking creature, but its destructive work on cotton plants can be devastating. When able to develop, the "squares" of the cotton plant mature during the summer and then break open into white, fluffy balls of cotton near picking time in the fall. If the weevil has invaded the squares to lay its eggs, however, the squares fail to mature properly and therefore do not produce usable cotton. In *All God's Dangers: The Life of Nate Shaw,* the boll weevil is described as "a very creepin fellow, he gets about too; he'll ruin a stalk of cotton in a night's time."[12] Before the weevils' work was done, they had put in many a good night's work.

The weevil's march of devastation began in the 1890s, when it first entered the United States from Mexico. After crossing the border into Texas, it proceeded on a northeastern course. By the turn of the century it had nearly reached Louisiana, and by 1920 it had made its way into North Carolina and Florida. Not all cotton-growing areas were equally hard-hit, but when boll weevils arrived their impact on cotton production could be swift and dramatic. That was certainly the case for cotton farmers in Greene County, Georgia. In 1919 roughly twenty thousand bales of cotton were ginned in Greene County, a nearly unprecedented crop. As the weevil penetrated central Georgia, the cotton crop in Greene County shrank to thirteen thousand bales ginned in 1920 and reached a nadir of only 333 bales in 1922.[13] Many of the farmers whose crops were ruined by the boll weevil were unable to turn a profit and were forced to relocate—especially those who barely made it from year to year during the best of times. Some looked for alternative arrangements in nearby areas that had not yet been affected by the weevil or had recovered from a previous infestation. Others made more dramatic transitions away from the agricultural life altogether. Whatever their destinations, however, there can be little doubt that the boll weevil represented a powerful push factor for many southern farm families.

Nature stuck a second blow when devastating flooding occurred in parts of the South in 1916 and 1917. Like the boll weevil infestation, the floods had a serious impact on agricultural production and displaced legions of farmers—especially tenants who could no longer produce a crop on the flooded land. Despite the obviously temporary nature of the disruption, many Mississippi landlords were unable or unwilling to "carry" tenants who had been rendered idle and therefore unproductive by the natural disaster. Henderson Donald described how the floods in Alabama resulted in increased migration: "During the spring and summer of that year [1916] the rivers overflowed their banks and the water therefrom destroyed the crops throughout a large portion of the state. This made it necessary for both farmers and tenants to find other means of livelihood. The customary advances in money and provisions to the Negro tenants were cut off and in many cases the owners of large plantations were compelled to advise their Negro laborers to move away."[14]

A final, internal pressure for migration began to build after World War I as the size of the southern rural population continued to grow. The rural South maintained relatively high levels of fertility well into the twentieth century (chapter 4). There was also some progress in reducing mortality, even though death rates in the rural South remained higher than those in other parts of the country. As a result of persistently high fertility and falling mortality, the rural population grew sharply from natural increase. As Gunnar Myrdal pointed out, "The agricultural South is over-populated, and this over-population affects Negroes much more than whites. . . . In this Black Belt the over-population has—on the whole—been steadily increasing."[15] Although the consequences of rapid population growth would become more severe in later periods, the effects could be felt even in the early post–World War I years as increasing soil erosion and the development of a labor surplus caused many farmers to think about moving on.

As the pressures for out-migration continued to build, events outside the South increased the attractions of the North. The single most important change in this respect was the virtual cessation of immigration from Europe. As World War I intensified, the previously heavy flow of migrants was disrupted as hostile nations sought to hold on to potential combatants and international travel became logistically difficult. The immediate impact of the war on U.S. immigration was profound; the number of Europeans admitted to the country plummeted from 1,058,391 in 1914 to only 197,919 in 1915.[16]

Following the war, an intensified nativist mentality combined with the protectionist interests of organized labor to create strong pressure for anti-immigration legislation. In previous decades the United States had allowed racist sentiments (again coupled with economic paranoia) to result in immigration policies that effectively restricted the entry of Chinese, Japanese, and other Asian nationalities. Less enthusiasm had existed, however, for the restriction of immigration from Europe. After the national origin of European immigrants shifted toward the south and east, however, concern grew over the implications of immigration for the "complexion" of American society. At the same time, respected scientists were telling the country that the new foreign stock was biologically, intellectually, and culturally inferior to the northern and western Europeans who had dominated earlier waves of immigration.[17]

For those who were not persuaded by the xenophobic arguments of the eugenicists and nativists there was always the straightforward and appealing argument that immigrants took jobs away from native-born Americans. Combined, these concerns resulted in the imposition of immigration quotas that sharply reduced the number of migrants from southern and eastern Europe. The U.S. Congress took a first stab at establishing a quota system when it passed the Quota Act of 1921, which set a ceiling on immigration from each country defined as 3 percent of the foreign-born population from that country as of 1910. In addition, the law allowed for roughly 350,000 "quota immigrants" each year. Finding the new restrictions unsatisfactory, anti-immigration forces revised the law by passing the Immigration Quota Act of 1924. That law altered the formula for determining the ceiling on immigration to 2 percent of the foreign-born population from each country as of 1890. Subsequent refinements to the new quota laws imposed even more stringent limits on the potential for legal immigration. Although immigration from Europe persisted after the restrictive laws were established, its scale diminished substantially.[18]

With the flow from the immigration spigot reduced to a relative trickle, northern employers were forced to find a substitute for the immigrant labor force on which they had relied for so long. That need was especially critical during the war years as northern industries accelerated production in order to provide the materiel required to fight the European war. They turned their attention to the South and its previously untapped pool of workers, and labor agents spread out to lure workers northward. They promised wages that were unheard of in the South, especially in agricultural areas, and even promised to arrange for the migrants' transportation to the North.

Despite the efforts of southern states to restrict the activity of labor agents—by charging exorbitant fees for a license to operate or, in some cases, by threatening the agents with physical violence—the strategy of northern industrialists was successful. A south-to-north migration stream of unprecedented strength developed between World War I and the Great

Depression. Eventually, that stream would result in a dramatically altered geographic and residential distribution of the U.S. population.[19]

The first large-scale relocation of blacks from the South to the North in U.S. history is now called the Great Migration. Because many push factors that encouraged blacks to leave the South (e.g., economic deprivation, political disenfranchisement, and violence) had existed previously, the timing of the Great Migration is best explained by the emergence of opportunities in the northern economy. The central importance of that economic promise is evident in the letters of migrants and potential migrants that were collected by Emmett Scott and published in a 1919 issue of the *Journal of Negro History*.[20] A good example is the letter written by a farmer from Fort Gaines, Georgia, who was searching for northern employment in the face of recent agricultural disasters:

> *Dear Sir:* Replying to your letter dates Oct. 6th [1916] the situation here is this: Heavy rains and Boll weavel has caused a loss of about nine thousand bales of cotton which together with seed at the prevailing high prices would have brought $900,000.00 the average crop here being eleven thousand bales, but this years' crop was exceptionally fine and abundant and promised good yeald until the two calamaties hit us.
>
> Now the farmer is going to see that his personal losses are minimised as far as possible and this has left the average farm laborer with nothing to start out with to make a crop for next year, nobody wants to carry him till next fall, he might make peanuts and might not, so taking it alround, he wants to migrate to where he can see a chance to get work.[21]

Expectations for greater freedom, and reduced exposure to the risk of violence, were also instrumental in decisions to relocate. One letter-writer from Troy, Alabama, expressed well the combined economic and non-economic motives operating on potential migrants:

> *Dear Sirs:* I am enclosing a clipping of a lynching again which speaks for itself. I do wish there could be sufficient presure brought about to have federal investigation of such work. I wrote you a few days ago if you could furnish me with the addresses of some firms or co-opporations that needed common labor. So many of our people here are almost starving. The government is feeding quite a number here would go any where to better their conditions. If you can do any thing for us write me as early as posible.[22]

At the same time that the push and pull forces operating on southern farmers were intensifying, some key obstacles to migration became less daunting. First, and most important, expanding opportunities for high-wage employment in the North helped weaken restrictions on mobility among blacks in the plantation economy that Mandle and other scholars have described. The lack of alternatives had long been a central element of the tight grip that southern planters used to retain their low-cost, compliant work force.

A second factor in the weakening of obstacles to migration was the more efficient spread of information about the alternative opportunities that did exist. Information about the advantages of potential destinations plays a critical role in affecting the motivation to move and influencing decisions of where to move. Northern labor agents were very effective at letting those considering migration know about employment opportunities outside the South, including information about specific employers. The "black press," especially the *Chicago Defender*, was also instrumental in publicizing northern opportunities. During the Great Migration the *Defender* was relentless in extolling the virtues of northern life and contrasting them to the economic and social inequality of the South. After initial hesitance, the newspaper became a strong advocate for the migration of blacks and made effective use of stories and illustrations describing the horrors of southern lynching and the injustices of debt peonage. It even went so far as to organize the "Great Northern Drive" of May 15, 1917, during which a massive exodus of African Americans was supposed to occur. Although contraband in many areas of the South, the *Chicago Defender* enjoyed wide albeit surreptitious circulation. As a result, its anti-South, pro-North, and pro-migration message was no secret to most southern blacks.

As the war and subsequent events led to increasing geographic mobility prior migrants became another important conduit for information about potential destinations. They also served as a source of support for newly arriving relatives and friends. Many provided temporary accommodations as new arrivals sought their own places to live. In addition, some were able to introduce newcomers to potential employers or at least help identify the most promising employment opportunities. Such assistance was able to reduce significantly the monetary and psychological costs of relocation and thereby partially neutralize an important obstacle to migration.

More and more southern farmers began moving to nearby cities between World War I and the Great Depression, and the flow of southern migrants to the North grew to massive proportions. Between 1910 and 1920, for example, the state of Mississippi lost 129,000 blacks through net outmigration; South Carolina, Georgia, and Alabama each lost more than seventy thousand. The loss of white population from these states was even greater in absolute terms, although a smaller proportion of the states' white populations. Mississippi lost 198,000; South Carolina, 79,300; Georgia, 94,000; and Alabama, 111,700.[23] Many of these migrants were leaving southern farms.

## Migration during the Great Depression

Conventional wisdom dates the beginning of the Great Depression from the stock market crash that occurred in October of 1929. In fact, the depression had arrived considerably earlier in the lives of southern farmers. That was due to a mix of interrelated factors that worked against their economic security. First, although southern farmers had always been subject to year-to-year fluctuations in the prices paid for their crops, they experienced a more long-term decline in the ratio of farm income to retail prices beginning around 1920. That deterioration in purchasing power had a deleterious effect on the standard of living and reduced access to credit. Second, long-term abuse of the southern soil took a brutal toll on the fertility of the land and required increasing amounts of fertilizer just to maintain the same level of productivity. Third, continued population growth in the rural South created a larger and larger surplus population that could no longer be sustained by the limited amount of arable land at the same time that increasing farm mechanization began to alter labor demands in southern agriculture. Finally, non-farm employment opportunities for farmers began to dry up as the depression began to spread to other sectors of the southern economy, denying access to wages that traditionally had supplemented family incomes.

For the most part, southern farmers had not been prosperous—even in the best of times. The hardships caused by the Great Depression pummeled an already staggering population and drove it even closer to economic distress and failure. T. J. Woofter and Ellen Winston have described the devastating effects of the depression on rural Americans, especially southerners, in *Seven Lean Years*. During the hardest period, between 1931 and 1937, "the effects of industrial collapse were piled upon the effects of agricultural disadvantage."[24] Landless tenants and croppers were particularly vulnerable.[25] As Woofter and Winston describe depression-era conditions in the cotton-intensive areas of the Southeast ["Eastern Cotton States"]:

> Living conditions are often deplorable. In 1934 almost one in four of all houses of white farmers and almost one in three of all houses of Negro farmers in the Eastern Cotton States had no sanitary facilities whatsoever. Food is scant in

quantity and poor in quality, and a diet too largely composed of meal, salt pork, and molasses results in high sickness and death rates. In 1930 the seven Eastern Cotton States had almost two and one-half times as many deaths from pellagra, a dietary disorder, as all the rest of the states in the registration area together. High birth rates continue to add to an already excessive rural population.[26]

The deterioration of conditions among southern farmers brought on by the Great Depression increased substantially the strength of push factors motivating them to relocate. So, too, did some of the New Deal policies of the federal government that were intended to improve conditions for the farmers. The Agricultural Adjustment Act (AAA) of 1933 had probably the greatest impact on dislocation; one program within the act encouraged giving the exhausted soil a rest by withdrawing parts of farms from cultivation. In return, the federal government paid participating farmers to compensate them for the income they were losing. Although the government intended for tenant farmers to be included in the compensation scheme, those plans frequently were thwarted at the local level. Instead, landlords withdrew tenant land from production, forcing thousands of families to move even further down the agricultural ladder and either become wage laborers or leave farming altogether. All the while, the landlords continued to profit from the idle land.[27]

Compounding the problem of dislocation caused by the withdrawal of acreage from cultivation was the decision by many landlords to use their government subsidies to buy tractors and further mechanize crop production. Depending on the specific crop involved, tractors effectively reduced the need for laborers; Pete Daniel has estimated that the 111,399 tractors introduced into cotton-growing states displaced somewhere between one hundred thousand and five hundred thousand farm families.[28] Farm owners—especially wealthier ones—benefited nicely from the AAA and were able to weather the economic storm brought on by the Great Depression. Most tenants and croppers, however, were not so fortunate.

Many southern farmers decided to move in response to the deteriorating conditions during the depression; still others were forced to move because of economic insolvency or federal policy. The depression also had a powerful effect on the pull of alternative opportunities available elsewhere, however. Industrial production and manufacturing activity felt the effects of the depression somewhat later than the agricultural sector, but when they did the impact was dramatic. In 1926 the U.S. unemployment rate stood at only 1.8 percent; by 1933 it had soared to more than 25 percent.[29]

A former tenant farmer near Clarkesdale, Mississippi, stands in front of his children and a tractor. With the introduction of farm machinery such as tractors, many share-croppers were displaced and the labor value of their children reduced. (Photo by Dorothea Lange, Library of Congress, LC-USF34-17479-E)

The strong demand for labor that had helped drive the massive migration of the pre-depression era had evaporated.

Still, Americans continued to move, even in the grimmest of times. Displaced farmers were forced to find another way to make a living. Some simply moved to non-farm dwellings in the countryside and worked for wages on nearby farms. Others sought to improve their fortunes in southern cities or in the North or West, even though the depression made it less

A family of black farm laborers became interstate migrants as they moved from Arkansas to Mississippi. (Photo by Dorothea Lange, Library of Congress, LC-USF34-18952-E)

likely that those destinations could offer much hope of economic betterment. Indeed, the flow of south-to-north migrants continued during the depression years, although at a slower pace.

## Southern Farmers on the Move during the Great Depression

When the U.S. population was enumerated by the census in 1940 the country was still mired in the Great Depression. Even if the seven lean years were over, fat years had not yet returned. It was in 1940 that the Bureau of the Census introduced a line of inquiry that had not been included in previous censuses but would be repeated in all subsequent ones: People were asked to report information about where they were living at some time in the recent past, in this case 1935. By comparing current residence in 1940 with previous residence in 1935, it is possible to examine in some detail the migratory behavior of Americans during the later years of the Great Depression. That information can be used to determine a number of important facts about all individuals. Did they change residences between 1935 and 1940? If they moved, it is also possible to determine whether they crossed a county line or a state line or moved from a farm and what distance (in miles) they moved if they crossed a county line. To some extent other characteristics of individuals can be incorporated to describe race and class differences in these migration-related behaviors. I use these data for the 1940 census to examine two general types of migration by southern farmers. First, I describe the migration histories of married couples who lived on southern farms in 1940. Second, I expand the focus beyond those couples to compare the characteristics of all individuals who left southern farms between 1935 and 1940 with those who remained behind.[30]

### Recent Migration History of Southern Farm Couples

Where did the individuals identified as "southern farm couples" in 1940 live in 1935 and how extensive was their mobility between 1935 and 1940? Did levels of migration differ significantly by race and class? Was it more common for "movers" to travel relatively short distances or to undertake longer treks? How do mobile and sedentary couples differ, if at all?

Although relatively little attention has been devoted to the migration patterns of southern farmers during the depression, scattered evidence suggests that renters (especially sharecroppers) moved more frequently than owners and, within classes, that whites were more mobile than blacks. In his detailed study of farm tenancy in the Cotton South, T. J. Woofter noted the relatively high levels of mobility of renters and ascribed it to the plantation-style of farming that was so prevalent: "The lack of written contract between tenant and landowner, and the fact that the tenant has no legal claim and receives no recompense for improvements he may make on the property, deprive the cotton tenant farmer of that incentive which leads to stability."[31] In language similar to that Jay Mandle would use forty years later, Woofter offered an explanation for the lower mobility of southern black farmers: "The relative stability of the Negro families may indicate that Negroes are less free to circulate territorially than whites and that their stability is the result of conditions to some extent forced upon them by circumstance. The Negro is certainly in a less favorable bargaining position than the white."[32] Similar conclusions were reached by Arthur Raper and his colleagues based on their extensive investigations of southern farm life during the Great Depression.[33]

Evidence gleaned from the 1940 census is only partially consistent with contemporary descriptions of mobility among southern farmers. Considerable mobility occurred between 1935 and 1940; fully 59 percent of all farm couples changed residences at least once during those five years. Consistent with previous descriptions, renters were significantly more mobile than owners; 76 percent of tenant couples and 36 percent of owner couples moved between 1935 and 1940. In contrast with previous evidence, however, race differences in residential mobility were quite small, controlling for class. Roughly three-quarters of farm renters of both races moved, whereas 36 percent of white owners and 34 percent of black owners did so.[34] Perhaps previous inferences of greater mobility for African American farmers ignored the substantial class variation in migration. If owners and renters are lumped together, for example, 66 percent of black couples and 57 percent of white couples moved during this five-year period. The much higher percentage of renters among African American farm couples accounts for their higher overall level of residential mobility.[35]

What was the nature of mobility for the sizable percentage of farm couples that did move between 1935 and 1940? Farm-to-farm movement was clearly dominant, accounting for at least 80 percent of all moves regardless of race or class (table 14). Among recent movers, however, whites were more likely to have non-farm origins, as were owners of both races. The latter differential may reflect a period before the 1940s when couples saved to muster the financial resources for a downpayment on a farm. That is, during a period of "asset accumulation" they may have lived in non-farm dwellings and perhaps been engaged in non-agricultural employment.

Most mobile farm couples also moved within a relatively small geographic area, with the majority of migrants of both races and classes remaining in their county of origin. Only about one in ten of all black couples who moved crossed a county line, with a slightly higher percentage of inter-county moves among renters than owners. Although whites were somewhat more likely than African Americans to move from one county to another (15.2 percent), intra-county mobility was still the norm. White renters also exhibited a somewhat stronger propensity for inter-county

*Table 14.* Characteristics of Moves for Couples Living on Southern Farms in 1940 Who Moved between 1935 and 1940, by Race and Class

|  | Farm Origin 1935[a] | Different County, 1935[a] | Median Distance Moved (miles)[b] |
|---|---|---|---|
| Black owners | 91.3% | 8.1% | 28 |
|  | (301) | (412) | (26) |
| Black renters | 95.9% | 10.1% | 31 |
|  | (2,906) | (3,976) | (359) |
| All black couples | 95.4% | 9.9% | 30 |
|  | (3,207) | (4,388) | (385) |
| White owners | 84.6% | 12.8% | 38 |
|  | (2,574) | (3,506) | (375) |
| White renters | 89.6% | 16.3% | 37 |
|  | (5,981) | (7,793) | (1,173) |
| All white couples | 88.1% | 15.2% | 37 |
|  | (8,555) | (11,299) | (1,548) |

*Source:* 1940 Integrated Public Use Microdata Series, Social History Research Laboratory, University of Minnesota.

*Note:* Number of cases in parentheses.

a. Reported as percentage of migrants.

b. Intercounty moves only.

migration than white owners (16.3 percent and 12.8 percent, respectively). Among couples who did change their county of residence between 1935 and 1940, the average (median) move was only between thirty and forty miles, with whites moving somewhat longer distances than blacks.[36]

The image that emerges from the evidence available in the 1940 census is one of a highly mobile population that confined its moves to a relatively restricted geographic area. Most farm couples changed residences between 1935 and 1940, and the large majority of those who did move remained in the same county and had farmed before they moved. Although the specifics of that image may differ somewhat from earlier descriptions of the mobility of southern farmers, the broader picture is generally consistent with those descriptions.

It is clear from the evidence available in the 1940 census that residentially mobile farm couples belonged, disproportionately, to the renting class—and that was true for both blacks and whites. Further contrasts between the characteristics of mobile and sedentary farm couples suggest only modest differences (table 15). On the one hand, movers were considerably younger than stayers. Among blacks, for example, the husbands in residentially mobile couples were about five years younger than husbands

*Table 15.* Comparison on Selected Characteristics of Movers and Stayers among Southern Farm Couples, by Race and Class, 1940

|  | Husband's Age (mean years) | Husband's Schooling (mean years) | Wife's Schooling (mean years) | Family Size (mean) | Number of Cases |
|---|---|---|---|---|---|
| Black owners |  |  |  |  |  |
| Movers | 48.5 | 4.2 | 5.3 | 4.9 | 449 |
| Stayers | 54.0 | 4.1 | 5.2 | 5.0 | 854 |
| Black renters |  |  |  |  |  |
| Movers | 39.5 | 3.6 | 4.7 | 4.8 | 4,240 |
| Stayers | 45.3 | 3.4 | 4.4 | 5.4 | 1,558 |
| White owners |  |  |  |  |  |
| Movers | 45.4 | 7.2 | 8.0 | 4.6 | 3,768 |
| Stayers | 53.1 | 6.9 | 7.6 | 4.5 | 6,767 |
| White renters |  |  |  |  |  |
| Movers | 39.2 | 6.2 | 7.0 | 4.7 | 8,329 |
| Stayers | 43.9 | 6.4 | 7.2 | 4.9 | 2,481 |

*Source:* 1940 Integrated Public Use Microdata Series, Social History Research Laboratory, University of Minnesota.

in residentially stable couples, regardless of class. That age difference is consistent with migration patterns for other time periods and populations, which typically are characterized by greater mobility among younger groups. On the other hand, there do not appear to have been large or consistent differences between movers and stayers in educational attainment or family size.

Because age, education, and family size are interrelated, the crude comparisons presented in table 15 may not reveal the true differences between movers and stayers. Older couples are more likely than younger couples, for example, to have fewer years of schooling and larger families. A better idea of the net differences in migration status by a particular characteristic (e.g., education or family size) can be obtained by simultaneously controlling for other characteristics (e.g., age). That can be accomplished through a multivariate logistic regression analysis that uses husband's age, husband's education, and family size (plus race and class) to predict migration status (movers versus stayers).[37] The results from such an analysis are reported in table 16 and indicate the influence of each characteristic on migration status, net of all other variables included in the equation.[38]

Consistent with the previous evidence, younger couples and renters were much more likely than older couples and owners to move between 1935 and 1940. Furthermore, once all other variables are controlled, it appears that residential mobility was significantly more common for couples with

Table 16. Coefficients from Logistic Regression
Analysis of Migration History (Movers vs.
Stayers) for Southern Farm Couples, 1940

| Independent Variable | Coefficient |
| --- | --- |
| Race (black) | –0.19*** |
| Class (renter) | 1.51*** |
| Husband's age | –0.03*** |
| Husband's schooling | –0.03*** |
| Family size | –0.04*** |
| Intercept | 1.47*** |
| Number of cases = 27,627 | |

*** denotes statistical significance at p ≤ .001

fewer children and less education. Those differences were not apparent in table 15, no doubt because of the relationships among age, education, and family size. Furthermore, black couples were significantly less likely to have moved between 1935 and 1940, once race differences in class, age, schooling, and family size are taken into account.

A better idea of the full implication of these differentials in residential mobility can be gained by using the results of the analysis to estimate the probability of moving for two contrasting groups of couples. I have defined "migration-prone" couples as those who rent their farms and are one standard deviation below the mean on husband's age, husband's schooling, and family size. Conversely "migration-averse" couples are those who own their farms and are one standard deviation above the mean on husband's age, husband's schooling, and family size. Separate comparisons between these two groups are made for blacks and whites. For blacks, the probability of moving for the migration-prone group was .823; for the migration-averse, .213. For whites, the probabilities were .853 and .246, respectively.

To be sure, these definitions of migration-prone and migration-averse couples represent arbitrary combinations of characteristics. Nonetheless, the probabilities illustrate that the combined social and economic characteristics of farm couples could have had a striking impact on their migration behavior—resulting in differentials of residential mobility that vary by a factor of nearly four. It should be recognized that by increasing the assumed differentials on age, schooling, and family size the contrast between the two groups could be made even more dramatic. Yet the underlying conclusion remains the same: The migration histories of southern farm couples varied markedly according to their personal characteristics as well as their location in the class structure.[39]

*Leaving the Farm, 1935–40*

Some people residing on farms in 1935 decided to abandon farm life altogether and, when enumerated in the 1940 census, were living in non-farm
dwellings. Twelve percent of African Americans and 15 percent of whites
who resided on southern farms in 1935 no longer did so in 1940. Some
had moved from a farm to a non-farm dwelling in a rural area within the
same county; others left the countryside altogether and moved to towns
and cities in the South. Still others severed their southern roots entirely and
moved north or west.

A common type of off-farm migration saw struggling tenants leaving the
agricultural economy for mill work, although that type of movement was
much more common for whites than for blacks. Oral histories collected
by the Federal Writers' Project include a number of stories describing such
experiences. One FWP interviewer related the migratory experience of a
white man living in South Carolina: "He says that he came to Newberry
Cotton Mills with his father and mother when he was fourteen years old,
they having come here from a farm in the piney woods section of the Dutch
Fork, because they were not making anything much on the farm and they
thought they might do better in the mill."[40] A white woman, also in South
Carolina, recalled her family's decision to leave the agricultural economy
and turn to mill work, although the move proved to be only temporary:
"When I was thirteen, pa decided it would be better to move to a mill town
where us children could work. We came to Columbia, and I got work in a
weave room at fifty cents a day. But even with us children at work, we had
a hard time. And pa wasn't satisfied. He loved to farm and wanted to go
back to the country. Then his aunt died and left him a little money. That
decided him to go back and start farming again."[41]

The vast majority of off-farm migrants remained in the South—blacks
(91 percent) as well as whites (85 percent).[42] Among those who left the
region, whites were most likely to go west (56 percent), whereas the primary destinations for black inter-regional migrants were in the north central region (54 percent) or the Northeast (33 percent). Relatively few white
inter-regional migrants ventured to the Northeast (6 percent), and blacks
were relatively unlikely to migrate west (13 percent). The most popular
states outside the South chosen by black migrants were New York and
Illinois; whites were most likely to end up in California or Ohio.

Although the typical move for off-farm migrants was within the South,
and even within the same state, many made moves that represented a

significant break with their pasts. Nearly half, blacks and whites alike, changed their counties of residence between 1935 and 1940, and roughly half of inter-county migrants moved to a different state. Furthermore, nearly one in three black migrants and one in four white migrants ended up in metropolitan areas in 1940. The average (median) distance moved for those who crossed a county line was about seventy-one miles for blacks and eighty-eight miles for whites, nearly twice the average distance traveled by southern farm couples who had moved between 1935 and 1940.

An idea of the selectivity of off-farm migration can be gained by comparing the characteristics of migrants and non-migrants, as was done earlier for southern farm couples. On average, off-farm migrants were slightly more likely to be female than were non-migrants. Off-farm migrants were also about six years younger than those who remained on southern farms, consistent with the earlier observation that residentially mobile farm couples were younger than sedentary couples. Finally, migrants of both races had completed about one year of schooling more than their sedentary counterparts.

In general, these comparisons suggest only relatively minor differences between the characteristics of those individuals who abandoned southern farms between 1935 and 1940 and those who stayed behind. Once again, however, in order to estimate the net influence of each characteristic on off-farm migration it is useful to conduct a logistic regression analysis that simultaneously considers all relevant characteristics as predictors of migration history. All of the predictors, except gender, are related statistically significantly to migration off of southern farms between 1935 and 1940 (table 17). Off-farm mobility was more common for younger white males with more years of schooling. The substantive implications of these statistical relationships can be demonstrated even better by determining the probability of migration for two ideal types: the migration averse and the migration prone (as was done for farm couples earlier). In this case, the migration averse are females who have ages that are one standard deviation above the mean and educations one standard deviation below the mean. The migration prone are males who have ages one standard deviation below the mean and schooling one standard deviation above the mean. The probability of moving off of a southern farm between 1935 and 1940 for migration-prone blacks was .209; for migration-averse blacks, .074. For whites, the probabilities were .232 and .083, respectively.

The combined influence of these characteristics on off-farm migration is more modest than was observed for the similar estimates made for the

*Table 17.* Coefficients from Logistic Regression Analysis Comparing Movers (20 and Older) between 1935 and 1940 to Those Who Stayed on Southern Farms

| Independent Variable | Coefficient |
| --- | --- |
| Race (black) | –0.13*** |
| Gender (male) | 0.02 |
| Age | –0.03*** |
| Schooling | 0.05*** |
| Intercept | –1.05*** |
| Number of cases = 80,214 | |

*** denotes statistical significance at $p \leq .001$
*Note:* Movers are defined as those who moved to the North (farm or not) or to a non-farm in the South.

migration history of farm couples. The probability of migration for the migration prone and the migration averse differed by a factor of roughly three for both blacks and whites. An African American with migration-prone characteristics, for example, had nearly a 21 percent chance of leaving the farm between 1935 and 1940. In contrast, an African American with migration-averse characteristics had only about a 7 percent chance of doing so. In sum, even though those who were younger and better educated were more likely to abandon southern farms, having those characteristics was certainly no guarantee of off-farm mobility.

## Occupations of Off-Farm Migrants

How did migrants make a living once they had abandoned southern farms? Not surprisingly, only a relatively small percentage of off-farm migrants reported agricultural occupations, which is understandable given the relative paucity of those who moved to farms outside the South. Of those black migrants reporting an occupation in 1940, only about one in four continued to work in agriculture, most as farm laborers. It is likely that many within this group were former tenant farmers who were forced by agricultural changes in the South to move to non-farm residences but who continued working as wage hands on nearby farms. That was a common occurrence as federal policies and increased farm mechanization displaced tenant farmers and increased the demand for agricultural wage workers. Most black migrants reporting non-agricultural occupations held jobs as unskilled laborers or operatives. An even smaller 16 percent of white male migrants maintained agricultural employment after moving off farms. Of

course, the panoply of occupations available to those whites was much
wider than for blacks. Although many whites who entered non-agricultural occupations also worked as unskilled laborers, it was much more
common for white migrants than African Americans to become craftsmen
or proprietors. Although they, too, had abandoned southern farms, black
men continued to suffer the consequences of severe occupational discrimination in the larger American economy.

The occupational distributions for female migrants who left southern
farms between 1935 and 1940 suggest two racial differences. First, black
women were much more likely than white women to report an occupation of any kind; roughly half of black women and one-quarter of white
women were gainfully employed. That is consistent with the relatively well-
known pattern of greater labor force participation among African American women that has persisted historically. Second, nearly 70 percent of
employed black women reported "domestic service" occupations—house-
keepers, laundresses, and servants for private families. Again, that occupational concentration agrees with many earlier descriptions of the history
of work for African American women in the United States.[43]

Movement away from farms involved a substantial shift into the non-
agricultural economy for blacks and whites alike. It is equally clear that
white migrants enjoyed greater access to the wider variety of jobs in the
non-farm marketplace. Even if their initial non-farm job was relatively
unskilled and undesirable, there was potential for upward occupational
mobility. That was far less true for black migrants, for whom the repertoire of first non-farm jobs was much more restricted and upward mobility a long shot at best.

## Conclusion

The population of southern farmers experienced considerable residential
mobility between 1935 and 1940. Most couples living on southern farms
in 1940 had moved at least once since 1935. Tenant families were especially likely to move, as were less-educated younger couples with smaller
families. The typical move by these farm couples did not cross county lines,
and those that did covered a distance of only thirty to forty miles. In addition, many southerners abandoned their farms entirely between 1935 and
1940. The majority remained in the South, but many relocated to new
counties. Off-farm migration was significantly more common among the
younger and better-schooled population.

These patterns of mobility were the result of various push and pull factors—in the South and North or West—that affected the motivation to move. Changes in the southern agricultural economy as a result of depression, federal policy, mechanization, and soil exhaustion displaced many families. Although inter-regional migration slowed considerably during the depression, some southerners continued to search for opportunity in northern and western cities. Those southern farmers who abandoned the region between 1935 and 1940 perpetuated a migration stream that had evolved from a trickle to torrent during and after World War I. That same stream continued to carry them northward and westward in huge numbers during and after World War II. Before the massive interregional migration had run its course, the African American population had experienced a fundamental redistribution. A population that historically had been southern and rural grew more likely to reside outside of Dixie and became disproportionately urban. There are some who claim that the legacy of the era of interregional migration is more than demographic—that southern migrants, especially rural folk, carried with them a cultural heritage that had a profound effect on life in northern and western cities. That is the issue to be considered in chapter 7.

# 7

# To the City

To this point my discussion has focused nearly exclusively on the family lives of farmers in the South—how they married, built families, made a living, kept their families together, and changed residences. In this chapter I will change that focus significantly and follow those southern farmers from the countryside of Dixie to inner cities outside the South. Although the southern farm experience remains important within this changed focus, it does so more as a backdrop than as the centerpiece for the discussion. The transition is legitimate because the migratory behavior of the farmers resulted in a pronounced southern presence in northern cities.[1]

It is natural to wonder, then, how the experiences of these migrants, with a distinct background and cultural heritage, differed from those of their new neighbors who did not share in the southern experience—at least so recently as the migrants. What interests me is whether southern migrants to the North were more likely than native northerners to experience family disorganization. In other words, did a "southern legacy" threaten the stability of family life in northern cities? There is a strong tradition in the sociological literature that claims there was. Indeed, it has become conventional social science wisdom to assume that the families of migrants were at greater risk in their new urban milieu. Surprisingly, however, little effort has been expended to examine that assumption critically. Finally, I also depart from the approach used in previous chapters by extending the temporal focus to the present. By definition, a legacy must have time to develop, and it is better to take a long view when attempting to discern its existence and persistence.

## Leaving the South

During and after World War II, southern migrants were increasingly likely to head northward and westward in search of opportunity. Definite migration streams carried them to specific destinations in the North and West. The Illinois Central Railroad provided residents of the Mississippi Delta with convenient access to Chicago.[2] Families from around Abbeville, South Carolina, followed one another to Philadelphia.[3] A newer stream of migration took farmers from parts of Texas and Oklahoma to the West Coast, especially California. Because most of these migrants were pursuing economic opportunities they did not enjoy in the South, and because the northern opportunities were located disproportionately in cities, their mobility established a strong linkage between the rural South and the urban North.

Individual migrants were driven by personal motives and ambitions—a better job, higher wages, improved schools, more freedom, or safety from mobs. The connection that their relocation created between the rural South and urban North, however, was the result of larger social and economic forces far outside their control. World War I created a labor vacuum in northern cities by fueling wartime production and cutting off the immigration of low-wage workers from southern and eastern Europe. World War II had a similar stimulating effect on northern industries, while immigration remained relatively low as a result of restrictive legislation adopted in the 1920s. For the first time during the 1940s, southern migrants began to move westward in large numbers as the armaments industry expanded rapidly in California. In the South, New Deal programs encouraged the reorganization of agricultural production by paying landowners to let land lay fallow, resulting in the displacement of thousands of tenant farm families. Other New Deal policies led directly to the increased mechanization of southern farming, which further displaced tenants and agricultural wage workers. With the introduction of mechanical cotton harvesters in the 1940s, southern agricultural production was fundamentally altered. The demand for tenants and wage laborers dwindled dramatically, and many were driven from the bucolic South to the metropolitan North.[4]

The scale of the northward migration was truly impressive, especially for African Americans (fig. 10). Blacks began to leave the South in significant numbers only after 1910, especially after the beginning of World War I. Between 1910 and 1930 the percent of southern-born blacks living outside the region grew from 5 to 13 percent. Migration slowed somewhat during

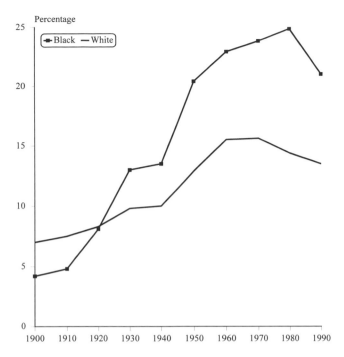

Figure 10. Percentage of Southern-Born Population Living Outside the South, by Race, 1900–1990. (*Sources:* 1900–1970 data
from U.S. Bureau of the Census [1975]; 1980 and 1990 data
from Integrated Public Use Microdata Series, Social History
Research Laboratory, University of Minnesota.)

the Great Depression but soared after World War II, and by 1950 more than
20 percent of southern-born blacks resided in the North or West. At the peak
of the migration roughly a quarter of the blacks born in the South had moved
to the North or West. It is little wonder that the inter-regional migration
responsible for this trend has been termed the "Second Black Diaspora." The
evidence for whites suggests a generally parallel pattern of movement from
the South, although at a more modest level.[5]

## The Southern Migrants

The impact that these southerners had on northern cities, and their experiences after arriving, depended on the characteristics of the migrants themselves. Naturally, a stream of displaced, unskilled, illiterate, agricultural
workers would be expected to have a different effect on their places of

destination than would migrants who were disproportionately well-educated urbanites.

Prior work has provided somewhat conflicting portraits of southern migrants. Carter Woodson claimed that blacks migrating before the Great Migration were drawn disproportionately from the "talented tenth" of the southern black population and were more likely to be educated and have some type of occupational skill than those who remained.[6] As the pace of northward migration intensified, however, the portrait of the migrants painted by many contemporary observers began to change. In her study of migrants to Philadelphia around 1920, Sadie Farmer Mossell observed, "With few exceptions the migrants were untrained, often illiterate, and generally void of culture."[7] E. Franklin Frazier's extensive writing about African American families in Chicago gives the definite impression that the majority of migrants to that city were drawn from the rural South and arrived with rough edges and very little human capital: "The movement of Negroes from the rural South to cities has probably been the most significant episode in Negro life since emancipation."[8] He also notes that "among the migrants there were thousands of ignorant and impoverished peasant families released from the customary controls of rural southern communities."[9] Finally, Charles Johnson offers a similar description in the report compiled for the Chicago Commission on Race Relations following the race riot of 1919: "Much of the adjustment was a double process, including the adjustment of rural southern Negroes to northern urban conditions. It is to be remembered that over 70 per cent of the Negro population of the South is rural. This means familiarity with rural methods, simple machinery, and plain habits of living."[10] Johnson further cites a study of migrants to Chicago done by the Chicago School of Physics and Philanthropy that showed that 58 percent of the families were from rural locations.

More recent scholars have also described a southern migrant population with largely rural origins. Like Frazier and Johnson before him, James Grossman focused on Chicago for his study of black migration to the North. His discussion reinforces the description of southern migrants offered by contemporary observers: "The movement had to have drawn heavily upon the impoverished farmers and laborers who constituted the overwhelming proportion of black southerners."[11] Grossman also notes that the migrants were no doubt positively selected from the southern population as a whole.

Nicholas Lemann's examination of the lives of southern migrants to Chicago after World War II implies a continuation, perhaps even intensification, of the migration stream described by Du Bois, Mossell, Frazier, Johnson, Grossman, and others. Lemann's migrants are disproportionately rural southerners who were forced to move after the introduction of mechanical cotton pickers left them without jobs. The economic dislocation caused by increasing farm mechanization was especially severe for sharecroppers, who, Lemann suggests, represented a large share of migrating southerners. Lemann further asserts that the composition of the southern migratory population had significant dysfunctional consequences for northern cities.[12]

Other scholars have presented evidence that forces us to hesitate before uncritically accepting the conventional wisdom about the characteristics of southern migrants. Horace Hamilton and Stanley Lieberson have concluded, for example, that better-educated southern blacks were more likely to migrate than were their less-educated neighbors. Lieberson found a much higher net out-migration rate for literate blacks from World War I through about 1930. Hamilton, observing a continuation of this pattern, infers a higher probability of migration among the more educated segments of the southern black population into the post–World War II era.[13] If educated southern blacks were more likely to move North, how could the migrant population be as rural, agricultural, and uncultured as so many social scientists and commentators have claimed?

Drawing upon the earlier work by Lieberson and others, Carole Marks insists that prior descriptions of black southern migrants as predominantly agricultural refugees were largely wrong. For her, migrants were the "displaced mudsills" of southern industrial development rather than a suddenly superfluous agricultural labor force. That is a key distinction because Marks's explanation implies a more urban, educated, and skilled migratory population. She asserts that the stream of south-to-north migrants was more diverse than has been inferred from previous research and describes them as "representatives of a fledgling class of artisans and urban nonagricultural laborers as well as some farm owners and relatively prosperous tenants."[14]

How can these largely contradictory portraits of southern migrants possibly be reconciled? The solution to this puzzling paradox probably lies in the difference between two perspectives on the migration—the view of migrants as a segment of the population from which they originated and the view of migrants as perceived by the receiving population. Hamilton, Lieberson, and Marks are likely correct when they argue that more educated and skilled southern blacks were over-represented among migrants.

Although the well educated were more likely to move North than were other groups of southerners, they were a relatively small segment of the southern black population. Even as late as 1940, for example, more than 40 percent of all southern black households were located on farms and 51 percent of the population resided in rural areas. Also in 1940, southern blacks had completed an average of only five years of schooling, and only 6 percent held high school diplomas.[15] Thus, as Grossman noted, the sheer size of the rural and unschooled southern population during the first half of the century virtually assured that they would dominate the northward migration stream, even if their probability of moving was somewhat lower than their better educated, more skilled, neighbors.

From the perspective of the residents of the northern cities it is therefore understandable that the migrants might have seemed rough and unsophisticated "human flotsam which was tossed into the city streets by successive waves of migration from the South."[16] The contrast between these two different perspectives of the migrants—from the point of view of their place of origin versus the point of view of their destination—can be illustrated by referring to educational differentials. In 1940 black migrants averaged two years of schooling more than similar blacks they left behind in the South but one and one-third fewer than those they joined in the North and West.[17]

## The Migrants' Reception in the North

Before the massive influx of southerners, the northern black population was quite small. In 1910, for example, slightly more than one million African Americans lived outside the South, only about forty thousand of them in Chicago. By 1940 the Great Migration had swelled the non-southern black population to 3.2 million, and more than 270,000 blacks lived in Chicago alone.[18] Other northern and western cities experienced similar growth in African American populations during the same period.

Some within the native-northern black population resented the arrival of the southern migrants and believed that the burgeoning black communities threatened their social, economic, and political well-being. Although still unable to enjoy the full rights and privileges of American citizenship, northern blacks generally were well aware of the advantages they enjoyed over southern blacks. These advantages were made abundantly clear by the black press, the *Chicago Defender,* for example, which provided extensive coverage of the insults of life under Jim Crow and the brutality of

Children playing on the sidewalk in the South Side of Chicago rather than working in the cotton fields as their parents likely did. (Photo by Russell Lee, Library of Congress, LC-USF33-12980-M3)

Two black men sit on a park bench in Chicago rather than in front of a rural country store in the South. By 1941 the African American population of Chicago had swelled to more than a quarter of a million as a result of migration from the South. (Photo by Russell Lee, Library of Congress, LC-USF33-13008-M4)

Some migrants headed west, rather than north, like this field worker in California's Imperial Valley. His shoes, made from the tire on which he sits, suggest that his move to California was not followed quickly by prosperity. (Photo by Dorothea Lange, Library of Congress, LC-USZ62-50849)

southern lynchings. Of Chicago, Frazier noted that "many members of this class of Negroes in northern cities [longtime residents] viewed with alarm . . . the influx of the ignorant masses from the plantations into their communities."[19] Drake and Cayton mention that some of the black "Old Settlers" in Chicago even blamed the migrants for the race riot of 1919, which began when a young black swimmer was stoned by whites for straying outside of the designated "black" area of a local beach.[20] Similar perceptions also existed among native northern blacks in other cities. Sadie Farmer Mossell, for example, mentions that established blacks in Philadelphia blamed the influx of southern migrants for the deterioration of living conditions for all blacks there.[21]

Two factors are responsible for the often disdainful reception of southern migrants by northern blacks. First, their arrival created a clash of cultures within black communities. The rural and agricultural backgrounds of some migrants marked them as rubes whose awkward and unsophisticated behavior reflected poorly on the native northerners. Second, the scale of in-migration to northern cities threatened to disrupt the racial status quo. In general, northern whites were able to tolerate their black neighbors as long as there were not too many of them—and as long as they remained "in their place." Yet as their numbers grew, primarily from the influx of migrants unfamiliar with the etiquette of the status quo, whites grew more and more uneasy.

It was likely the growth of the black population more than the cultural background of the migrants that concerned most northern whites. A minuscule black population could be contained and tolerated relatively easily. Rapidly expanding black communities were more difficult to deal with. Northern whites often turned to violence in their initial responses to the Great Migration. Race riots erupted in many cities, including East St. Louis, Chicago, and Springfield, Illinois, and claimed scores of victims—black and white. Arsonists burned the houses of many black families who dared to move into traditionally white neighborhoods. White gangs brutalized blacks who were not burned out of their homes or who simply wandered into the wrong neighborhoods. Although perhaps failing to match the viciousness of their southern counterparts in their levels of anti-black violence, northern whites were still effective in terrorizing the black community when doing so served their purposes.

Although violence can be an extremely useful technique for controlling minority populations, it is most effective when buttressed by institutional measures. The brutality of southern lynching, for example, would likely have occurred even more frequently if blacks had not also been "controlled" through the adoption of the plantation agricultural system and Jim Crow legislation. These aspects of southern social organization acted in concert to restrict social, economic, and political opportunities, thereby reducing the perceived need for mob violence. Similarly, the long-term response of northern whites to the black migration evolved to include a variety of measures to segregate newcomers residentially. Restrictive covenants, discriminatory real estate practices, urban renewal programs, and other measures assured that blacks in northern cities remained concentrated in certain areas and away from whites.[22] As manufacturing employment and the white population relocated to the suburbs, central cities became more and more isolated from the mainstream community. Jobs grew more scarce and life grew more brutal. Over time, many of these areas became ghettos, suffering from high levels of poverty, violence, drug and alcohol addiction, and disrupted family life.[23] Southern migrants were blamed for many of these social ills.

## The "Dysfunctional" Impact of Southern Migrants

As the pace of migration from the South accelerated and the size of the black population in northern cities swelled, criticism of the newcomers intensified. Native northerners, black and white alike, blamed them for a variety of social ills plaguing urban areas—worsening crime, delinquency, alcoholism, and venereal disease—and often attributed those difficulties to the rural, peasant origins of the migrants.

It was the perception that urban family life was becoming more disrupted and disorganized that received the most commentary, however. Concern grew over the instability of marital unions within the black community. Desertion and divorce were on the rise, more and more families were headed by women, and more children lived with only one parent. Premarital and non-marital sexual activity became increasingly common, as did the number of illegitimate births. Social scientists expressed alarm over a finding that 16.5 percent of African American babies born in the Birth Registration Area in 1943 had unmarried mothers.[24] Although that percentage seems trivial compared with the corresponding figure of two-thirds in the early 1990s, it was nevertheless deemed large enough to be a cause for concern at the time. Many fingers pointed to the southern migrants. It was widely believed that these "deviant" behaviors—desertion, non-marital sexuality, and illegitimacy—were inherent elements in the culture of the plantation South, especially among sharecroppers. That line of argumentation is most obvious in the work of E. Franklin Frazier.

According to Frazier, southern black families were a result of the slavery experience. Families were matriarchal institutions with great tolerance for non-marital sexual relations, illegitimacy, and unstable marital unions. All of these characteristics were part of the general adaptation of African Americans to the conditions of slavery. The same basic family pattern persisted into the post-slavery era. According to Frazier, marriage and parenthood remained somewhat independent, "Motherhood signifies maturity and the fulfillment of one's function as a woman. But marriage holds no such place in the esteem of many of these women."[25] Frazier believed that black families in the rural South were able to survive despite high levels of marital instability and illegitimacy because of the extensive support provided by extended family members, churches, lodges, and other institutions.[26]

Subsequently, according to Frazier, rural migrants carried their culture and family patterns with them to the northern cities, with two important results. First, the simple transplantation of the southern rural family pattern increased the levels of marital instability, illegitimacy, and non-marital sexual contact within the black community. That "composition effect" accounts partially for the trends in family patterns that caused concern among contemporary observers. Second, within their new social milieu migrants could not depend on the same kinds of familial support that they enjoyed in the rural South. Consequently, family patterns that previously were acceptable and accommodated became dysfunctional and problematic. "When one views in retrospect the waste of human life, the immorality, delinquency, desertions, and broken homes which have been involved in the development of Negro family life in the United States," Frazier maintains, "they appear to have been the inevitable consequences of the attempt of a preliterate people, stripped of their cultural heritage, to adjust themselves to civilization."[27]

Although Frazier was no doubt the most prominent proponent for this perspective, he was definitely not alone. As early as the 1890s, W. E. B. Du Bois had made similar observations about migrants to Philadelphia and their influence on family patterns: "The lax moral habits of the slave régime still show themselves in a large amount of cohabitation without marriage."[28] St. Clair Drake and Horace Cayton also echoed many of Frazier's sentiments in their study of the black community in Chicago ("Bronzeville") during the 1940s. They describe similar family patterns and attribute much of the blame to the deleterious impact of southern migrants. Regarding the instability of unions, they contend that "an old southern pattern is intensified and strengthened in Bronzeville. Unstable common-law marriages of relatively short duration alternate with periods of bitter disillusionment on the women's part. The end result is often a 'widow' and her children, caused either by a husband's desertion or by a wife's impetuous dismissal of him."[29]

Drake and Cayton also saw illegitimacy as a social problem that had originated in the southern rural culture of African Americans: "This [tolerant] attitude toward illegitimacy is imported from the South, where on the plantations the masses of the Negro people have historically considered a child a welcome gift, another 'hand' to help make a crop. It is only in the cities that children became 'handicaps,' and illegitimate ones, liabilities."[30] Thus, it was a relatively well-established intellectual tradition that led more recent social commentators to also blame southern migrants, especially those with rural origins, for alarming trends in the family lives of African Americans.[31]

The same thread of reasoning runs through Daniel Patrick Moynihan's warning about the increasingly precarious status of black families.[32] Moynihan, who drew heavily from the work of Frazier, referred to a "tangle of pathology" that surrounded black families in northern cities and attributed "matriarchal" black family structure to a "legacy of slavery." He was criticized severely for implying that a cultural "defect" rather than structural barriers (i.e., economic and social discrimination) was responsible for the characteristics of black families. Despite a flurry of books and articles in response to Moynihan, his identification of a southern origin ("legacy of slavery") for the problems of embattled black families in northern cities has remained a largely untested reassertion of Frazier's conclusion of thirty years before.[33]

The work of earlier social scientists, from Frazier to Moynihan, is clearly evident in the work of Nicholas Lemann. Lemann presents a compelling portrait of a number of families and individuals who migrated from rural Mississippi to Chicago after the introduction of mechanized cotton picking in the 1940s. He tells a disturbing story of extensive marital instability, family disruption, and illegitimacy in housing projects. Eerie similarities connect Lemann's description with the work of Frazier during the 1930s, however the problems he describes are much more severe. Like Frazier, Lemann argues that those problems are largely due to the transplantation of a southern "sharecropping culture" to northern cities, a culture that was "the national center of illegitimate childbearing and of the female-headed family."[34] Those who migrated from that culture encountered the most difficulty in the urban North: "People who had grown up in the sharecropper system—rural, poorly educated, often from unstable families—tended to fare worst."[35]

These are powerful indictments against the migrants, and there is little question that the family life of African Americans in northern cities has undergone a profound transformation. Marriage has become an endangered institution, and non-marital births have become the norm.[36] But is there more than the coincidence of two social trends (migration and family change) to suggest that it was the Great Migration that led to those changes in family life?

Frazier and others present primarily anecdotal evidence to support their contention that migrants are responsible for the deterioration of urban family life. Individual personal experiences and histories are recounted to illustrate the acceptance of illegitimate childbearing or the instability of unions. Drake and Cayton, for example, tell of "Old Ben" and "Baby Chile," two southern migrants living in Bronzeville. They are not married, and Baby Chile has a daughter, "Fanny Mae," by another man. Baby Chile stabs Old Ben with a paring knife after he fails to buy Fanny Mae a Christmas present. The union between Old Ben and Baby Chile is obviously temporary because Baby Chile is interested in starting a "relationship" with "Slick," the apartment building custodian who lives with them. The story of Old Ben and Baby Chile includes virtually all of the important failings of the southern migrant's family life—marital instability, illegitimacy, and sexual promiscuity. But were these characteristics really more typical among migrants than others?

Frazier attempts to offer more convincing evidence to support his argument when he contrasts different residential "zones" within Chicago's black community. His analysis suggests that there is more family instability—illegitimacy and desertion—in the zone with the highest percentage of migrants. It is unclear, however, whether those migrants are from the South or even whether it is they who are having illegitimate children or deserting spouses.

In one of the only empirical studies of the different family patterns of migrants and non-migrants in northern cities, Lieberson and Wilkinson conclude that migrants had more stable families than non-migrants. Using data from the 1960 U.S. Census, they find that "southern blacks living in the North and West differ from their Northern-born compatriots on a variety of attributes. Perhaps the most striking of these is the greater level of family stability found among migrants."[37] Migrants, both male and female, were more likely to have ever married, and, if married, they were more likely to live with their spouse.[38] That evidence contradicts the earlier anecdotal evidence provided by Frazier, Drake and Cayton, and others—at least for the late 1950s.

Was the rural South really the "national center of illegitimate childbearing and of the female-headed family"? Field studies conducted there during the 1930s and 1940s paint a grim picture of the family lives of black sharecroppers. The observations of Hortense Powdermaker, Arthur Raper, Charles Johnson, and others do suggest that marital unions were fragile and illegitimate births common within this population.[39] Early public health studies also showed relatively high rates of venereal disease among the southern black population, suggestive of multiple sex partners and poor hygiene.[40] None of these studies, however, provided the empirical evidence on which to base a conclusion about Lemann's assertion.

Evidence presented in earlier chapters of this book provides some basis for comparing the family patterns of southern farmers with those in the North. The description of marriage patterns in chapter 3 indicated that the southern farm population was definitely not avoiding marriage. In 1940 they were more likely to ever marry, and married earlier, than blacks in the North. Comparative evidence on family structure and stability in chapter 5 showed that black children living on southern farms in 1940 were more likely than their northern counterparts to live with two parents and less likely to have a mother who had never been married. Although admittedly sketchy, these contrasts do not suggest significantly greater instability among southern farm families than among black families in the North.

Thus, prior work on the subject, although it contains tantalizing clues, provides an inadequate foundation on which to base a conclusion regarding the hypothesized dysfunctional effect of black southern migrants on family life in the urban North.

## Family Life among Migrants and Non-Migrants in the Urban North

If, in fact, the families of southern migrants suffered from greater disruption than those of long-term northern residents, then one would expect migrants to have fewer children living in two-parent households, more marriages disrupted by divorce or desertion, and higher levels of non-marital childbearing. The living arrangements of children and women, as described by the post–World War II decennial U.S. Censuses, can be used to determine whether migrant families were more likely to exhibit these characteristics. It is useful to take the long view by examining migrant–non-migrant differences in family structure from 1940 through 1990, because family characteristics can change over time. Black families in inner cities have attracted the most attention among social scientists, therefore it is reasonable to focus on the family structure of African Americans living in the central cities of metropolitan areas in the North and West.

### Living Arrangements of Children

The living arrangements of black children in the urban North, regardless of migration history, remained stable through 1960. Three-quarters of all children living with their mothers also had a father present in 1940, and that percentage dropped only slightly to 72 percent in 1960. By 1970, however, the percentage of children living with both parents had dropped to 59 percent, and to only 33 percent by 1990. That temporal pattern alone appears incompatible with an explanation for family change among African Americans that assigns primary responsibility to the disruptive influence of southern migrants. Why should the consequences of southern migration to northern cities be so much more evident after 1960? Indeed, when southern- and northern-origin children are compared, migrants are more likely than non-migrants to live with both parents.[41] That differential is present in all six decades (fig. 11).

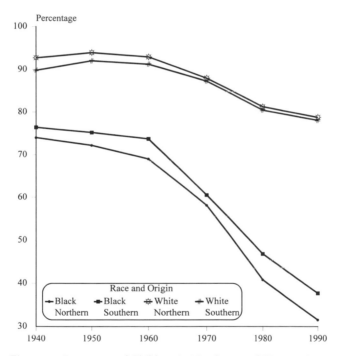

Figure 11. Percentage of Children in Northern and Western Central Cities Living with Two Parents, by Race and Regional Origin, 1940–90. (*Source:* Integrated Public Use Microdata Series, Social History Research Laboratory, University of Minnesota. Only children living with their mothers are considered, to allow better classification by regional origin; see n. 41, p. 209.)

The living arrangements of white children shifted more modestly after World War II. The percentage of white children living with both parents, for example, fell from 93 percent in 1960 to 79 percent in 1990. As a result of these divergent trends for blacks and whites, the race differential in children's living arrangements increased dramatically by 1990, when African American children in northern cities were nearly two and one-half times more likely than white children to live with only one parent. In contrast to the evidence for blacks, whites with southern origins were less likely to live with both parents, although the difference by regional origin was slight for whites, especially after 1960.

Thus, in recent decades decline in the percentage of children living with both parents has been a phenomenon that disproportionately affects African Americans. Although children with southern and northern origins alike have experienced the same general decline, there is a persistent "southern advantage" for these children in northern cities. Increasing "orphanhood" can be rejected as a cause of the decline in paternal presence because these decades saw a general increase in life expectancy for black males. Therefore, the trends in the living arrangements of children after World War II are more likely the result of two changes in the status of mothers: an increase in the extent of marital disruption from causes other than mortality or an increase in the frequency of non-marital motherhood.

### Living Arrangements of Married Women

Is the precipitous decline in the percentage of African American children living with both parents the result of increasing spousal desertion and marital instability, and are migrant children more likely to live with two parents because their parents' marriages are more durable? Trends in the living arrangements of married black women since the 1940s parallel closely trends in the living arrangements of children. After little change in marital disruption between 1940 and 1960 the percent of married women living with their spouse dropped sharply, from 71 percent in 1960 to less than half in 1990. Clearly, the increasing fragility of marriages among African Americans in northern cities increased the exposure of children to living in one-parent families.

Although migrants and non-migrants alike experienced increasing marital disruption, a "southern origin" once again conferred some advantage for greater family stability (fig. 12). With the exception of 1950, ever-married women born in the South were more likely to live with their husbands than were their northern-born counterparts. That is further evidence

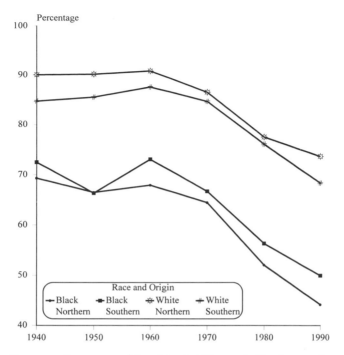

Figure 12. Percentage of Ever-Married Women in Northern and Western Central Cities Living with Spouse, by Race and Regional Origin, 1940–90. (*Source:* Integrated Public Use Microdata Series, Social History Research Laboratory, University of Minnesota. Widows were excluded; women ages 20–49 are included.)

contradicting explanations for family change in the urban North that are based on the importation of cultural norms and values from the rural South. Furthermore, it suggests that greater marital stability among southern-born women is no doubt partially responsible for the higher proportion of these children living with their fathers.

Marital disruption also increased substantially among white women between 1940 and 1990, but white marriages remained significantly more stable than black marriages. In 1990, for example, roughly three-quarters of married white women lived with their spouse, whereas fewer than half of all married black women were doing so. In a further divergence from the family patterns for African Americans, white women with southern origins were less likely than non-migrants to be living with their husbands. The latter difference, of course, is also consistent with the larger proportion of non-migrant white children who were living with both parents.

## Motherhood among Never-Married Women

It is also possible for children to not have a father present in the household because they were born to unmarried women. Thus, non-marital childbearing is a second proximate determinant for the living arrangements of children. Certainly, Frazier, Drake and Cayton, Lemann, and others have cited illegitimacy as an important component of the southern-migrant explanation for family change in northern cities.

The trends in non-marital childbearing for African American women after World War II are striking.[42] After remaining relatively low through 1960, the percent of mothers who had never been married skyrocketed from fewer than 3 percent in 1960 to more than 35 percent in 1990. Once more, the evidence on non-marital childbearing suggests that it was not southern migrants who were primarily responsible for family disruption in northern cities (fig. 13). Although the frequency of non-marital births increased sharply

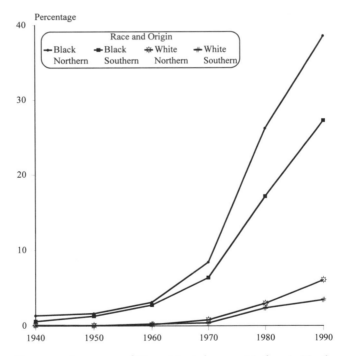

Figure 13. Percentage of Never-Married among Mothers in Northern and Western Central Cities, by Race and Regional Origin, 1940–90. (*Source:* Integrated Public Use Microdata Series, Social History Research Laboratory, University of Minnesota.)

among both migrants and non-migrants after 1960, women with southern origins had lower levels of illegitimacy than their northern-born counterparts in each decade. Furthermore, the differential in non-marital childbearing by migration history grew steadily after 1960 until in 1990 non-migrant mothers were 42 percent more likely than migrant mothers to have never married. Clearly, the large gap in non-marital motherhood for northern- and southern-origin women in 1980 and 1990 must have contributed substantially to the corresponding, and large, difference in the percentage of children not living with their fathers.

Non-marital motherhood among white women remained minuscule until 1980, when it increased to only 3 percent. Even as late as 1990 black mothers were roughly six times as likely as white mothers to never marry. In contrast to the differences by migration history for the living arrangements of children and married women, non-marital motherhood was slightly higher among the southern-origin white population.

It appears that increases in both marital disruption and non-marital childbearing have contributed to the declining proportion of African American children living with two parents since 1940. But which of the two proximate determinants has had the strongest impact on the living arrangements of young children? Between 1940 and 1990 the contribution of non-marital childbearing to paternal absence among black children grew dramatically. In 1940 less than 10 percent of children living in households without fathers were doing so because their mothers had never married; by 1990 that figure had risen to more than 50 percent (fig. 14). In contrast, the contributions of widowhood and marital disruption have both declined since 1940. Although the latter continues to remain a potent force in determining whether African American children co-reside with their fathers, it was less important than non-marital motherhood in 1990. Among whites, non-marital childbearing has also become a more important reason for children not living with a father (fig. 15). Unlike the situation for blacks, however, marital disruption remains the most important reason for children residing separately from fathers. It accounts for a larger percentage of one-parent families in 1990 than it did in 1940.

## The Beliefs of Southern Farmers

Evidence from U.S. Censuses taken after World War II strongly suggests that the families of southern migrants were not at greater risk of disruption than the families of those African Americans with deeper roots in the

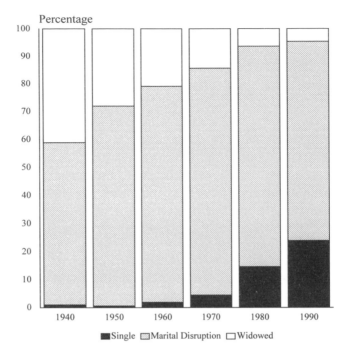

Figure 14. Marital Status of Mothers of Black Children in Northern and Western Central Cities Living without Fathers, 1940–90. (*Source:* Integrated Public Use Microdata Series, Social History Research Laboratory, University of Minnesota. Children are the unit of analysis, so mothers are counted for each child they have between the ages of 0 and 14 years.)

urban North. Traditional arguments also describe important attitudinal differences between migrants and non-migrants, however, claiming that there was something unique about the culture of southern farmers, especially sharecroppers. Within this culture, impulsive behavior is considered likely to overwhelm rational, calculated behavior; profligacy is more common than frugality; and immediate pleasure is seen as a more powerful motivation than deferred gratification. It is largely these attitudinal characteristics that purportedly put migrants from the farm South at greater risk of such social pathologies as crime, alcoholism and drug abuse, venereal disease, poverty, and family breakdown. Yet little or no direct evidence of such attitudinal differences between southern farmers and others has been presented.

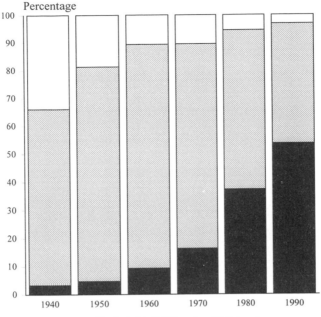

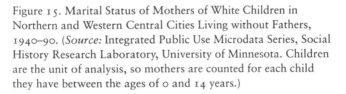

Figure 15. Marital Status of Mothers of White Children in
Northern and Western Central Cities Living without Fathers,
1940–90. (*Source:* Integrated Public Use Microdata Series, Social
History Research Laboratory, University of Minnesota. Children
are the unit of analysis, so mothers are counted for each child
they have between the ages of 0 and 14 years.)

Unfortunately, there is a serious scarcity of systematic attitudinal information for the periods and population groups of interest, although scattered attitudinal evidence was collected by early investigators of life in the
rural South. Charles Johnson, for example, conducted surveys of roughly
two thousand black children there during the early 1940s, including selected attitudinal items.[43] Hortense Powdermaker also gathered attitudinal information in her study of a small town in rural Mississippi.[44] The
original data collected by Johnson, Powdermaker, and a few others are no
longer available, however. Even if they were, they would not provide a basis
for comparing evidence with that for other population groups from whom
they gathered no information.

Although less than ideal, evidence from more recent social surveys can be used to explore the attitudes of southern farmers. The Panel Study of Income Dynamics (PSID) is one such survey that has included relevant attitudinal items and enough subjects to compare the responses of southern farmers and others.[45] In the 1972 cycle of the PSID, heads of families were asked a variety of questions that tapped a diversity of attitudes and beliefs, including some relevant to the long-held assumption about the unique worldview of southern farmers. From those questions, I have selected five that are particularly useful for distinguishing present versus future orientations, willingness to defer gratification, and belief in individual responsibility for life events. Responses to these questions can be used to determine whether southern farmers differed from others in (1) believing that they were able to carry out plans they had made; (2) believing that what happened to them was their own doing; (3) preferring saving to spending; (4) thinking a great deal about the future; and (5) disagreeing that people get good things undeservedly.

Overall, the attitudes of black southern farmers in 1972 were similar to the attitudes of blacks living elsewhere (table 18).[46] The only dimension on which the southern farmers differed significantly from the other groups (southern non-farmers and non-southerners) was their greater tendency to believe that life's events are not their own doing.[47] Although that difference might appear to suggest that southern farmers are less willing to assume responsibility for important life events (successes or failures), it is not

*Table 18.* Selected Attitudes about the Future by Race and Residence, 1972

| | Black | | | White | | |
|---|---|---|---|---|---|---|
| Percentage Who | Southern Farm | Southern Non-Farm | Non-South | Southern Farm | Southern Non-Farm | Non-South |
| Usually carry out plans | 46.8 | 39.5 | 42.0 | 65.0 | 69.0 | 67.1 |
| Think that what happens to them is their own doing | 65.7 | 72.5 | 73.2 | 79.4 | 85.1 | 83.8 |
| Prefer saving to spending | 53.8 | 53.5 | 44.1 | 44.0 | 39.4 | 37.5 |
| Think a lot about the future | 41.2 | 45.8 | 43.2 | 36.5 | 41.6 | 41.5 |
| Do not believe that people get good things undeservedly | 45.2 | 46.8 | 42.6 | 56.9 | 60.3 | 54.9 |

*Source:* Panel Study of Income Dynamics.
*Note:* Residential differences in attitudes are determined while income is held constant (see n. 46, p. 210).

accompanied by similar inter-group differences on the other items. The same residential difference exists for whites.

Responses to other questions in the PSID survey indicated that southern farmers were also more religious than the other two groups. That may have accounted for their somewhat fatalistic belief that life events were outside of their control. Other than a somewhat stronger sense of fatalism, when compared with the other population groups southern farmers were just as likely to (1) carry out plans they have made; (2) think about the future; (3) believe that good things happen to people because they deserve them; and (4) prefer saving money to spending it. In fact, they were significantly more likely than non-southerners to prefer saving to spending. Virtually the same residential differentials were observed for whites.

Although the attitudinal information from the PSID must be considered at best suggestive, it clearly does not provide support for the hypothesis that southern farmers held attitudes significantly different from those observed for other population groups. Nor does it suggest that the attitudes and beliefs of southern farmers put them at greater risk of family disruption or disorganization. One might argue, though, that their northward migration was selective for those with more dysfunctional attitudes, leaving a more conventional population of southern farmers by 1972. If that were the case, then one would also expect the behavioral comparisons made earlier in the chapter to show greater family disruption for southern migrants. In fact, however, adult native northerners were more likely to live apart from their spouses and native northern children were less likely to live with both parents. Combined, the behavioral and attitudinal evidence presented in this chapter points to the inescapable conclusion that southern migrants to the North were participants in—but certainly not the cause of—the dramatic transformation experienced by urban black families during the last half of the twentieth century.

## Conclusion

The evidence since the mid-1940s is unequivocal in its description of changes in family patterns of African Americans living in northern cities. Consistent with the observations of earlier investigators such as Frazier, Johnson, Drake, and Cayton, sharp increases occurred in the percentage of children who lived apart from their fathers, married women not living with spouses, and mothers who had never been married. Yet the data yield no support for the argument that southern migrants were responsible for this transformation in family life. In fact, on virtually every dimension and during all periods it was children or women with southern origins who reported the most stable or conventional family patterns. Southern-born and northern-born alike experienced the same trends. That suggests that the forces responsible for the weakening dominance of traditional family life (co-resident married couples, children living with two parents, and infrequent non-marital motherhood) affected all African Americans living in the central cities of the North. Although those with a southern heritage were somewhat buffered from such forces, apparently all were vulnerable. But why was family disruption less common among those with southern origins?

The evidence of a southern advantage in family patterns is consistent with earlier findings that southern migrants, when compared with northern-born blacks, had higher rates of labor force participation, lower levels of unemployment, higher incomes, and lower levels of poverty and welfare dependency.[48] To the extent that economic status is related to family stability, the southern advantage, therefore, makes sense. Yet why should migrants have compared favorably with non-migrants on these economic characteristics despite their lower levels of education? Perhaps it was because their economic opportunities in the North compared favorably with their recollections of the southern labor market, with its lower wages and more powerful racial discrimination.[49] Or perhaps, as new arrivals in the northern city, they had not yet had time to become permanently discouraged by the new obstacles that they did face in the urban marketplace.

Selective migration may also have contributed to the economic and family-related advantages of southern migrants. We know that migrants were more educated than the sedentary southern population. Perhaps that means that the migrants also were disproportionately selected from the more ambitious, determined, and future-oriented segments of the southern black population. Alternatively, return migration could have been more common for prior migrants who experienced either economic failure or family disruption in the North.

Although it is plausible that selective return migration contributed to the differences by regional origin for residents in the North, it alone likely can not explain the differences in family structure between migrants and non-migrants in the North.[50] Another possible, although still untested, hypothesis is that something about southern culture predisposed migrants to more stable family life in the North. Southern migrants, for example, may have been more religious than their northern-born counterparts in northern cities. Religion and the church were definitely an important part of their lives, and there is evidence to suggest that they continued to be important in the North.[51] Perhaps religion decreased the likelihood of marital disruption and nonmarital motherhood among migrants. Yet such a hypothesis clearly contradicts the assumptions about the nature of black families in the rural South that were made by investigators from Frazier through Lemann.

Although the precise mechanisms responsible for greater family stability among southern migrants have not been identified by the empirical evidence presented in this chapter, that evidence does show that it is time to abandon the long-held belief that the migrants carried with them a dysfunctional family culture, like so much extra baggage. Why inner-city migrants and non-migrants alike have experienced such severe family dislocation in recent decades will be touched upon in the epilogue.

# Epilogue:
## A New Plantation?

The twentieth century has been one of profound demographic changes for the African American population. One of the most dramatic has been substantial geographic redistribution. At the beginning of the century, nine out of ten African Americans lived in the South; by the end of the century, only a little more than one in two were southerners. During the same period the black population living in rural areas plummeted from three-quarters to only 13 percent of the total.[1] Within the South, blacks abandoned agricultural pursuits rapidly after the Great Depression. Farm households accounted for more than 40 percent of all African American households in the South in 1930 but had dwindled to only about 10 percent of the total by 1960 (fig. 1). As a result of these changes, the average black family of 1990 was exposed to a much different social and economic milieu than was the average black family in 1910 or even 1940. That transformation was also reflected in the shifting emphasis of social science research concerned with the African American population. The rural-agrarian emphasis that characterized the work of the North Carolina School of scholars during the 1920s and 1930s has gradually given way to a preoccupation with life in inner cities.[2]

It has been a major theme of this book that African American families have been shaped—for better or for worse—by the social, economic, and cultural environment within which they are located. That is, individuals and couples tend to make decisions about family-related behaviors that seem appropriate and adaptive given their circumstances and prospects. When it comes to family patterns, macro-level conditions determine the medium within which micro-level processes are carried out. That is not an original interpretation of the social world; indeed, it is a relatively accurate description of what the discipline of sociology is all about. Although it is wise to avoid conceptual models of demographic behavior that are overly environmentally deterministic, it is also naive to believe that demographic behavior is immune to the influences of the larger social structure. More people will choose to marry at a young age where early marriage carries some social or economic advantage for individuals. More couples will choose to have only a small number of children where family limitation provides them with some social or economic benefit. Marital unions will be more fragile where disrupted marriage has no cultural stigma or where alternatives to marriage are more abundant. These generalizations are as true of sharecroppers who lived in the Mississippi Delta during the 1930s as they are of urbanites living on the South Side of Chicago in the 1990s. Indeed, as different as those two environments may seem, there are intriguing parallels in the macro-level social forces that have affected the family patterns of African Americans.

## Macro-Level Forces and Southern Farm Families

A plantation system of agricultural organization, especially the dominance of sharecropping, was a dominant force shaping the lives of southern blacks during the first half of the twentieth century. Concentrated in the southern countryside, the economic opportunities for the large majority of African Americans were extremely limited by the plantation organization. Most black farmers were tenants, and the potential for escaping tenancy was limited. Racial discrimination and Jim Crow restrictions assured that even blacks with adequate human capital had relatively few economic opportunities outside plantation agriculture.[3] Southern whites erected barriers to black land ownership, and blacks were routinely denied access to most non-agricultural occupations. As Nicholas Lemann argues, the plantation economy, especially sharecropping, was an efficient form of segregation, and when reinforced by other forms of racial discrimination it severely restricted the opportunities available to blacks.[4]

Two consequences of the plantation system had profound implications for African American families. First, it discouraged the mechanization of southern farming.[5] Second, it was based on a system of domestic production. As a result, southern agricultural production relied heavily on the labor of family members, including children.[6] Dependence on the family labor force in turn encouraged early marriage and high fertility (chapters 3 and 4). Although an appropriate and even rational response to the prevailing social and economic conditions, that demographic behavior had important long-term, negative consequences. Most important, early marriage and large families interfered with the accumulation of human capital that might have increased the likelihood of escaping the oppressive conditions of southern agriculture.

The same basic social and economic conditions prevailed for southern blacks for decades, making the environmental pressures on family life much the same in 1940 as they had been in 1880. Although they seemed to be a permanent feature of southern agriculture and destined to last forever, the conditions eventually changed. When they did, so did the social pressures affecting black families. Largely as a result of New Deal policies, southern landowners began making decisions that fundamentally altered the organization of agriculture. Most important was the introduction of mechanized farming techniques that reduced dependence on family labor. As farm owners began to use tractors, mechanical harvesters, and other equipment, they were able to cultivate larger tracts of land and no longer needed to rely on tenant families. Sharecropping families were displaced, and the structural foundation supporting the economic rationality of early marriage and large families began to crumble.[7]

As oppressive as the plantation system had been for most black farmers, its collapse left them without a definite niche in the rural economy and forced them to confront a new challenge. What were they to do, now that southern landowners no longer needed them to occupy their land year-round and their labor was no longer so important in generating profits? Some moved downward on the agricultural ladder and became wage laborers, working seasonally for a few dollars a day. Others moved to southern towns and cities, where they encountered a new kind of structural impediment—occupational discrimination. Many, of course, moved to northern cities, where a much different social and economic atmosphere has developed.[8]

## Macro-Level Forces and Inner-City Families

Despite the obvious and significant differences between the rural South before World War II and the urban North at the century's close, many inner-city black residents face conditions reminiscent of those experienced on southern plantations.[9] Like sharecropping families during the first half of the twentieth century, the family life of inner-city blacks since the 1960s has been shaped by powerful structural conditions. In the urban North, residential segregation replaced the southern plantation economy as the most powerful force shaping the lives of African Americans. Northern blacks are heavily concentrated in large metropolitan areas, where they are further concentrated in certain neighborhoods—usually inner cities.

The extent of this residential segregation can be demonstrated by the Index of Dissimilarity, a statistical measure that describes the percentage of blacks that would need to move in order to achieve an even racial distribution throughout the city. In 1940 the Index of Dissimilarity for northern cities was 87.0.[10] By 1990 the level of segregation had declined only modestly to 78. Those levels of residential segregation mean that many black residents of northern cities live in areas that are virtually all black and that their chances of interacting with whites outside of the workplace are low.

According to sociologists Douglas Massey and Nancy Denton, persistent and severe racial residential segregation isolates many blacks in urban America and magnifies the deleterious effects of poverty through what they refer to as "concentration effects." One, family-related, consequence of these social forces is the creation of an "oppositional culture" in some inner-city neighborhoods. Part of that culture is the belief of some young African Americans that "if whites speak Standard American English, succeed in school, work hard at routine jobs, marry, and support their children, then to be 'black' requires one to speak Black English, do poorly in school, denigrate conventional employment, *shun marriage, and raise children outside of marriage.*"[11]

Although it is not necessary for the residential separation of blacks and whites in metropolitan areas to undermine the life chances of African Americans, other social forces have assisted racial segregation in producing that undesirable effect. Historically, high levels of residential segregation have increased the dependence of black workers on jobs available in or near their neighborhoods. As long as those jobs were available, black couples in inner cities could marry and build families, much like other urbanites. Indeed, the evidence presented in chapter 7 suggests that family patterns among northern blacks remained stable until after 1960 despite high levels of segregation in northern cities (figs. 11, 12, and 13). Through 1960, a clear majority of black children in northern cities lived with both parents, most ever-married women lived with their spouses, and only a trivial percentage of mothers had never been married. Like southern tenant farmers before them, however, the structural forces affecting inner-city blacks were subject to change.

After 1960 the economies of northern urban areas changed profoundly. Blue-collar and manufacturing industries abandoned central cities in favor of suburbs and non-metropolitan areas. In exchange, the urban economy offered greater opportunities for well-educated, highly skilled workers in the financial and information-processing sectors.[12] As a consequence, labor force participation rates fell, and unemployment rates among young African American men rose to extraordinary levels. Just like the southern tenant farmers of the previous generation, inner-city black males were displaced from their jobs as a result of decisions made by those who controlled the important economic capital—landowners in the former situation, corporate leaders in the latter.

The loss of blue-collar jobs from inner cities had an exaggerated impact on the economic opportunities for black men because of occupational discrimination that excluded them from a variety of alternative, well-paying jobs. Those who offered less human capital (education and job skills) to potential employers were especially likely to suffer the consequences of the changing inner-city economy.

Extensive and persistent joblessness among inner-city males has had implications for family life in northern cities. Unable to provide much financial security to prospective spouses, an unemployed black male is considered unmarriageable. The shortage of marriageable black men—largely as a result of economic transformations in inner cities—has led black women to the retreat from marriage. There is also some evidence that recent trends in income among blacks have been more favorable for women than for men, further reducing the attractiveness of many males as potential marriage partners.[13] These divergent income trends could lead to greater economic independence for black women and raise their expectations (or demands) in a prospective spouse.[14] As a result, the average age at marriage and the proportion single have risen sharply among African American women in inner cities.

Taken alone, one might predict that the faltering economic fortunes of black men in inner cities and the resulting retreat from marriage by black women also would significantly reduce the motivation for parenthood. After all, most economic theories of fertility predict that reproductive decisions are based heavily on the balance of costs and benefits associated with children and the ability of prospective parents to support their children financially.[15] Such predictions would not be entirely accurate, however, because non-marital fertility has replaced marital fertility as the norm in an inner-city setting. That behavior presents a challenge for social scientists in search of explanations for the fact that more than two-thirds of black babies are born to unmarried women and that the rate of childbearing by young single black women has risen since the mid-1980s.[16] Either the young black women who bear children out of wedlock are behaving irrationally or they are responding to a set of motivational factors to which non-marital motherhood is a predictable response. Because there is limited potential for social scientists to provide explanations for irrational behavior, it is more fruitful to focus on the possible factors motivating the choice of parenthood. What might those factors be, and how are they related to the socioeconomic milieu of inner cities?

Arline Geronimus proposes one possible explanation for the "positive value" of non-marital childbearing for some young women that is based on the unique structural and cultural conditions of inner cities.[17] First, teenage motherhood, in general, serves as a rite of passage to adulthood among young women for whom alternative opportunities are blocked, especially for those who did not thrive in school. In contrast, young women with exceptional academic skills, and therefore greater potential, pursue more conventional routes to social and economic independence. Second, Geronimus contends that early childbearing may be an adaptive response to the reality of inner cities, where marriageable men are in short supply and many black women must plan for a future of economic independence. In that setting, it is preferable for black women to complete their childbearing at an early age, when they can count on a larger kin-based support group to help with child care. Later, when the women are older and their child care demands less intense, they will be in a better position to participate in the labor force more actively.

Although Geronimus's explanation may seem to be based more heavily on cultural differences between inner-city and mainstream populations, it also hinges on an important structural underpinning. That is, it assumes both a scarcity of marriageable men because of male joblessness and blocked social and economic opportunities for many young women in inner cities. It is, therefore, an adaptive response to the structural conditions they face, much like early marriage and high fertility was a rational response to plantation agriculture in the South. Like the demographic response of rural southerners, the behavior of young, unmarried mothers in inner cities also has negative consequences for the black community. At the very least, it means that a larger percentage of inner-city African American children grow up in households with only one parent whose income may not exceed the poverty level. The significant long-term disadvantages of such living arrangements have been well documented: reduced educational attainment, greater probability of non-marital parenthood, more delinquent involvement, and higher levels of unemployment and poverty.[18]

Reminiscent of the experiences of rural southerners during and after the Great Depression, government policy may once again have combined with economic forces to create conditions that affect the family life of African Americans in inner cities. New Deal policies in the 1930s offered southern landowners an opportunity to turn to an alternative form of agricultural production, which destroyed the tenancy system and the family patterns it helped to shape. After 1960, government assistance programs such as Aid to Families with Dependent Children (AFDC) offered single mothers an alternative form of financial independence.

Yet in many ways the eligibility requirements of these programs have penalized those who would seek a stable union (marriage or cohabitation) with their child's father. Some have suggested that the availability of such governmental assistance, combined with limited social and economic potential for many young inner-city women, created an atmosphere in which non-marital childbearing has its own economic rationality. As Elijah Anderson, an African American sociologist who has conducted an extensive ethnographic study of an inner-city neighborhood in Philadelphia observes, "It has become increasingly socially acceptable for a young woman to have children out of wedlock—significantly, with the help of a regular welfare check."[19]

Anderson's conclusion is a controversial one because it seems to support the arguments of conservative commentators such as Charles Murray, who claim that Great Society welfare programs have contributed to an increase in non-marital childbearing since the 1960s.[20] According to Murray and others, welfare programs provide an alternative route to independent living for young women, thereby increasing the motivation for non-marital motherhood and reducing its negative consequences.

Anderson's observation is also controversial because a sizable body of empirical research has failed to demonstrate a strong association between welfare programs such as AFDC and out-of-wedlock births.[21] For example, those studies point out that the real value of AFDC payments declined since the 1970s, at the very time that non-marital fertility increased. Based on that information, most social scientists have rejected the politically incorrect idea that welfare policy has an impact on family-related behaviors such as non-marriage and out-of-wedlock childbearing. Yet it is not clear that the kinds of empirical studies that have been done on this topic are sensitive enough to detect the type of process Anderson inferred. That is, they usually have been based on highly aggregated analyses of cross-sectional patterns or time series that do not focus on the population for whom the risk of non-marital childbearing is greatest and for whom even the modest income from AFDC payments may seem attractive in comparison with other limited alternatives. Anderson's conclusion seems less controversial, however, when it is realized that one does not need to embrace the conservatives' nearly exclusive emphasis on welfare policy as the cause of non-marital childbearing to acknowledge that government policies are an active ingredient in the stew of macro-level forces that influence individual family-related behavior. They played a role historically in the rural South and have almost certainly done so in the urban North more recently.[22]

Structural conditions and the cultural adaptations to them are not permanent, although it might seem so after they have persisted for decades. The macro-level forces shaping contemporary inner-city families could change, just as the system of southern agricultural production changed earlier in the century. Residential segregation could weaken, making the populations of inner-cities less dependent on the shrinking supply of good jobs in their communities and reducing the concentration effects that intensify the deleterious impact of poverty in segregated neighborhoods. Or, the flow of good jobs away from inner-cities could reverse direction, providing residents with employment opportunities they have not enjoyed since the 1950s and thereby reversing the retreat from marriage by black women. Government welfare policies could evolve so they encourage marriage or discourage non-marital motherhood.[23] Finally, a new African American diaspora could develop, with inner-city residents abandoning their communities for destinations that offer greater economic opportunity.

To be sure, all of these scenarios may seem implausible in light of current conditions. It would be wise to remember, however, that every one of them has occurred in the past, affecting the family lives of those who have been the major focus of this book. Segregation on tenant farms in southern agriculture gave way to a regionally and residentially redistributed black population. Changes in the urban economy created opportunities for southern blacks where there had been few. Government policies and programs were introduced that had important implications for families, although not always positive. And discouraged and disenchanted families moved in massive numbers as they searched for opportunities that were not available in their own communities.

Perhaps the "new urban plantation" that shapes the lives and families of so many African Americans will eventually succumb to one, or more, of these potential changes—much as happened to southern plantations of the past. All of these changes would be accompanied by seismic jolts to the social order, as were the social transformations that led to the demise of southern plantations. That alone should not make them implausible scenarios for the future.

## A Final Word

Historical inquiry offers a buffer of time that tends to reduce the sensitivity of some subject matter. Although my discussion of the structural and cultural forces affecting family life in the farm South may generate some disagreement, for example, it is unlikely to be deemed controversial. Such is probably not the case for my speculation about the structural and cultural influences on family life among blacks in inner cities, the "new plantation"—especially my willingness to entertain the notion that welfare policies do affect childbearing by unmarried women.

Aside from the merits of the argument, one reason for the potentially different responses to my discussion of the historical and current influences on the black family concerns the unstated rules of social science discourse. If, in writing of the nature of black families in the early twentieth century, I conformed to the intellectual conventions of that period, the tone of this book would likely be much different. The dogma of "scientific racism" that was popular at the time would argue for biological explanations that assumed the inherent inferiority of African Americans or perhaps the inheritance of a "primitive" cultural heritage from Africa. I would have been considered somewhat of a maverick or even a crackpot to ignore those explanations in favor of more sociological explanations such as those I have discussed. In writing about the nature of African American families now, however, I am expected to conform to contemporary intellectual conventions. In the social sciences, those conventions strongly discourage the use of explanatory frameworks that blame the victim. According to this convention, for example, it is acceptable to explain the retreat from marriage among black women in terms of increasing joblessness among black men as a result of the disappearance of jobs from inner cities. Neither the women choosing not to marry nor the unemployed men are responsible for the structurally determined demographic outcome. In contrast, it is unacceptable to suggest that young unmarried women may deliberately choose to become mothers in order to be eligible for a guaranteed income from public assistance. Pointing out that this decision is made only because alternative routes to economic independence may have been blocked by forces outside of a young woman's control adds context to the explanation but still leaves the impression that she played an active role in the demographic outcome.

The status of "victim" seems to be conferred selectively on those individuals who occupy a disadvantaged position in the social hierarchy. It thereby selectively absolves individuals of responsibility for behaviors that have negative consequences for themselves or society. Thus, for instance, dysfunctional behaviors by members of the "underclass" are viewed through a different lens than are the dysfunctional behaviors of the "plunderclass," who pursue greater wealth and prestige with little regard for the larger social consequences of their greed. It is currently acceptable to attribute personal responsibility to members of the latter group but not to members of the former. With no buffer of time to protect them, explanations that violate prevailing intellectual conventions are far more likely to generate controversy and perhaps even outrage.

Finally, a historical perspective helps us to appreciate the impermanence of the social world. Without a historical perspective it is too easy to assume that what is will always be. Certainly, those southern farmers who contributed personal histories to the Federal Writers' Project would never have anticipated the dramatic social and economic changes that were on the horizon during the depression. Conversely, a historical perspective can reveal continuities across generations and the reoccurring influence of certain kinds of social forces, even within very different milieus. Economic transformation, government policy, and racial discrimination have affected African American family patterns in the southern countryside and the northern ghetto alike. It is my hope that this historical treatment of black families has successfully described many of those social forces and their consequences—not only among southern farmers between 1910 and 1940 but also for those who made their way north during and after the Great Depression.

# Appendix:

## Southern Black Farm Families in the 1910 and 1940 U.S. Censuses

The chapters in this book provide an in-depth description of farm families during the first part of the twentieth century (chapters 2–6) and among families in the urban North during the post World War II period (chapter 7). An important ingredient of such a portrait is statistical information with which family characteristics can be summarized, comparisons drawn (for example, between blacks and whites), and changes described. Although I rely on statistical information from a variety of sources, the heaviest burden falls on the 1910 and 1940 U.S. decennial censuses.

A number of factors justify the selection of these particular censuses as the primary source of quantitative evidence for the investigation of southern farm families. First, both contain a wealth of information that can be used to describe farm households and their members. Second, they bracket well the era of primary interest, a period of important social, economic, and demographic changes (chapter 1). The 1910 census is useful for describing the characteristics of farm families as they were during the first decade of the century, so is an appropriate point of departure. It is reasonable to close the era with the 1940 census in light of powerful forces that intensified in the rural South following 1940—massive out-migration of population, mobilization for World War II, significant agricultural reorganization, and an inchoate civil rights movement, although any boundaries for a historical era are certain to be somewhat arbitrary. Third, and perhaps most important, high-quality public-use samples of reasonable size are available for both the 1910 and 1940 censuses. Those samples are the primary source of statistical evidence on farm families during this period.

## Public-Use Samples for 1910 and 1940

Public-use samples of the U.S. Census have become increasingly common as sources of information for historical research. The Bureau of the Census began creating public-use samples as a routine part of the decennial census in 1960 and continued to do so through the 1990 census. In addition, public-use samples have also been constructed for many censuses before 1960, including 1850, 1860, 1870, 1880, 1900, 1910, 1920, 1940, and 1950. These versatile data files have proven instrumental in the study of a wide variety of social, economic, and demographic characteristics of the American past, including fertility, mortality, family structure, occupational status, educational consumption, and ethnic variation.[1] The most important advantage of public-use samples over more traditional census data available from printed documents and reports is their ability to provide information at the more micro level. They can be used to describe the characteristics of households, families, or even individuals rather than states, cities, or counties.

Historical public-use samples (those before 1960) have been constructed by sampling from the original manuscripts on which census enumerators recorded the information they had gathered from households. Although the specific design for creating such samples has varied, they are intended to produce a nationally representative sample of American households, including information about who resided in those households. The specific content of the samples necessarily varies across decades as a result of changes in the information collected during the census. Typical information gathered about the entire household includes location (state, county, and city); type of dwelling (farm or non-farm); and tenure status (owned versus rented). Individual-level information generally includes such common characteristics as race, sex, age, occupation, education or literacy, and marital status.

The federal government requires a seventy-two-year waiting period before the information gathered about individuals during a census is made publicly available. After that time, everything recorded during census enumeration, including names and addresses, can be obtained. Before the waiting period has elapsed, however, certain restrictions on access to information are imposed by the Bureau of the Census to protect the confidentiality of individuals included in public-use samples. Most commonly, the restrictions prohibit revealing the location of households when the population size of a geographic unit (e.g., county or city) is too small. Therefore, only historical public-use samples for censuses that occurred before 1930 are currently free from rules of confidentiality. Public-use samples for censuses after 1930 must include protection of the confidentiality of individuals. Unfortunately, confidentiality restrictions can impose a number of limitations on the versatility of the samples.

The public-use sample for the 1910 census, completed in 1989, was created at the University of Pennsylvania's Population Studies Center under the direction of Samuel H. Preston. It was the second historical public-use sample project for Preston, who also directed construction of the 1900 public-use sample at the University of Washington's Center for Studies in Demography and Ecology. The 1910 sample is substantially larger than its predecessor from 1900 and contains information for 366,239 Americans residing in 88,814 households.[2]

The 1910 public-use sample includes several key pieces of information about households and individuals that are useful for describing the characteristics of southern black farm families early in the twentieth century. At the household level, we know the state and county in which a residence was located as well as whether it was a farm or a non-farm dwelling, if it was owned or rented, and, if owned, whether it was mortgaged or owned free and clear. At the person level, adult women were asked to report the number of children they had borne as well as the number still living at the time of the census. Both men and women reported their marital status and the number of years they had been married. It is possible to determine whether children attended school, and, for older children, whether they worked. Because the 1910 public-use samples were created after the required seventy-two-year waiting period, they are completely free to report the geographic location of households, regardless of the size of cities or counties in which they were located.

S. Philip Morgan and Douglas Ewbank of the University of Pennsylvania have created a special "oversample" of households headed by blacks in selected southern states that is intended primarily to supplement the number of urban blacks in the 1910 public-use sample. Because the southern African American population was predominately rural in 1910, the original sampling design yielded relatively few southern blacks living in cities. This oversample created by Morgan and Ewbank includes information about 5,533 additional households and the 23,599 persons residing in them.[3]

The 1940 public-use sample was the product of a joint project involving the Center for Demography and Ecology at the University of Wisconsin and the U.S. Bureau of the Census. The Bureau of the Census's participation was required because access to the information collected during the 1940 census was still subject to confidentiality restrictions when the project began. As a result of both a growing population and a larger sampling fraction, the 1940 public-use sample is substantially larger than the 1910 sample. Containing information for 1,351,732 individuals living in 391,034 households, it is a 1 percent sample of all U.S. households at that time, whereas the main 1910 public-use sample is a sample of every 1 in 250 households.

Like its 1910 counterpart, the 1940 public-use sample includes a wide variety of information describing both households and individuals. Both levels of data, however, are subject to certain limitations. At the household level there are constraints caused by the absence of certain geographical information withheld to satisfy the still-operative confidentiality restrictions. Most important, the 1940 public-use sample does not identify a household's county of residence. In lieu of counties, the sample reports the household's state economic area (SEA), which is a larger geographic unit composed of counties or groups of counties that share important social and economic characteristics.[4] SEAs were created for use with the 1950 census, when 501 state economic areas were identified. Because some SEAs in 1940 did not have populations large enough to satisfy the confidentiality restrictions, they were combined with other SEAs within the same state.[5] In addition, in contrast to other historical public-use samples, the 1940 sample does not distinguish rural from urban households. The latter restriction is not problematic for this study, which focuses primarily on farm households that are identified in the 1940 public-use sample (PUMS). Neither is the absence of county location a significant problem, although it does prevent efforts to link county-level characteristics that could be used to describe the social and economic environment of local areas with households or individuals located in those areas.

A different type of limitation affects the individual-level data in the 1940 public-use sample. Like the 1910 sample, the 1940 data includes separate records for each household and all persons residing there. In a deviation shared only with the 1950 public-use sample, however, the 1940 data also include what is referred to as a "sample line record." Each household includes only one "sample line person." Unfortunately, only sample line persons were asked to report certain items that are important for the study of farm families. For example, only ever-married sample line females, fourteen or older, reported their age at marriage and the number of children they had borne. All other women (those who were not the household's sample line person) were not asked to report on these important characteristics. As a result, the samples appropriate for certain descriptive purposes are smaller than they would have been had all information been requested of all persons.

As valuable as the 1910 and 1940 public-use samples were when originally created, they have been improved even further by an ambitious project carried out at the Social History Research Laboratory at the University of Minnesota. Under the direction of Steven Ruggles and Russell Menard, the Integrated Public Use Microdata Series (IPUMS) was created by combining data from all currently available public-use microdata samples from decennial censuses. The IPUMS provides researchers with national-level information with which to trace longitudinal patterns for a wide variety of personal and household characteristics, including family patterns. In addition to the information originally collected by census enumerators, the IPUMS project has constructed a variety of additional variables that are extremely useful for studying households and families, including the location of spouses in the household, the location of father and mother in the household, the number of own children living in the household, and the age of the eldest and youngest children in the household.[6] Throughout this book, descriptions and analyses based on public-use samples use the IPUMS, and that includes the information for 1910 and 1940 presented in chapters 2 through 6 as well as that for more recent years presented in chapter 7.

At this point the IPUMS does not include the black oversample for 1910. In some analyses for 1910, however, where the 1910 IPUMS file is compatible with the 1910 black oversample, the farm households in the oversample are included. In all cases the quantitative evidence presented is virtually identical with and without the oversample. The descriptive tables presented in this appendix do not include households from the oversample.

The public-use samples of historical censuses are a rich matrix from which to mine information about black farm families. They can enrich substantially descriptions of a variety of family-related characteristics and processes, such as marriage patterns, childbearing, family structure and stability, schooling, and work. They also facilitate comparisons between black families and white ones as well as descriptions of changes over time. Still, certain limitations to such census data must be acknowledged. Although they are powerful tools for reporting the objective characteristics of households and individuals, they tell nothing about the thoughts, ambitions, attitudes, or frustrations felt by those who ultimately compose the families involved. Nor are they revealing of linkages or dependencies that had developed between households and families in the same locale. Finally, as all data collected from individuals by other individuals, they are subject to error and misreporting. To partially compensate for these limitations I have incorporated supplementary information to help provide a fuller perspective to the numbers derived from the public-use samples. Especially valuable in this effort are the oral histories gathered by the Federal Writers' Project during the 1930s, one of Franklin Roosevelt's New Deal programs designed to assist out-of-work writers during the Great Depression. Included in the archives of the Federal Writers' Project are many stories of the lives of southern farmers—black and white, tenant and owner. These stories are extremely valuable for providing a richer context for the parallel stories told by numbers from the census.[7] Where appropriate I also rely on the writing of contemporaries to supplement the statistical evidence.

## Construction of the Southern Farm Study Sample

From the 1910 and 1940 public-use samples I have extracted all southern farm households. It is important to recognize that designation as "farm household" according to the census is based on whether a dwelling unit was reported as a farm. Thus, eligibility for inclusion in the study sample is based on the characteristics of the residence and not on the occupation reported by the household head or any other member of the household. As a result, some farm households were located in urban areas and were not headed by individuals who reported "farmer" as their primary occupation (chapter 2). Conversely, some non-farm households were located in rural areas and were headed by farmers. Despite these potential problems, the majority of farm households fit the traditional description of a dwelling located on land cultivated for profit, with at least some family members engaged in farming.

All individuals living in farm households are included in the core study sample. When discussing the characteristics of farm households, I usually draw from information on the household record or characteristics of the individual identified as the household head. When referring to individuals residing on farms, I typically

include all persons enumerated within farm households, regardless of their relationship to the household head. That is an important distinction because there are
far more farm individuals than there are farms. Age restrictions are imposed for
some analyses, of household heads and other individuals, to make the sample more
appropriate for the particular topic under consideration. When used, these age
restrictions are described in the text or the tables.

Although my primary interest is in the family lives of southern black farm families, white farm families are also included in most analyses for purposes of comparison. The "race" of farm families is determined by the reported race of the
household head. Therefore, when discussing the characteristics of black farm households, I am referring to those households in which a black person was enumerated as head, regardless of the race of other household members.[8] When focusing
on black individuals in families residing on farms, no consideration of the race of
the household head is made, only the race of individuals or family members. The
majority of households included members who were of the same race.

## Characteristics of Farm Households in the Core Study Sample
### Size of Sample

The primary study sample derived from the 1910 census includes 11,790 farm
households, 3,442 of them headed by blacks and 8,348 headed by whites. Within
those households resided 17,976 black and 43,357 white individuals.[9] The 1940
study sample consists of 37,127 total households, 9,903 with blacks as heads and
27,224 with whites as heads. Those households included 49,125 black individuals and 124,634 white individuals. The larger number of households in the 1940
sample can be due to growth in the number of farm households during this thirty-
year period or the larger sampling fraction used in 1940.

### State Distribution

Most black-operated farms were located within the Black Belt region of Alabama,
Georgia, Louisiana, Mississippi, North Carolina, and South Carolina during both
periods (table A-1). Texas and Arkansas also supplied a sizable number of black
farm households for the core study sample. In contrast, black farmers were less
common in Florida, Kentucky, Tennessee, and Virginia. A somewhat different
pattern emerges for white farm households, which were more heavily concentrated
in Kentucky, North Carolina, Tennessee, Oklahoma, and Texas.

### Tenure Status

The limited opportunities for farm ownership among blacks is apparent in the
evidence on tenure status of farms (table A-2). In 1910 only about one in four of
all farms operated by blacks were occupied by owners. Between 1910 and 1940
the likelihood of ownership for blacks declined, and only one in five of all farms
operated by blacks were owned in the latter period. Although farm ownership was

*Table A-1.* State Distribution of Southern Farm Households by
Race, 1910 and 1940

| | Black | | White | |
|---|---|---|---|---|
| | 1910[a] | 1940 | 1910 | 1940 |
| Alabama | 9.6% | 10.9% | 6.4% | 7.1% |
| Arkansas | 8.6 | 7.5 | 6.3 | 6.9 |
| Delaware | 0.0 | 0.2 | 0.5 | 0.4 |
| District of Columbia | 0.0 | 0.0 | 0.0 | 0.0 |
| Florida | 2.1 | 2.2 | 1.5 | 2.0 |
| Georgia | 12.1 | 11.4 | 7.6 | 7.1 |
| Kentucky | 1.6 | 1.0 | 11.7 | 10.2 |
| Louisiana | 8.2 | 8.7 | 3.1 | 4.1 |
| Maryland | 1.1 | 1.0 | 2.1 | 1.7 |
| Mississippi | 14.6 | 18.4 | 4.6 | 5.2 |
| North Carolina | 9.7 | 8.9 | 8.3 | 9.1 |
| Oklahoma | 1.1 | 1.4 | 8.2 | 7.4 |
| South Carolina | 9.3 | 10.6 | 3.3 | 3.3 |
| Tennessee | 5.3 | 3.7 | 10.0 | 9.4 |
| Texas | 10.2 | 8.8 | 15.0 | 15.8 |
| Virginia | 6.5 | 5.3 | 6.7 | 6.1 |
| West Virginia | 0.0 | 0.1 | 4.7 | 4.1 |
| Total | 100.0 | 100.0 | 100.0 | 100.0 |
| Number of households | 3,442 | 9,903 | 8,348 | 27,224 |

*Sources:* 1910 and 1940 Integrated Public Use Microdata Series, Social History Research Laboratory, University of Minnesota.
   a. Does not include black oversample.

the majority status for whites in both periods, there was little reason for rural whites
to be sanguine about their opportunities for moving up the agricultural ladder.
Indeed, between 1910 and 1940 the percentage of white farm owners dropped from
61.8 to 52.4 percent—a decline of 15 percent. The forces operating on the southern rural economy (e.g., increasing mechanization and New Deal farm policy) were
having a powerful effect on the rural white class structure, and more and more white
farmers were shifted to the more tenuous status of sharecroppers.

## Household Size

A popular conception of farm households has multiple generations living under
the same roof—grown children of the middle generation taking care of their elderly parents, and several children from the newest generation helping their own
parents with household chores. Often that image also includes a mix of "lateral"
family members such as aunts, uncles, nephews, and nieces and even boarders or
lodgers. All of these co-resident relatives and non-relatives would have added up
to a farm household of considerable size as well as complexity. The numbers in
table A-2 contradict somewhat that popular conception.

*Table A-2.* Selected Information on Southern Farm Households by
Race, 1910 and 1940

|  | Black | | White | |
|---|---|---|---|---|
|  | 1910[a] | 1940 | 1910 | 1940 |
| Farms owned | 24.0% | 20.4% | 61.8% | 52.4% |
| Farms rented | 76.0 | 79.6 | 38.2 | 47.6 |
| Size of household |  |  |  |  |
|   Average (mean) | 5.0 | 4.5 | 5.1 | 4.4 |
|   Standard deviation | 2.8 | 2.7 | 2.4 | 2.2 |
| Farm households |  |  |  |  |
|   Headed by females | 8.2 | 11.7 | 5.1 | 7.4 |
|   Headed by males | 91.8 | 88.3 | 94.9 | 92.6 |
| Age of heads |  |  |  |  |
|   Average (mean) | 42.1 | 44.4 | 43.6 | 46.6 |
|   Standard deviation | 14.3 | 15.5 | 14.0 | 15.0 |
|   Median | 40.0 | 43.0 | 42.0 | 46.0 |
|   < 15 years | 0.0 | 0.0 | 0.0 | 0.0 |
|   15–24 years | 9.3 | 8.5 | 6.7 | 5.2 |
|   25–34 years | 25.9 | 22.8 | 24.2 | 20.3 |
|   35–44 years | 23.4 | 21.6 | 25.0 | 21.6 |
|   45–54 years | 20.2 | 19.2 | 20.7 | 22.0 |
|   55–64 years | 13.3 | 14.8 | 15.3 | 16.7 |
|   65+ years | 8.0 | 13.1 | 8.2 | 14.2 |
| Number of cases | 3,442 | 9,903 | 8,348 | 27,224 |

*Sources:* 1910 and 1940 Integrated Public Use Microdata Series, Social History
Research Laboratory, University of Minnesota.
  a. Does not include black oversample.

In 1910 the average southern farm household, black or white, contained roughly
five members. By 1940 average household size had fallen to about four and one-
half family members for both black and white households. A number of factors
may have contributed to that change but likely the most influential were lowered
marital fertility among farm couples and migration out of farming. The evidence
for both 1910 and 1940 also suggests somewhat more variation around these average household sizes for blacks, as reflected in their larger standard deviation (e.g.,
$\sigma = 2.8$ for blacks and $\sigma = 2.4$ for whites in 1910). That greater diversity could be
due to a frequently observed pattern of childbearing for blacks during this era, with
proportionately more women concentrated at the lowest and highest parities (chapter 4). A stronger propensity for African American households to incorporate non-
nuclear family members could also have contributed.

## Characteristics of Family Heads

One individual has been designated as "family head" for each family in the 1910
and 1940 public-use samples. Typically, the husband and father is considered the

head of the family—when he is present. A relatively wide variety of other configurations are also possible, however, including single-parent heads (male or female), unmarried childless heads, or extended families headed by grandparents. The identification of family head was not done randomly and generally reflects the location of power and control within each family.

In 1910 more than 90 percent of black and white farm families were headed by males. It was somewhat more common for black women to head families than it was for their white counterparts (8.2 percent versus 5.1 percent), although the patterns of headship were similar for blacks and whites during the earlier period. By 1940 the probability of a farm family being headed by a female increased for both races, but more so for African Americans than for whites. Nearly 12 percent of all African American farm families were headed by women in 1940. The level of female headship among whites also increased by 1940 (to 7.4 percent) but remained below that observed for blacks, even in 1910.

The median age for heads of African American farm families in 1910 was forty; heads of white families were somewhat older, with a median age of forty-two.[10] The racial difference in the distribution of heads of households across specific age ranges is especially sharp in the youngest and oldest groups. Fully 9.3 percent of black household heads were younger than twenty-five compared to only 6.7 percent for whites. The racial difference is reversed at the older ages, where 23.5 percent and 21.3 percent of white and black household heads, respectively, were fifty-five or older. Between 1910 and 1940 the average age increased by three years for blacks and by four years for whites. Focusing on the extreme age groups for blacks and whites alike, the proportion of heads of households younger than twenty-five fell by 1940, whereas the proportion fifty-five and older increased.

## Characteristics of Farm Residents in the Core Study Sample

Household heads are not the only residents of southern farms worth studying; there were roughly four other co-resident individuals living on each farm (table A-2). Indeed, in the chapters of this book I often invoke the full sample of farm residents rather than just household heads to describe the family life of southern farmers. Therefore, it is useful to consider the characteristics of the farm population in general.

### Race and Sex

There are 61,333 total residents of southern farms available from the 1910 public-use sample (table A-3). Of that total, 17,976 (29.3 percent) are black, and 43,357 (70.7 percent) are white. The black farm population is split evenly between males and females, but the white population has proportionately more males (51.8 percent) than females (48.2 percent). The 1940 public-use sample yields a total sample of 173,759 farm residents, including 49,125 (28.3 percent) African Ameri-

*Table A-3.* Age and Sex Distributions of Individuals on Southern Farms by Race, 1910 and 1940.

| Age (in years) | Black | | | | White | | | |
| | 1910[a] | | 1940 | | 1910 | | 1940 | |
| | Male | Female | Male | Female | Male | Female | Male | Female |
|---|---|---|---|---|---|---|---|---|
| 0–4 | 15.0% | 15.6% | 12.5% | 13.4% | 14.1% | 15.3% | 10.2% | 10.5% |
| 5–9 | 16.3 | 15.1 | 13.3 | 13.3 | 14.2 | 14.1 | 11.1 | 11.4 |
| 10–14 | 13.9 | 14.5 | 13.0 | 12.9 | 12.9 | 12.4 | 12.0 | 12.0 |
| 15–19 | 11.7 | 11.7 | 11.7 | 11.4 | 11.2 | 11.3 | 11.6 | 11.5 |
| 20–24 | 7.7 | 9.2 | 8.8 | 9.3 | 8.4 | 8.9 | 8.7 | 8.1 |
| 25–29 | 6.5 | 7.3 | 7.1 | 7.5 | 6.4 | 7.0 | 7.1 | 7.2 |
| 30–34 | 4.9 | 5.1 | 5.5 | 5.6 | 5.9 | 6.1 | 6.1 | 6.3 |
| 35–39 | 5.0 | 5.2 | 5.0 | 5.4 | 5.6 | 5.7 | 5.4 | 6.0 |
| 40–44 | 3.8 | 3.9 | 4.2 | 4.4 | 4.4 | 4.2 | 5.0 | 5.4 |
| 45–49 | 3.6 | 3.5 | 3.9 | 4.1 | 3.5 | 3.6 | 4.9 | 5.1 |
| 50–54 | 3.7 | 2.8 | 3.8 | 3.4 | 4.1 | 3.3 | 4.7 | 4.5 |
| 55–59 | 2.7 | 1.8 | 3.1 | 2.6 | 3.1 | 2.7 | 3.7 | 3.7 |
| 60–64 | 2.1 | 1.7 | 2.6 | 2.1 | 2.6 | 2.2 | 3.3 | 3.0 |
| 65–69 | 1.5 | 0.9 | 2.6 | 2.1 | 1.7 | 1.5 | 3.0 | 2.4 |
| 70–74 | 0.9 | 0.7 | 1.5 | 1.1 | 0.9 | 0.7 | 1.6 | 1.4 |
| 75–79 | 0.5 | 0.4 | 0.6 | 0.6 | 0.5 | 0.6 | 0.8 | 0.8 |
| 80–84 | 0.2 | 0.3 | 0.4 | 0.3 | 0.2 | 0.2 | 0.5 | 0.4 |
| 85+ | 0.2 | 0.2 | 0.3 | 0.4 | 0.2 | 0.1 | 0.2 | 0.3 |
| | 100.0 | 100.0 | 100.0 | 100.0 | 100.0 | 100.0 | 100.0 | 100.0 |
| N | 8,977 | 8,999 | 24,596 | 24,529 | 22,439 | 20,918 | 64,666 | 59,968 |
| | (49.9%) | (50.1%) | (50.1%) | (49.9%) | (51.8%) | (48.2%) | (51.9%) | (48.1%) |

*Sources:* 1910 and 1940 Integrated Public Use Microdata Series, Social History Research Laboratory, University of Minnesota.

a. Does not include black oversample.

cans and 124,634 (71.7 percent) whites. The gender balance for both blacks and whites remained stable between 1910 and 1940, with blacks maintaining an even representation of males and females and whites holding steady at about 52 percent male and 48 percent female.

## Age

Age distributions of the southern farm population in 1910 were generally similar for blacks and whites. In a familiar pattern observed for populations with relatively high fertility, both blacks and whites exhibit a heavy concentration of individuals at younger ages and declining numbers at older ages. The black population is especially "young," with nearly 45 percent of all persons at age fourteen or below. Whites are not far below blacks in the youthfulness of the farm population, with about 42 percent of all individuals younger than fifteen. To put these figures in better perspective, only 32 percent of the entire U.S. population was concentrated at these young ages in 1910.

Some age groups in 1910 exhibit sex imbalances, which may have had implications for the family lives of southern farmers. Both blacks and whites, for example, show a significant deficit of females at older adult ages, fifty to seventy-four. These deficits can be summarized by another demographic tool, the "sex ratio," which describes the number of males present for every hundred females within a given age range. An even division by sex generates a sex ratio of 100. Sex ratios greater than 100 reveal an "excess" of males, whereas those below indicate a scarcity of males. The sex ratios for black and white farm residents aged fifty to seventy-four in 1910 are 137 and 127, respectively.

There are a number of possible explanations for the relative paucity of females. It was likely more difficult for unmarried women to succeed financially in the farm economy. Therefore, when marriages were disrupted (e.g., through death or separation) women were more likely than men to move to small towns or cities or at least to non-farm dwellings in rural areas.[11] Maternal mortality may have been another factor contributing to the masculine sex ratios among older adults. Fertility was high among the southern farm population, and health care was crude at best. Women were repeatedly exposed to the risk of infections and injuries associated with childbearing—some with fatal consequences. It is important to note that both of these forces would have operated against the countervailing pressure of higher male mortality among older adults.

A gender imbalance of another type is observed for farm blacks but not for whites in the young-adult ages of twenty to thirty-four. At these ages there was an excess of black females, as indicated by the sex ratio of 88 (compared with a ratio of 102 for whites). Many first marriages occur at this age range, so it is noteworthy that black women faced a relatively constricted pool of potential mates—decreasing the likelihood of marriage. Perhaps it was a harbinger of the same type of situation they would face in the inner cities of the 1990s.[12] Once again, the deficit of black males in the young-adult ages can be explained in a number of ways, including selective migration and a relatively high risk of mortality.

In general, the same patterns of age and sex concentration persisted between 1910 and 1940, yet in every case they had become somewhat more subtle by the later period. Both the black and white southern farm populations remained relatively young in 1940. The percent of the population younger than fifteen dropped substantially, however, from 45 to 39 percent for blacks and from 42 to 34 percent for whites (the national average was 26 percent). Declining farm fertility was probably largely responsible for this aging of the population.

Males continued to dominate numerically among the older adult population in 1940, with sex ratios of 118 and 122 for whites and blacks, respectively. Young-adult black females still faced a "marriage squeeze" caused by a shortage of young-adult black men. The severity of the sex imbalance at these ages lessened considerably, however, as the sex ratio rose from 88 to 95 males per every 100 females between the ages of twenty and thirty-four. In contrast, the sex ratio for whites at the prime marriage ages rose from 102 in 1910 to 109 in 1940.

## Families in the Urban North

Chapter 7 shifts the focus of the book to the family patterns of southern migrants in northern cities and requires data beyond the core study sample used to examine southern farm families. Fortunately, the IPUMS is versatile enough to accommodate this regional and temporal change in focus. Households in central cities of northern and western metropolitan areas form the basis of the analysis, which examines the living arrangements of children and women from 1940 through 1990. Additional information about the use of the IPUMS for those analyses is presented in the text of chapter 7, including age restrictions imposed, measurement of migration history, and the specific measures of living arrangements of women and children.

# Notes

## Chapter 1: Black Farm Families in the American South and Beyond

1. Burton (1985) argues that black and white families in the rural South were both strongly patriarchal despite common references to a matriarchal black family organization.

2. See, for example, Kirby (1987), Mandle (1978), and Ransom and Sutch (1977).

3. Kousser (1974); Woodward (1951, 1966).

4. Anderson (1988); Lieberson (1980); Margo (1990).

5. Tolnay and Beck (1995).

6. U.S. Bureau of the Census (1995: table 649, p. 411).

7. Of course, there were also a population of free blacks in the rural South during the antebellum period. Although they certainly enjoyed greater freedom and opportunity than slaves, their social and economic circumstances did not nearly approach equality with whites.

8. Nor were they willing to see the "superior" gene pool of the white population polluted through intermarriage and interbreeding. Southern whites' concerns about racial amalgamation became a regional hysteria after emancipation.

9. Newby (1965); Woodward (1966).

10. Wright (1990).

11. Higgs (1977).

12. U.S. Bureau of the Census (1985).

13. U.S. Bureau of the Census (1975:465).

14. See Genovese (1976) and Stampp (1965) for good although somewhat conflicting discussions of slavery and slave life.

15. Ransom and Sutch (1977:44–51).

16. See, for example, Moynihan (1965) and Frazier (1966).

17. Burton (1985:160); Gutman (1976).

18. Burton (1985:160)

19. See, for example, Shifflett (1975).

20. See, for example, Burton (1985).

21. See, for example, Blassingame (1977).

22. Steckel (1985).

23. Burton (1985:ch. 4).

24. See Ransom and Sutch (1977) for a thorough discussion of the rise of tenant farming in the South following the Civil War. Other good treatments of the economic status of blacks in the post–Civil War agricultural economy include Flynn (1983), Jaynes (1986), Mandle (1978), McKenzie (1994), Novak (1978), Reid (1981), and Schwartz (1976).

25. U.S. Bureau of the Census (1902, 1975).

26. See Landale and Tolnay (1991) and Tolnay (1984) for analyses that consider the effect of farm tenancy on the timing of marriage.

27. Hagood (1939:143).

28. See Burton (1985:chs. 6–7) for a thorough discussion of family life and structure among African Americans during the postbellum era in one southern community: Edgefield, South Carolina.

29. Tolnay (1995a).

30. See, for example, Cain (1977) and Mueller (1976). Cain concludes that male children in rural Bangladesh become "net producers" at age twelve, that they compensate for their own cumulative consumption at age fifteen, and that they compensate for their own and one sister's cumulative consumption at age twenty-two. Mueller concludes that children in peasant agricultural societies have a net "negative economic value" until they become parents themselves.

31. Federal Writers' Project (1939[1969]:73).

32. Preston and Haines (1991).

33. Burton (1985); Kirby (1987); Mandle (1978); Newby (1989).

34. Tolnay and Beck (1995:154); U.S. Bureau of the Census (1975:465).

35. See Higgs (1977) for an argument that stresses the social and economic progress of African Americans following emancipation. According the Higgs, the competitive marketplace created opportunities for blacks and moderated somewhat the extent of economic discrimination.

36. Raper (1936[1971]:141); see also Kirby (1987:242).

37. Tolnay and Beck (1995).

38. Tolnay and Beck (1995:151–53).

39. Daniel (1985); Kirby (1987).

40. See Daniel (1985) and Kirby (1987) for discussions of changes in southern agriculture during this era.

41. Tolnay (1995a).

42. Kester (1936[1969]).

43. Good treatments of the Southern Tenant Farmers' Union can also be found in Grubbs (1971), Kirby (1987), and Mitchell (1979).

44. Anderson (1988); Lieberson (1980); Margo (1990).

45. Tolnay and Beck (1995).

46. The quotation is from the *Journal of Negro History* 4, no. 3 (1919): 419–20.

47. The migration of blacks from the South to the North is discussed in more detail in chapter 7. Good general treatments of the migration can be found in Fligstein (1981), Grossman (1989), Henri (1975), and Marks (1989).

48. See, for example, Ewbank (1987) and Tolnay (1987). These estimates of fertility and mortality are based on the age-specific rates that prevailed in 1900 and 1940. They assume that as women grew older they were exposed at each age to the respective age-specific fertility and mortality rates.

49. U.S. Bureau of the Census (1945).

50. Tolnay (1987).

51. Couples had access to a variety of contraceptive techniques, including abstinence, spermicidal jellies and foam powders, diaphragms, and condoms. Abortion was also an option, although mechanical procedures were often dangerous and abortifacients unreliable. See Himes (1936).

52. Tolnay and Glynn (1994).

53. See Tolnay (1995a) for an analysis of class differentials in the fertility of southern farmers in 1910 and 1940, including a discussion of the different reproductive motivations affecting owners, tenants, and wage laborers.

54. See, for example, Anderson (1988), Lieberson (1980), and Margo (1990).

55. See Ewbank (1987) and Preston and Haines (1991) for informative treatments of the historical mortality patterns of African Americans.

56. Kirby (1987:242).

57. U.S. Bureau of the Census (1985:13–14).

58. For a rural-agrarian emphasis, see, for example, Hagood (1939), Johnson (1934, 1941a), Johnson, Embrey, and Alexander (1935), Raper (1936[1971], 1943), Raper and Reid (1941), and Woofter and Winston (1939). For the study of African Americans in northern inner cities, see, for example, Anderson (1990), Drake and Cayton (1962), Frazier (1932, 1966), Lemann (1991), Massey and Denton (1993), Taeuber and Taeuber (1965), and Wilson (1987).

59. Tucker and Mitchell-Kernan (1995:10–11).

60. Wilson (1987); Farley (1988); Murray (1984); Massey and Denton (1993).

61. See, for example, Drake and Cayton (1962), Du Bois (1899[1990]), Frazier (1932, 1966), and Mossell (1921).

62. See Drake and Cayton (1962) and Frazier (1932) for good examples of such evidence.

63. See, for example, Lemann (1991) and Moynihan (1965).

Chapter 2: Making a Living

    1. Jones (1988:19).

    2. Daniel (1981, 1985).

    3. See the appendix for a description of the samples of farmers for 1910 and 1940 and the distributions of households by state.

    4. Daniel (1985:4).

    5. Federal Writers' Project (1939[1969]):13.

    6. This description of tobacco cultivation draws heavily from Daniel (1985).

    7. Daniel (1985:25).

    8. Daniel (1985:28–29).

    9. Daniel (1985:42).

    10. Johnson (1941a:56).

    11. See also the descriptions of housing in the rural South by Kirby (1987:174–81) and Raper (1936[1971]:59–75).

    12. Raper (1936[1971]:52).

    13. Rosengarten (1974:16–17); see also Kirby (1987:46).

    14. See, for example, Flynn (1983:122–25).

    15. By "families" I mean married couples living on farms and their co-resident children, if any. A thorough description of the 1910 and 1940 census data used here appears in the appendix. In this analysis and elsewhere throughout the book I use the 1910 and 1940 public-use microdata samples (PUMS) as refined by the Integrated Public Use Microdata Series Project at the Social History Research Laboratory at the University of Minnesota.

    16. Of course, occupational data from the census paints an incomplete picture of the contributions made by these individuals. That is especially true of those made by women and children, which may not have been reflected in the occupational data collected by the census. It is also true for husbands because only a single occupation was reported for each individual even though some males held a variety of jobs throughout the year. Nonetheless, such data do allow a partial glimpse of the productive activities of family members.

    17. See Burton (1985) for a discussion of the patriarchal character of families in the rural South.

    18. The percentages of married men reporting their occupation as farmer in 1910 were: black owners, 89.6 percent; black renters, 96.4 percent; white owners, 90.1 percent; and white renters, 93.5 percent.

    19. The percentages of married men reporting their occupation as farmer in 1940 were: black owners, 75.5 percent; black renters, 68.3 percent; white owners, 69.8 percent; and white renters, 62.8 percent.

    20. Raper (1943:166).

    21. In citing the personal histories drawn from the Federal Writers' Project, I have adopted the style used by Pagnini (1992). Each interview in the collection is rep-

resented by a letter or letters identifying the state in which the interview took place and a number unique to an individual interview within the state. For example, the interview quoted here is NC-417. An S preceding the state-identifying letters means that the interview is from a supplement added to the original manuscripts. Interviews quoted from *These Are Our Lives* (Federal Writers' Project 1939[1969]) and *Such as Us: Southern Voices of the Thirties* (Terrill and Hirsch 1978) are attributed only to those sources.

22. Faulker et al. (1982:91).

23. Hagood (1939:4).

24. Raper (1936[1971]:74–75).

25. See, for example, Wilson (1987:76).

26. It is impossible to know whether "dressmakers" and "laundresses" worked on or off of the farm. Most likely they took in work that they performed in their own homes. Because they were earning off-farm income, however, I include them in the off-farm category.

27. Federal Writers' Project, SC-60.

28. Federal Writers' Project (1939[1969]:78).

29. See, for example, Link (1992).

30. Federal Writers' Project, SC-1.

31. Hagood (1939:211–12).

32. Federal Writers' Project, S-NC-52.

33. Anderson (1988:196–97).

34. Anderson (1988) provides a thorough discussion of the history of education for southern blacks during the early part of the twentieth century. See also Margo (1990).

35. The census data on children's schooling reported in tables 2 and 3 have certain limitations. The specific question asked in 1910 was whether a child had attended school since September of 1909. In 1940 children were asked whether they had attended school since March of 1940. Any attendance, no matter how brief, deserved an affirmative response. As a result, the description of educational patterns for farm children likely overstates somewhat the amount of schooling they were receiving. Unfortunately, neither the 1910 nor 1940 census included a question about a student's duration of schooling (e.g., months in school) during the past year.

36. The evidence for school enrollment in table 2 is restricted to children from ten to fourteen to simplify the presentation. Those are the ages at which school enrollment reached its highest levels during these years, so they offer a reasonable basis for residential and racial contrasts. More detailed age patterns in schooling for southern farm children are presented in table 3.

37. The occupational information in table 2 is reported only for older children to allow comparisons between 1910 and 1940. Although occupation data are available for children as young as ten in 1910, census enumerators in 1940 were instructed to record occupations only for individuals fourteen and older.

38. Only children of married couples who headed farm households are included in table 3 in order to focus the discussion around the roles of children who still lived within farm families. Without such a selection, children living away from home to work could inflate the percentage of children reporting occupations and deflate the percentage attending school.

39. As with the census data for the occupations of farm women, caution must be exercised when interpreting the information that was gathered for children. Not all enumerators were equally diligent about recording children as "family farm laborers" when it was appropriate. Thus, the census data surely underestimate the true extent of child labor in such households. The same is likely true regarding work for wages that children did away from the farm. Periodic work on a neighboring farm may not have been considered an "occupation" by the census-takers.

## Chapter 3: The Married Life

1. See, for example, Burton (1985), Jones (1988), and Kirby (1987).

2. See, for example, Davis, Gardner, and Gardner (1941:327–28).

3. Based on information from the 1910 and 1940 IPUMS files.

4. See, for example, Burton (1985:262).

5. Hajnal (1965).

6. Haines (1990).

7. For research that examines the association between societal marriage patterns and land availability, see Easterlin, Alter, and Condran (1978), Forster and Tucker (1972), Guest (1981), and Landale (1989).

8. See, for example, Burton (1985).

9. Because males usually are somewhat older than females at the time of their first marriage, I use ages eighteen to twenty-two for females and twenty to twenty-four for males to measure the prevalence of early marriage.

10. I calculated the median age at first marriage from the percentages single by single years of age for the respective population group, using a technique described by Shryock and Siegel (1976:292–93). It takes into account both the percentages never marrying and the speed with which the percent single declines among young women (especially those between fifteen and twenty-five).

11. It is possible that selective off-farm migration of unmarried individuals also contributes to these small percentages never married by forty-five to fifty-four. Such migration was especially likely for females who had failed to marry at younger ages and were from farm households. I have restricted this analysis of permanent non-marriage to ages forty-five to fifty-four to partially reduce the possibility of selective mortality and migration at older ages.

12. Substantial heterogeneity within the non-farm population reduces somewhat the utility of this comparison. For example, non-farm households ranged from rural families working primarily in the agricultural economy to residents of large south-

ern cities. No distinction is made between farmers and non-farmers among northern blacks because of the very small number of black farmers in the North.

13. See, for example, Daniel (1985), Fite (1984), and Kirby (1987).

14. These percentages refer to the adult population eighteen and older. They have been derived from the 1910 and 1940 IPUMS files.

15. Dixon (1971); see, for example, Landale and Tolnay (1991).

16. Oppenheimer (1988).

17. South and Lloyd (1992a); see also Lichter et al. (1992).

18. Landale (1989); Landale and Tolnay (1991).

19. By "closed" I mean that there was no migration into or out of the southern farm population. Therefore, the age distribution of the population would be influenced only by the number of births in any year and subsequent deaths experienced by the birth cohort.

20. Hajnal (1965).

21. Blacks were roughly twice as likely to be tenants in 1910—76.0 percent versus 38.2 percent for whites (table A-2). By 1940 the differential in tenancy had declined as landlessness grew for both races, especially among whites (79.6 percent for blacks versus 47.6 percent for whites in 1940).

22. Raper (1936[1971]:141).

23. Landale and Tolnay (1991). Although the same relationship was found for whites and blacks, males and females, it was somewhat weaker for white males.

24. Tolnay (1984).

25. These average values of farms have been drawn from ICPSR (1994: MRDF no. 0003). They were computed by dividing the total value of farm land and buildings in a county by the number of farms. To identify the extreme high- and low-value counties I limited consideration to only those with at least twenty-five farms in 1910 or 1940. Prices are reported in 1910 dollars, with the 1940 values adjusted by the change in the consumer price index between 1910 and 1940 for all consumer items (U.S. Bureau of the Census 1975).

26. Landale and Tolnay (1991).

27. Tolnay (1984).

28. See, for example, Tolnay (1987).

29. The issue of the economic value of children was discussed in greater detail in chapter 2.

30. Dixon (1971:222).

31. See Link (1992:ch. 10) for a discussion of attempts, largely unsuccessful, to change the role of women in southern rural society during the Progressive Era.

32. Burton (1985) notes that southern blacks faced a much different environment in towns and cities. He argues that the opportunities for black men in urban areas were severely constrained, forcing black women to be more fully engaged in the urban labor market. That made it more difficult for black men to rear and

support families in town and cities and resulted in a higher prevalence of female-headed households.

33. This is not to deny the important contributions made by some southern women outside of the agricultural economy. The strong voices of Jessie Daniel Ames and Ida B. Wells, two anti-lynching advocates during the early twentieth century, are good examples of exceptions to this generalization.

34. The sex ratio is determined by dividing the number of males in an area by the number of females. A value greater than 1 indicates a surplus of males; a value less than 1 suggests a deficit of males. The sex ratio is race-specific.

35. For 1910, counties are used to define the area of residence. Because county of residence is not available in the 1940 Public Use Sample, I have substituted state economic areas (SEAs). State economic areas are counties, or groups of counties, that share the same general socioeconomic environment.

36. See, for example, Landale and Tolnay (1991), Lichter et al. (1992), South and Lloyd (1992a), and Wilson (1987).

37. The specific values for levels of farm tenancy one standard deviation above the mean were 96.4 percent for males and 94.4 percent for females. Levels one standard deviation below the mean were 52.2 percent for males and 54.1 percent for females.

38. The original distribution of the average value of farm land within counties was highly skewed because of a few extreme values. Therefore, I have taken the natural logarithm of the variable. The coefficients in table 5 represent the effect of land value after it has been transformed.

39. The specific values for average farm cost at levels one standard deviation above the mean were $4,352 for males and $3,959 for females. At one standard deviation below the mean, the values were $1,055 for males and $1,056 for females. These average farm costs are substantially below those reported earlier in the chapter because of the different nature of the averages reported. Earlier in the chapter I reported averages for southern counties, where the average farm cost in each county was weighted equally. For the averages reported from the logistic regression analysis each county is represented as many times as there are individuals from that county included in the sample. Clearly, the difference between these two types of averages suggests that southern farmers were more heavily concentrated in areas where farms were worth considerably less.

40. The percent tenancy for counties one standard deviation above the average are 91.9 percent for males and 92.1 percent for females. For counties one standard deviation below the mean, the values are 56.1 percent for males and 57.4 percent for females.

41. In lieu of a more sophisticated examination of the possible determinants of permanent singleness among those forty-five to fifty-four, I compared individuals who had ever married with those who had never married on selected factors in 1910 (e.g., literacy, blindness, and deafness) and 1940 (educational attainment) that

might have affected their likelihood of marriage. I discovered no significant differences between the two groups on any characteristics in either year. Thus, despite their obvious deviation from conventional marital behavior in this society, the available evidence (admittedly scanty) does not suggest that the never-married population possessed significantly less human capital than their married counterparts.

42. Although a relatively high mortality for adult black males may have influenced family structure among African Americans it likely did not have a powerful effect on the supply of potential marriage partners in the ages when most marriages occurred (the early twenties).

## Chapter 4: Building the Southern Farm Family

1. Rice (1989).

2. See chapter 2 for a fuller discussion of the roles children performed on southern farms.

3. As used by demographers, "fecundity" refers to the biological capacity to produce live children, whereas "fertility" is the actual reproductive performance (usually of women).

4. Federal Writers' Project, NC-349.

5. Tolnay (1987:213–14). The total marital fertility rate is a summary measure based on age-specific marital fertility rates. It can be interpreted as the number of children the average married woman would bear throughout her lifetime if she survived and remained married from ages twenty to forty-nine and was exposed at each age to the prevailing set of age-specific fertility rates (in this case marital fertility rates in 1905–10 and 1935–40).

6. Of course, not all children borne by southern farm women survived to adulthood. Some families experienced infant and child mortality. Therefore, descriptions of completed family size based on the number of children born does not necessarily reflect the number of children in the household at the time of the census or the number of children raised to the age of independence.

7. The lower boundary of this age range was chosen because few women bear additional children after age forty-five. Therefore, we can be reasonably confident that these women were reporting their completed family sizes. The upper boundary was selected to minimize the influence of selective mortality. I have chosen women with a stable marital history (married once with spouse present) so that comparisons across groups and years will not be contaminated by differences, or changes, in marital stability. Of course, other things being equal, women with stable marital histories will have been exposed to the risk of childbearing more consistently than other women and therefore should have somewhat higher fertility. Although that difference should be recognized, it does not undermine the primary objective in this chapter, which concerns childbearing within marriage. The topic of marital stability will be taken up in chapter 5.

8. Henry (1961); Knodel (1977). See also Tolnay (1981, 1987) for further evidence supporting the conclusion that southern farm blacks were a natural fertility population near the turn of the twentieth century.

9. See, for example, Cutright and Shorter (1979), Farley (1970), McFalls and McFalls (1984), Tolnay (1989), Tolnay and Glynn (1994), and Wright and Pirie (1984).

10. See, for example, Farley (1970).

11. Once again, in order to minimize the impact of marital instability, consideration is restricted to women twenty to forty-four who had been married only once and were still living with their husbands. Group comparisons and changes across time in cumulative fertility are sensitive to differences in age and marital duration. What appears to be a difference, or change, in marital fertility might actually reflect variation in the degree of exposure to childbearing. In light of that possibility, I also examined average cumulative fertility levels after they had been standardized for age and marital duration. Standardization did not have a noticeable effect on the comparisons of cumulative fertility across groups or over time. Therefore the unstandardized averages are reported.

12. Of course, some of the women who were twenty to forty-four in 1910 also contributed to the completed family sizes of women who were forty-five to sixty-four in 1940 because they would have been fifty to seventy-four at the later date.

13. Morgan (1991).

14. McFalls and McFalls (1984) provide a thorough discussion of the relationship between disease and subfecundity or sterility. See also Cutright and Shorter (1979) and Wright and Pirie (1984) for discussions of the possible effects of disease on black fertility in the United States. Morgan (1991) mentions the possible fertility-related effects of abortion on childlessness historically in the United States.

15. Morgan (1991), Tolnay (1980), and Tolnay and Guest (1982) have made the same point in their studies of historical childlessness in the United States.

16. See especially Morgan (1991) and Tolnay and Guest (1982).

17. Morgan (1991:801).

18. See, for example, Cutright and Shorter (1979), Farley (1970), and Wright and Pirie (1984).

19. See, for example, Cutright and Shorter (1979), Farley (1970), Link (1992:230–31), McFalls and McFalls (1984), Tolnay (1989), Tolnay and Glynn (1994), and Wright and Pirie (1984).

20. The public-use microdata samples are not extremely rich in measures of individual-level socioeconomic characteristics. Measures of education and home ownership are available in both, however.

21. Once again I have used logistic regression analysis (chapter 3) as a vehicle for deriving predicted proportions childless for the different levels of these two

variables. For example, in 1910 I present the expected levels of childlessness for couples, owners as well as renters, in which the wives are literate and those in which the wives are illiterate. The same is done for 1940 except that estimated childlessness is derived for a high education category and a low education category. The former is fixed at the average number of years of schooling plus one standard deviation; the latter is the average number of years of schooling minus one standard deviation. The expected levels of childlessness, by categories for education and ownership, are estimated by holding all other variables constant at their average (mean) values. In addition to literacy (or schooling) and home ownership, marital duration (in years) is included in the analyses. That is done to allow for the strong negative relationship between marital duration and childlessness.

22. See Davis (1945) and Notestein (1945) for original articulations of demographic transition theory.

23. Henry (1961); Knodel (1977).

24. Preston (1978).

25. Ewbank (1987).

26. Daniel (1985); Kirby (1987).

27. Anderson (1988).

28. Johnson (1941a:19).

29. Kirby (1987:167), for example, argues that changes in the agricultural economy during the 1930s reduced the economic value of large families among southern farm families and led to a reduction in fertility.

30. For critiques of demand theories of fertility and arguments in favor of an alternative theoretical paradigm, see Cleland and Wilson (1987), van de Walle and Knodel (1980), and Watkins (1991).

31. See, for example, van de Walle and Knodel (1980).

32. Federal Writers' Project, NC-263.

33. Federal Writers' Project, NC-297.

34. Federal Writers' Project, AL-29.

35. Federal Writers' Project, NC-240.

36. Kirby (1987:166).

37. Kirby (1987:169–70).

38. Federal Writers' Project, NC-253.

39. Link (1992:89) also mentions beatings of women and children by fathers in the rural South.

40. Federal Writers' Project, NC-263.

41. See Tolnay, Graham, and Guest (1982) and Tolnay (1987).

42. Tolnay (1995b).

43. Tolnay and Glynn (1994).

44. Link (1992:112).

45. See, for example, Gutmann and Fliess (1993) or Tolnay and Glynn (1994).

## Chapter 5: Keeping the Family Together

1. Weeks (1995:278).

2. National Center for Health Statistics (1994); Preston and Haines (1991:70).

3. For example, Ewbank (1987:111) estimates the life expectancy for whites and blacks in South Carolina and North Carolina in 1920 to have been fifty-six and forty-five years, respectively. Thompson and Whelpton (1933:242–44) fix white and black life expectancies for the entire South in 1920 at about fifty-eight and forty-six years, respectively.

4. U.S. Bureau of the Census (1943b).

5. Federal Writers' Project, NC-227.

6. Federal Writers' Project, NC-249

7. Weeks (1995).

8. See, for example, Link (1992:112–14).

9. See, for example, Burton (1985:137).

10. Terrill and Hirsch (1978:269).

11. Federal Writers' Project, NC-212.

12. Johnson (1941a:21).

13. U.S. Bureau of the Census (1996:62).

14. U.S. Bureau of the Census (1996:66).

15. U.S. Bureau of the Census (1994:476).

16. Frazier (1932:33).

17. See, for example, Myrdal (1944), Raper (1936[1971]), and Woodson (1930).

18. Burton (1985); Shifflett (1975).

19. An additional line of attack on Moynihan's work argued that moral judgments about the normative family form are inappropriate. Rather than criticizing African American families as deviant, disorganized, or unstable, scholars should recognize it as an adaptive strategy in response to a hostile and racist socioeconomic climate. Reacting to forces largely outside of its control, the black community had evolved a family form that ensured survival. African American women in particular deserved credit for the heavy burden they were required to shoulder as the centers of their families. Partially as a result of this more culturally sensitive and tolerant perspective, social scientists began to avoid such terms as *illegitimacy* when referring to out-of-wedlock births. It also became more common to treat female-headed households as an alternative family form rather than a social problem.

20. Burton (1985:300–311).

21. Morgan et al. (1993:822).

22. Ruggles (1994).

23. Pagnini and Morgan (1996).

24. McDaniel (1994); McDaniel and Morgan (1996).

25. Many of the issues related to the marital and family stability of African

Americans will be explored in more depth in chapter 7, which focuses on northern urban areas.

26. See, for example, Watkins (1994).

27. Of course, the illegal importation of slaves from Africa continued after the slave trade was legally prohibited in 1808.

28. The history of black migration during the first half of the twentieth century will be discussed more fully in chapters 6 and 7.

29. To facilitate comparisons across groups (black versus whites) and over time (1910 versus 1940), current marital status is examined within the following age groups: twenty to thirty-four, thirty-five to forty-nine, and fifty to sixty-four.

30. It might seem unnecessary to consider gender differences when examining the current marital status of only ever-married individuals. After all, if a couple is divorced or separated does that not leave one divorced or separated male and one divorced or separated female? Only if there is no out-migration from the southern farm population can we assume such symmetry. There was such migration, however, and that fact warrants a cautionary note. When examining the distributions of detailed marital statuses for the farm population it must be kept in mind that they may have been influenced by differential migration. Perhaps the prevalence of widowhood or spouse separation is understated because those who experienced such disruptions were more likely to move to towns or non-farm rural locations. Short of complete marital and residential histories (which are not available from the census data), however, selective migratory processes cannot be factored into the analysis of marital stability.

31. The higher levels of widowhood reported by black women in 1910 are likely partially due to the tendency of some never-married women with children to report their marital status as widowed rather than single (Preston, Lim, and Morgan 1992).

32. In order to describe the degree of marital disruption caused by spousal separations I have divided the currently married population into those who resided with their spouse at the time of the census and those who lived apart. To be sure, not all of those living separately were in marital unions that had been permanently terminated. Some were away from home temporarily and would return shortly after the census was taken. At the same time, some spouses who were recorded as co-residing went their separate ways the day after they were enumerated. The census data provide only a snapshot perspective on the status of current marriages and must be interpreted with that limitation in mind. As I describe the prevalence of spousal separation, I refer to the percentages in tables 10 and 11 that appear in parentheses for the "married spouse present" and "married spouse absent" categories. These percentages are based only on the currently married population. That allows comparisons between races and across decades without having differentials and trends in widowhood distort the picture.

33. Pagnini and Morgan (1996).

34. See, for example, Johnson (1941a), Myrdal (1944), Powdermaker (1939), and Raper (1936[1971]).

35. Federal Writers' Project, LA-1.

36. Federal Writers' Project, NC-172.

37. Figures 8 and 9 summarize the living arrangements for children (presented in more detail in table 12). The evidence in table 12 and figures 8 and 9 is restricted to children fourteen and younger because of the greater likelihood of older children residing away from home in order to work—and sometimes living at their place of employment.

38. See, for example, McDaniel (1994), McDaniel and Morgan (1996), and Stack (1974).

39. McDaniel and Morgan (1996) controlled for "crisis conditions" such as illiteracy, female employment, and an absent husband and found that black mothers were still significantly more likely than white mothers to live apart from their children. They do not deny that such crises result in children living away from parents but argue that African cultural traditions also contribute to the significant race differential in child fosterage.

40. Lemann (1991:31).

41. Of course, there are many reasons why such an assumption may not be accurate. First, reported marital status and marital duration were easily manipulated to hide births that occurred outside of wedlock (see, e.g., Preston, Lim, and Morgan 1992). Second, and probably even more problematic, marriages that occurred subsequent to a non-marital birth will bias an estimate of non-marital childbearing downward based solely on the marital status of mothers. Even if precise estimates of the level of illegitimacy in this population are elusive, however, this approach may still be a way to provide useful information with which to gauge racial differences in non-marital childbearing and its change over time.

42. This conclusion is consistent with Burton's (1985) description of rural families in Edgefield County, South Carolina, in the late nineteenth century.

43. See, for example, Morgan et al. (1993), Moynihan (1965), and Ruggles (1994).

## Chapter 6: The Mobility of Southern Farm Families

1. Lee (1966).

2. Kousser (1974).

3. See, for example, Flynn (1983), Mandle (1978), and Ransom and Sutch (1977).

4. Anderson (1988); Johnson (1941b); Margo (1990).

5. This is the total number of blacks lynched by white mobs in the following ten states: Alabama, Arkansas, Florida, Georgia, Kentucky, Louisiana, Mississippi, North Carolina, South Carolina, and Tennessee (Tolnay and Beck 1995). See also

Tolnay and Beck (1992) for a description of how lynchings motivated southern blacks to migrate.

6. Newby (1989).

7. Kirby (1987) mentions that before 1930 the opportunities for non-farm work among black men were largely restricted to coal mines and tobacco warehouses and factories. Turpentine camps in south Georgia and Florida can also be added to that list.

8. U.S. Bureau of the Census (1995: table no. 5, p. 10).

9. Watkins (1994).

10. Mandle (1978).

11. For a good description of dept peonage in the South during the early twentieth century see Daniel (1972).

12. Rosengarten (1974:235–36).

13. Raper (1936[1971]:202).

14. Donald (1921:412).

15. Myrdal (1944:231).

16. U.S. Bureau of the Census (1975:105).

17. See, for example, Gould (1981) and Haller (1963).

18. See Hutchinson (1981) for a thorough history of U.S. immigration policy.

19. Campbell and Johnson (1981); Henri (1975); Marks (1989); Woodson (1918[1969]).

20. Many of the letters in the collection published by the *Journal of Negro History* were from correspondence to the *Chicago Defender,* a publication with a primarily African American audience.

21. Scott (1919:422).

22. Scott (1919:440).

23. U.S. Bureau of the Census (1975:93–95).

24. Woofter and Winston (1939:6).

25. See, for example, Johnson, Embree, and Alexander (1935), Raper (1936[1971], 1943), Raper and Reid (1941), and Woofter (1936).

26. Woofter and Winston (1939:124–25). The seven "Eastern Cotton States" are Alabama, Arkansas, Georgia, Louisiana, Mississippi, North Carolina, and South Carolina.

27. See, for example, Havens (1986) and Kirby (1987).

28. Daniel (1985:175).

29. U.S. Bureau of the Census (1975:126).

30. Certain limitations to the migration-related data available from the 1940 census should be noted. First, inferences of migration must be made by comparing where an individual lived in 1935 with their place of residence in 1940. Unfortunately, information about their other characteristics or statuses in 1935 is unavailable—for example, marital status, tenure status, occupation, or living arrangements. Second, inferences of geographic mobility can be made only for one

move between 1935 and 1940. Clearly, some individuals moved more than once during those five years. For those "multiple movers," however, mobility can be described only by comparing their 1935 and 1940 residences. Third, some of the questions regarding residence in 1935 have a large amount of missing data, which will be noted when those questions are considered. I am convinced that these relatively few limitations to the data are more than outweighed by the insights they can provide about the geographic mobility of the southern farm population during this important era.

31. Woofter (1936:114).

32. Woofter (1936:123).

33. Raper (1936[1971], 1943); Raper and Reid (1941); see also Campbell and Johnson (1981) and Kirby (1987:276–78).

34. Among the sample of farm couples, 82 percent of African Americans and 51 percent of whites were renters.

35. The special nature of the sample of farm couples must be kept in mind when interpreting these patterns of residential mobility. That is, they are couples who lived on southern farms in 1940. Families that moved from farm to non-farm residences (rural or urban) between 1935 and 1940 are excluded from consideration. The class distinctions are based on the couples' tenure status in 1940; their class location in 1935 is unknown.

36. The median distances reported in table 14 should not be overemphasized because the information was not available for most inter-county migrants. For example, the number of cases range from only 26 for black owners to 1,173 for white renters.

37. See chapter 3 for a description of logistic regression. A wife's education is not included in the analysis because it is highly correlated with her husband's education.

38. All of the coefficients in table 16 are statistically significant at p < .001, meaning that one can conclude with 99.9 percent certainty that their effect on migration status is real and not due to chance.

39. The expected probabilities described here assume the same causal processes for whites and blacks. That is, the logistic regression analysis reported in table 16 pooled blacks and whites and did not allow for the influence of the independent variables to vary by race. Somewhat different probabilities would be obtained if separate equations were estimated for black and whites and if race-specific means and standard deviations were used to identify the migration-prone and migration-averse groups. The expected probabilities are derived by inserting the appropriate value of each independent variable into the logistic regression equation, multiplying by the corresponding coefficient, and then summing across all variables (including the intercept). That yields a predicted log likelihood (L) that can be converted to a predicted probability using the following equation: $P_i = 1/(1 + e^{-L})$.

40. Federal Writers' Project, S-SC-76.

41. Federal Writers' Project, S-SC-68.

42. For the purposes of this discussion of the characteristics of off-farm mobility, "migrants" are defined as those individuals who lived on southern farms in 1935 but not in 1940. Non-migrants are those who reported a southern farm residence in both 1935 and 1940. Although I refer to the former group as "off-farm migrants," it should be recognized that a small percentage of them moved to farm residences in the North or West. By "off-farm migrants" I mean those who left southern farms between 1935 and 1940, regardless of the type of dwelling in which they lived in 1940.

43. Lieberson (1980); Ovington (1969).

## Chapter 7: To the City

Portions of this chapter appeared as "The Great Migration and Changes in the Northern Black Family, 1940 to 1990" (Tolnay 1997) and are used with permission.

1. Throughout this chapter I often use the inelegant term *non-South* to refer to all states outside the census-defined South. Occasionally, however, I revert to the use of *northern* to refer to cities in the North and West.

2. See, for example, Grossman (1989) and Lemann (1991).

3. Ballard (1984).

4. In *Going North,* Neil Fligstein (1981) provides an excellent description of the changes in the "social relations of production" and "technical relations of production" in southern agriculture during the first half of the twentieth century and how they affected migration. Nicholas Lemann (1991) discusses the impact of mechanical cotton pickers on migration from the South in *The Promised Land.* Other good treatments of the social and economic forces responsible for south-to-north migration during this period can be found in Campbell and Johnson (1981), Grossman (1989), Jones (1992), Kirby (1987), and Marks (1989).

5. In absolute numbers there were more southern-born whites living in the North. In 1970, for example, 7,376,464 (15.6 percent) of southern-born whites lived in the North or West. The comparable figures for blacks were 3,478,732 (23.8 percent) (U.S. Bureau of the Census 1975).

6. Woodson (1918[1969]).

7. Mossell (1921:216).

8. Frazier (1932:49).

9. Frazier (1932:73).

10. The Chicago Commission on Race Relations (1922:94).

11. Grossman (1989:33).

12. Lemann (1991).

13. Hamilton (1959); Lieberson (1978).

14. Marks (1989:167).

15. Information about the size of the black southern rural population in 1940 was drawn from U.S Bureau of the Census (1985:14). Figures for educational at-

tainment were drawn from page 93 of the same source and refer to the population twenty-five years of age and older.

16. Drake and Cayton (1962:577).

17. Tolnay (1998a).

18. Figures on total non-southern black population in 1910 and 1940 are from U.S. Bureau of the Census (1975); the black population of Chicago in 1910 and 1940 is from Drake and Cayton (1962:8).

19. Frazier (1932:238).

20. Drake and Cayton (1962:66).

21. Mossell (1921).

22. See Massey and Denton (1993) for an excellent discussion of the history of racial residential segregation in America and the various forces responsible for increasing segregation during the twentieth century.

23. See Wilson (1987) for a good discussion of the development of the black urban underclass.

24. For example, see Frazier (1966:257).

25. Frazier (1966:95).

26. Frazier (1966:255).

27. Frazier (1966:367).

28. Du Bois (1899[1990]:67).

29. Drake and Cayton (1962:584).

30. Drake and Cayton (1962:590).

31. Other social scientists also noted the unique family patterns of blacks in the rural South, especially sharecroppers (e.g., Johnson 1934; Myrdal 1944; Powdermaker 1939; Raper 1936[1971]). They did not, however, necessarily infer a strong connection between the migration of rural blacks and changing family patterns in the urban North.

32. Moynihan (1965).

33. Following the publication of Moynihan's book, a number of authors took issue with his conclusion that the black family was historically unstable and disrupted (e.g., Furstenberg, Hershberg, and Modell 1975; Gutman 1976; Lammermeier 1973; Shifflett 1975). Research using historical U.S. Census data, however, tends to vindicate part of Moynihan's argument (e.g., Morgan et al. 1993; Ruggles 1994).

34. Lemann (1991:31).

35. Lemann (1991:287).

36. See, for example, Cherlin (1992), Tucker and Mitchell-Kernan (1995), and Waite (1995).

37. Lieberson and Wilkinson (1976:222–23).

38. Other studies have compared the economic characteristics of black migrants and non-migrants living in the North. They have shown that migrants were more likely to be employed and had higher incomes and lower levels of poverty or wel-

fare dependency, even though they had lower levels of education (e.g., Long 1974; Long and Heltman 1975; Masters 1972). The reverse differential was observed for whites. Unlike Lieberson and Wilkinson (1976), these other studies did not examine family-related characteristics.

39. See, for example, Powdermaker (1939), Raper (1936[1971]), and Johnson (1934).

40. See Farley (1970) for a summary.

41. In lieu of information about past migration, which is not available for all censuses, the regional origin of children is distinguished by using the reported birthplace for them and their mothers. Children are considered to be of southern origin if they (or their mother) were born in the South. If neither the mother nor child was southern-born, then the child is classified as having northern origins. Only children living with their mothers are included to reduce a potential upward bias in the percentage of migrant children living with both parents. Because the birthplace of parents is included in the determination of whether children had southern origins, the odds of being classified as a migrant increases when both parents are present. To circumvent that problem I consider only the birthplace of the child and mother in determining whether they had southern origins. A possible limitation of this classification scheme is that the mother may have been the child of a southern-born parent who migrated to the North. Because the U.S. Censuses for 1940 through 1990 do not include the birthplace of parents on person records, it is impossible to include information for previous generations in making this distinction. Thus, those with southern origins may be considered relatively recent migrants from the South. By including only children living with their mother and thereby ignoring those living with neither parent, the evidence in figure 11 surely understates the overall percentage of children not living in two-parent households.

42. It is difficult to discern non-marital childbearing directly from the census data, because to do so requires reliable information about the marital status and marital duration of the mother as well as the date of birth for all children. Rather than trying to determine the legitimacy of each child co-residing with his or her mother, I use a relatively straightforward approach to describing recent trends in non-marital childbearing for residents of northern cities. The reported marital status for each mother of a child zero to fourteen years of age is used to compute the percentage of mothers who never married. As before, the mother's birthplace is used to distinguish southern-origin from northern-origin women. That evidence does not refer to the marital status of a mother at the time of her child's birth. It is based on her marital status at the time of census enumeration. Therefore, women who had children while unmarried but who subsequently married are not considered to have experienced non-marital fertility. As a result, these figures likely underestimate the true extent of non-marital childbearing in this population.

43. Johnson (1941a).

44. Powdermaker (1939).

45. The PSID is a longitudinal survey of Americans and their families that was initiated in 1968 with roughly eighteen thousand individuals. In subsequent years the sample size grew substantially (e.g., it was 37,500 in 1988) as a result of the creation of new families by those in the original sample, for example through the marriage of children or the divorce and remarriage of adults. See Hill (1992) for more information about the PSID.

46. The evidence was presented by race and residence in 1972, and no specific comparison can be made between migrants and non-migrants. Rather, the results are useful only for discerning whether significant attitudinal differences existed between southern farmers and others in 1972. The percentages in table 18 have been adjusted for differences in family income to avoid inferences of cultural differences across groups that are due to social class. That adjustment was made by conducting a logistic regression analysis. The dependent variables were dichotomies, scored 1 if the respondent fit the characteristic and 0 otherwise. On the righthand side of the equation were dummy variables representing the three residential groups and a continuous covariate measuring total family income. The coefficients produced by this analysis were used, in conjunction with the mean value of total family income, to generate an expected percentage for each residence group, holding total family income constant at the overall mean. Separate analyses were conducted for blacks and whites.

47. The significance of the inter-group differences were determined from the results of the logistic regression analysis used to generate the adjusted percentages in table 18.

48. See, for example, Gregory (1995), Lieberson and Wilkinson (1976), Long (1974), Long and Heltman (1975), and Masters (1972).

49. Wilson (1987:176).

50. Tolnay (1998b).

51. See, for example, Ballard (1984).

## Epilogue

1. U.S. Bureau of the Census (1975, 1990).

2. For the North Carolina School, see, for example, Hagood (1939), Johnson (1934, 1941a), Johnson et al. (1935), Raper (1936[1971], 1943), Raper and Reid (1941), and Woofter and Winston (1939). For a focus on inner cities, see Anderson (1990), Drake and Cayton (1962), Frazier (1932, 1966), Lemann (1991), Massey and Denton (1993), Taeuber and Taeuber (1965), and Wilson (1987).

3. Mandle (1978).

4. Lemann (1991:6).

5. See, for example, Ransom and Sutch (1977).

6. See, for example, Tolnay (1984).

7. Tolnay (1995a).

8. Throughout the previous chapters, a variety of other macro-level forces affecting southern farm families also have been discussed.

9. Of course, not all African American families are located in the inner cities of metropolitan areas. Many reside in city suburbs or even in non-metropolitan areas. Likewise, not all black families face the same challenges of those in inner cities, and many families of all residences are stable and resilient. The focus in this discussion, however, is a possible parallel between the forces affecting family life in the farm South and those affecting family life in inner cities.

10. This average is for the thirty northern metropolitan areas with the largest black populations. See Massey and Denton (1993:47).

11. Massey and Denton (1993:168), emphasis added; see also Massey (1996).

12. Kasarda (1985); Wilson (1987).

13. Wilson (1987).

14. See, for example, Farley (1988). Lichter et al. (1992) and Wilson (1987) infer a weaker effect of female economic independence on the marital behavior of black women.

15. See, for example, Easterlin (1975).

16. Smith, Morgan, and Koropeckyj-Cox (1995).

17. Geronimus (1987).

18. See, for example, McLanahan and Sandefur (1994) for a discussion of the consequences for children of growing up in single-parent households.

19. Anderson (1989:69).

20. Murray (1984).

21. See, for example, Bane and Ellwood (1994) and Ruggles (1997).

22. In one of the best studies on this topic, Lichter, McLaughlin, and Ribar (1997) show that welfare contributed to the rise in female-headed families between 1980 and 1990, especially among blacks. They conclude that other factors, especially local marriage markets and general economic conditions, however, had much stronger effects on the growth of female-headed families. See also Moffitt (1992, 1994).

23. Changes in the family-related impact of public assistance programs such as Aid to Families with Dependent Children was one of the stated reasons for the reform of federal welfare policy.

## Appendix

1. Susan Watkins's edited volume *After Ellis Island: Newcomers and Natives in the 1910 Census* (1994) is an excellent example of the variety of substantive questions that can be explored using historical public-use samples. Other examples include Elman (1993), Guest and Tolnay (1985), Landale (1989), Landale and Tolnay (1991), Morgan et al. (1993), Preston and Haines (1991), Ruggles (1994, 1997), Sassler (1995), and Tolnay (1995a).

2. The 1900 public-use sample includes information for 27,067 households and 100,438 persons.

3. For more information about the 1910 black oversample see Morgan and Ewbank (1990).

4. Bogue (1951).

5. See U.S. Bureau of the Census (1983:ch. 6) for a fuller description of the SEAs used in the 1940 public-use sample.

6. For more complete information about the IPUMS data see Ruggles and Sobek (1995) and the special winter 1995 issue of the journal *Historical Methods* devoted to the project (vol. 28, no. 1).

7. For an overview of the Federal Writers' Project, see Terrill and Hirsch (1978). Several interviews are also published in Federal Writers' Project (1939[1969]). Throughout this book many references are made to specific oral histories collected during the Federal Writers' Project. Most of these were obtained from Deana Pagnini.

8. In 1910 the census further distinguished between blacks and mulattoes. I have combined the two groups into a single category.

9. These figures for the number of households and individuals reflect the totals available in the 1910 IPUMS and do not include the black oversample. The oversample is used in some analyses where it is most compatible with the IPUMS.

10. The median divides the age distribution into two equal parts, with as many individuals above the median age as there are below the median age. In contrast, the mean is an arithmetic average that takes into consideration every person's age and therefore is more sensitive than the median to extreme (especially old) ages.

11. See, for example, Burton (1985:262).

12. See, for example, Lichter et al. (1992), South and Lloyd (1992a, 1992b), and Wilson (1987).

# References

Anderson, Elijah. 1989. "Sex Codes and Family Life among Poor Inner-City Youths." *The Annals of the American Academy of Political and Social Science* 501:59–78.

———. 1990. *Streetwise: Race, Class, and Change in an Urban Community.* Chicago: University of Chicago Press.

Anderson, James D. 1988. *The Education of Blacks in the South, 1860–1935.* Chapel Hill: University of North Carolina Press.

Ballard, Allen. 1984. *One More Day's Journey: The Story of a Family and a People.* New York: McGraw-Hill.

Bane, Mary Jo, and David T. Ellwood. 1994. *Welfare Realities: From Rhetoric to Reform.* Cambridge: Harvard University Press.

Blassingame, John W. 1977. *Slave Testimony: Two Centuries of Letters, Speeches, Interviews, and Autobiographies.* Baton Rouge: Louisiana State University Press.

Bogue, Donald J. 1951. *State Economic Areas.* Washington, D.C.: Government Printing Office.

Burton, Orville Vernon. 1985. *In My Father's House Are Many Mansions: Family and Community in Edgefield, South Carolina.* Chapel Hill: University of North Carolina Press.

Cain, Mead T. 1977. "The Economic Activities of Children in a Village in Bangladesh." *Population and Development Review* 3:201–27.

Campbell, Daniel M., and Rex Johnson. 1981. *Black Migration in America: A Social Demographic History.* Durham: Duke University Press.

Cherlin, Andrew J. 1992. *Marriage, Divorce, Remarriage.* Cambridge: Harvard University Press.

Chicago Commission on Race Relations. 1922. *The Negro in Chicago: A Study of Race Relations and a Race Riot.* Chicago: University of Chicago Press.

Cleland, John, and Christopher Wilson. 1987. "Demand Theories of Fertility Transition: An Iconoclastic View." *Population Studies* 41:5–30.

Cutright, Philips, and Edward Shorter. 1979. "The Effects of Health on the Completed Fertility of Nonwhite and White U.S. Women Born between 1867 and 1935." *Journal of Social History* 13:191–217.

Daniel, Pete. 1972. *The Shadow of Slavery: Peonage in the South.* Urbana: University of Illinois Press.

————. 1981. "The Transformation of the Rural South 1930 to the Present." *Agricultural History* 55:231–48.

————. 1985. *Breaking the Land: The Transformation of Cotton, Tobacco, and Rice Cultures since 1880.* Urbana: University of Illinois Press.

Davis, Allison, Burleigh B. Gardner, and Mary R. Gardner. 1941. *Deep South: A Social Anthropological Study of Caste and Class.* Chicago: University of Chicago Press.

Davis, Kingsley. 1945. "The World Demographic Transition." *The Annals of the American Academy of Political and Social Science* 237:1–11.

Dixon, Ruth B. 1971. "Explaining Cross-Cultural Variations in Age at Marriage and Proportions Never Marrying." *Population Studies* 25:215–33.

Donald, Henderson. 1921. "The Negro Migration of 1916–1918." *Journal of Negro History* 6:383–498.

Drake, St. Clair, and Horace R. Cayton. 1962. *Black Metropolis: A Study of Negro Life in a Northern City.* New York: Harper and Row.

Du Bois, W. E. B. 1899[1990]. *The Philadelphia Negro.* New York: Blom.

Easterlin, Richard A. 1975. "An Economic Framework for Fertility Analysis." *Studies in Family Planning* 6:54–63.

Easterlin, Richard A., George Alter, and Gretchen Condran. 1978. "Farms and Farm Families in Old and New Areas: The Northern States in 1860." In *Family and Population in Nineteenth-Century America,* 22–84. Ed. Tamara K. Hareven and Maris A. Vinovskis. Princeton: Princeton University Press.

Elman, Cheryl. 1993. "Turn of the Century Dependence and Interdependence: Roles of Teens in the Family Economies of the Aged." *Journal of Family History* 18:65–85.

Ewbank, Douglas. 1987. "History of Black Mortality and Health Before 1940." *Milbank Quarterly* 65, suppl. 1:100–128.

Farley, Reynolds. 1970. *Growth of the Black Population.* Chicago: Markham.

————. 1988. "After the Starting Line: Blacks and Women in an Uphill Race." *Demography* 24:477–95.

Faulkner, Audrey Olsen, Marsel A. Heisel, Wendell Holbrook, and Shirley Geismar. 1982. *When I Was Comin' Up: An Oral History of Aged Blacks.* Hamden: Archon Books.

Federal Writers' Project. 1939[1969]. *These Are Our Lives: As Told by the People and Written by Members of the Federal Writers' Project of the Works Progress Administration in North Carolina, Tennessee, Georgia*. New York: Arno Press.

Fite, Gilbert. 1984. *Cotton Fields No More: Southern Agriculture, 1865–1980*. Lexington: University Press of Kentucky.

Fligstein, Neil. 1981. *Going North*. New York: Academic Press.

Flynn, Charles L. 1983. *White Land, Black Labor: Caste and Class in Late Nineteenth-Century Georgia*. Baton Rouge: Louisiana State University Press.

Forster, Colin, and G. S. L. Tucker. 1972. *Economic Opportunity and White American Fertility Ratios*. New Haven: Yale University Press.

Frazier, E. Franklin. 1932. *The Negro Family in Chicago*. Chicago: University of Chicago Press.

———. 1966. *The Negro Family in the United States*. Chicago: University of Chicago Press.

Furstenberg, Frank, Theodore Hershberg, and John Modell. 1975. "The Origins of the Female-Headed Black Family: The Impact of the Urban Experience." *Journal of Interdisciplinary History* 6:211–34.

Genovese, Eugene D. 1976. *Roll, Jordan, Roll: The World the Slaves Made*. New York: Vintage.

Geronimus, Arline T. 1987. "On Teenage Childbearing and Neonatal Mortality in the United States." *Population and Development Review* 13:245–79.

Gould, Stephen Jay. 1981. *The Mismeasure of Man*. New York: Norton.

Gregory, James N. 1995. "The Southern Diaspora and the Urban Dispossessed: Demonstrating the Census Public Use Microdata Samples." *Journal of American History* 82:111–34.

Grossman, James R. 1989. *Land of Hope: Chicago, Black Southerners, and the Great Migration*. Chicago: University of Chicago Press.

Grubbs, Donald H. 1971. *Cry from the Cotton: The Southern Tenant Farmers' Union and the New Deal*. Chapel Hill: University of North Carolina Press.

Guest, Avery M. 1981. "Social Structure and U.S. Inter-state Fertility Differentials in 1900." *Demography* 18:465–86.

Guest, Avery M., and Stewart E. Tolnay. 1985. "Agricultural Organization and U.S. Educational Consumption in 1900." *Sociology of Education* 58:201–12.

Gutman, Herbert. 1976. *The Black Family in Slavery and Freedom*. New York: Pantheon.

Gutmann, Myron P., and Kenneth H. Fliess. 1993. "The Determinants of Early Fertility Decline in Texas." *Demography* 30:443–57.

Hagood, Margaret Jarman. 1939. *Mothers of the South: Portraiture of the White Tenant Farm Woman*. Chapel Hill: University of North Carolina Press.

Haines, Michael. 1990. "Western Fertility in Mid-Transition: Fertility and Nuptiality in the United States and Selected Nations at the Turn of the Century." *Journal of Family History* 15:23–48.

Hajnal, John. 1965. "European Marriage Patterns in Perspective." In *Population in History*, 101–43. Ed. D. V. Glass and D. E. C. Eversley. London: Arnold.

Haller, Mark H. 1963. *Eugenics: Hereditarian Attitudes in American Thought*. New Brunswick: Rutgers University Press.

Hamilton, Horace C. 1959. "Educational Selectivity of Net Migration from the South." *Social Forces* 38:33–42.

Havens, Eugene A. 1986. *Studies in the Transformation of U.S. Agriculture*. Boulder: Westview Press.

Henri, Florette. 1975. *Black Migration: Movement North, 1900–1920*. Garden City: Anchor Press/Doubleday.

Henry, Louis. 1961. "Some Data on Natural Fertility." *Eugenics Quarterly* 8:81–91.

Higgs, Robert. 1977. *Competition and Coercion: Blacks in the American Economy, 1865–1914*. New York: Cambridge University Press.

Hill, Martha S. 1992. *The Panel Study of Income Dynamics: A User's Guide*. Newbury Park: Sage Publications.

Himes, Norman Edwin. 1936. *Medical History of Contraception*. Baltimore: Williams and Wilkins.

Hutchinson, E. P. 1981. *Legislative History of American Immigration Policy, 1798–1965*. Philadelphia: University of Pennsylvania Press.

Interuniversity Consortium for Political and Social Research. 1994. *Historical, Demographic, Economic, and Social Data: The United States, 1790–1970*. Machine Readable Data File 0003. Ann Arbor: ICPSR.

Jaynes, Gerald David. 1986. *Branches without Roots: Genesis of the Black Working Class in the American South, 1862–1882*. New York: Oxford University Press.

Johnson, Charles S. 1934. *Shadow of the Plantation*. Chicago: University of Chicago Press.

———. 1941a. *Growing Up in the Black Belt: Negro Youth in the Rural South*. Washington, D.C.: American Council on Education.

———. 1941b. *Statistical Atlas of Southern Counties: Listing and Analysis of Socioeconomic Indices of 1,104 Southern Counties*. Chapel Hill: University of North Carolina Press.

Johnson, Charles S., Edwin R. Embree, and W. W. Alexander. 1935. *The Collapse of Cotton Tenancy: Summary of Field Studies and Statistical Surveys, 1933–35*. Chapel Hill: University of North Carolina Press.

Jones, Jacqueline. 1988. "'Tore Up and a-Movin': Perspectives on the Work of Black and Poor White Women in the Rural South, 1865–1940." In *Women and Farming: Changing Roles, Changing Structures*, 15–34. Ed. Wava G. Haney and Jane B. Knowles. Boulder: Westview Press.

———. 1992. *The Dispossessed: America's Underclasses from the Civil War to the Present*. New York: Basic Books.

Kasarda, J. D. 1985. "Urban Change and Minority Opportunities." In *The New Urban Reality*, 36–67. Ed. P. E. Peterson. Washington, D.C.: Brookings Institution.

Kester, Howard. 1936[1969]. *Revolt among the Sharecroppers*. New York: Arno Press.

Kirby, Jack Temple. 1987. *Rural Worlds Lost: The American South, 1920–1960*. Baton Rouge: Louisiana State University Press.

Knodel, John. 1977. "Family Limitation and the Fertility Transition: Evidence from the Age Patterns of Fertility in Europe and Asia." *Population Studies* 31:219–49.

Kousser, J. Morgan. 1974. *The Shaping of Southern Politics: Suffrage Restriction and the Establishment of the One-Party South*. New Haven: Yale University Press.

Lammermeier, Paul. 1973. "The Urban Black Family in the Nineteenth Century: A Study of Black Family Structure in the Ohio Valley, 1850–1880." *Journal of Marriage and the Family* 35:440–55.

Landale, Nancy S. 1989. "Agricultural Opportunity and Marriage: The United States at the Turn of the Century." *Demography* 26:203–18.

Landale, Nancy S., and Stewart E. Tolnay. 1991. "Group Differences in Economic Opportunity and the Timing of Marriage: Blacks and Whites in the Rural South, 1910." *American Sociological Review* 56:33–45.

Lee, Everett S. 1966. "A Theory of Migration." *Demography* 3:47–57.

Lemann, Nicholas. 1991. *The Promised Land: The Great Migration and How It Changed America*. New York: Alfred A. Knopf.

Lichter, Daniel T., Diane K. McLaughlin, and David C. Ribar. 1997. "Welfare and the Rise of Female-Headed Families." *American Journal of Sociology* 103:112–43.

Lichter, Daniel T., Diane K. McLaughlin, George Kephart, and David J. Landry. 1992. "Race and the Retreat from Marriage: A Shortage of Marriageable Men?" *American Sociological Review* 57:781–99.

Lieberson, Stanley. 1978. "Selective Black Migration from the South: A Historical View." In *The Demography of Racial and Ethnic Groups*, 119–41. Ed. Frank D. Bean and W. Parker Frisbie. New York: Academic Press.

———. 1980. *A Piece of the Pie: Blacks and White Immigrants since 1880*. Berkeley: University of California Press.

Lieberson, Stanley, and Christy A. Wilkinson. 1976. "A Comparison between Northern and Southern Blacks Residing in the North." *Demography* 13:199–224.

Link, William A. 1992. *The Paradox of Southern Progressivism, 1880–1930*. Chapel Hill: University of North Carolina Press.

Long, Larry H. 1974. "Poverty Status and Receipt of Welfare among Migrants and Nonmigrants in Large Cities." *American Sociological Review* 39:46–56.

Long, Larry H., and Lynne R. Heltman. 1975. "Migration and Income Differences between Black and White Men in the North." *American Journal of Sociology* 80:1391–409.

Mandle, Jay R. 1978. *The Roots of Black Poverty: The Southern Plantation Economy after the Civil War.* Durham: Duke University Press.

Margo, Robert. 1990. *Race and Schooling in the South, 1880–1950.* Chicago: University of Chicago Press.

Marks, Carole. 1989. *Farewell—We're Good and Gone: The Great Black Migration.* Bloomington: Indiana University Press.

Massey, Douglas. 1996. "The Age of Extremes: Concentrated Affluence and Poverty in the Twenty-first Century." *Demography* 33:395–412.

Massey, Douglas, and Nancy Denton. 1993. *American Apartheid.* Cambridge: Harvard University Press.

Masters, Stanley H. 1972. "Are Black Migrants from the South to Northern Cities Worse Off Than Blacks Already There?" *Journal of Human Resources* 8:411–23.

McDaniel, Antonio. 1994. "Historical Racial Differences in Living Arrangements of Children." *Journal of Family History* 19:57–77.

McDaniel, Antonio, and S. Philip Morgan. 1996. "Racial Differences in Mother-Child Coresidence in the Past." *Journal of Marriage and the Family* 58:1011–17.

McFalls, Joseph A., and Marguerite McFalls. 1984. *Disease and Fertility.* Orlando: Academic Press.

McKenzie, Robert Tracy. 1994. *One South or Many? Plantation Belt and Upcountry in Civil War–Era Tennessee.* New York: Cambridge University Press.

McLanahan, Sara, and Gary Sandefur. 1994. *Growing Up with a Single Parent: What Hurts, What Helps.* Cambridge: Harvard University Press.

Mitchell, H. L. 1979. *Mean Things Happening in This Land: The Life and Times of H. L. Mitchell, Co-founder of the Southern Tenant Farmers' Union.* Montclair: Allanheld, Osmun.

Moffitt, Robert A. 1992. "The Incentive Effects of the U.S. Welfare System: A Review." *Journal of Economic Literature* 30:1–61.

———. 1994. "Welfare Effects on Female Headship with Area Effects." *Journal of Human Resources* 29:621–36.

Morgan, S. Philip. 1991. "Late Nineteenth- and Early Twentieth-Century Childlessness." *American Journal of Sociology* 97:779–807.

Morgan, S. Philip, and Douglas Ewbank. 1990. *Census of Population, 1910 [United States]: Oversample of Black-Headed Households: User's Guide.* Philadelphia: University of Pennsylvania.

Morgan, S. Philip, Antonio McDaniel, Andrew T. Miller, and Samuel H. Preston. 1993. "Racial Differences in Household Structure at the Turn of the Century." *American Journal of Sociology* 98:798–828.

Mossell, Sadie Farmer. 1921. "The Standard of Living among One Hundred Negro Migrant Families in Philadelphia." *Annals of the American Academy of Political and Social Science* 97:169–222.

Moynihan, Daniel P. 1965. *The Negro Family: The Case for National Action.* Washington, D.C.: Office of Policy Planning and Research, U.S. Department of Labor.

Mueller, Eva. 1976. "The Economic Value of Children in Peasant Agriculture." In *Population and Development: The Search for Selective Interventions,* 98–153. Ed. Ronald G. Ridker. Baltimore: Johns Hopkins University Press.

Murray, Charles. 1984. *Losing Ground: American Social Policy, 1950–1980.* New York: Basic Books.

Myrdal, Gunnar. 1944. *An American Dilemma: The Negro Problem and Modern Democracy.* New York: Harper and Row.

National Center for Health Statistics. 1994. *Vital Statistics of the United States, 1990, Life Tables.* Public Health Service. Washington, D.C.: Government Printing Office.

Newby, I. A. 1965. *Jim Crow's Defense: Anti-Negro Thought in America, 1900–1930.* Baton Rouge: Louisiana State University Press.

———. 1989. *Plain Folk in the New South: Social Change and Cultural Persistence, 1880–1915.* Baton Rouge: Louisiana State University Press.

Notestein, Frank W. 1945. "Population—The Long View." In *Food for the World,* 36–57. Ed. T. W. Schultz. Chicago: University of Chicago Press.

Novak, Daniel A. 1978. *The Wheel of Servitude: Black Forced Labor after Slavery.* Lexington: University Press of Kentucky.

Oppenheimer, Valerie K. 1988. "A Theory of Marriage Timing." *American Journal of Sociology* 94:563–91.

Ovington, Mary White. 1969. *Half a Man: The Status of the Negro in New York.* New York: Hill and Wang.

Pagnini, Deanna L. 1992. "American Fertility Transition: Rural Family Building Patterns in the Early Twentieth Century." Ph.D. diss., University of North Carolina, Chapel Hill.

Pagnini, Deanna L., and S. Philip Morgan. 1996. "Racial Differences in Marriage and Childbearing: Oral History Evidence from the South in the Early Twentieth Century." *American Journal of Sociology* 101:1694–718.

Powdermaker, Hortense. 1939. *After Freedom.* New York: Viking Press.

Preston, Samuel H. 1978. *The Effects of Infant and Child Mortality on Fertility.* New York: Academic Press.

Preston, Samuel H., and Michael R. Haines. 1991. *Fatal Years: Child Mortality in Late Nineteenth-Century America.* Princeton: Princeton University Press.

Preston, Samuel H., Suet Lim, and S. Philip Morgan. 1992. "African-American Marriage in 1910: Beneath the Surface of Census Data." *Demography* 29:1–16.

Ransom, Roger, and Richard Sutch. 1977. *One Kind of Freedom: The Economic Consequences of Emancipation.* New York: Cambridge University Press.

Raper, Arthur. 1936[1971]. *Preface to Peasantry.* Chapel Hill: University of North Carolina Press.

———. 1943. *Tenants of the Almighty.* New York: Macmillan.

Raper, Arthur, and Ira Reid. 1941. *Sharecroppers All.* Chapel Hill: University of North Carolina Press.

Reid, Joseph D. 1981. "White Land, Black Labor, and Agricultural Stagnation: The Causes and Effects of Sharecropping in the Postbellum South." In *Market Institutions and Economic Progress in the New South, 1865–1900,* 33–45. Ed. Gary M. Walton and James F. Shepherd. New York: Academic Press.

Rice, Sarah. 1989. *He Included Me: The Autobiography of Sara Rice.* Athens: University of Georgia Press.

Rosengarten, Theodore. 1974. *All God's Dangers: The Life of Nate Shaw.* New York: Avon.

Ruggles, Steven. 1994. "The Origins of African-American Family Structure." *American Sociological Review* 59:136–51.

———. 1997. "The Effects of AFDC on American Family Structure, 1940–1990." *Journal of Family History* 22:307–25.

Ruggles, Steven, and Matthew Sobek. 1995. *Integrated Public Use Microdata Series: Version 1.0.* Minneapolis: Social History Research Laboratory, University of Minnesota.

Sassler, Sharon. 1995. "Trade-Offs in the Family: Sibling Effects on Daughters' Activities in 1910." *Demography* 32:557–75.

Schwartz, Michael. 1976. *Radical Protest and Social Structure: The Southern Farmers' Alliance and Cotton Tenancy, 1880–1890.* New York: Academic Press.

Scott, Emmett J. 1919. "Letters of Negro Migrants." *Journal of Negro History* 4:290–340.

Shifflett, Crandall. 1975. "The Household Composition of Rural Black Families: Louisa County, Virginia, 1880." *Journal of Interdisciplinary History* 6:235–60.

Shryock, Henry S., and Jacob S. Siegel. 1976. *The Methods and Materials of Demography.* New York: Academic Press.

Smith, Herbert L., S. Philip Morgan, and Tanya Koropeckyj-Cox. 1995. "A Decomposition of Trends in the Nonmarital Fertility Ratios of Blacks and Whites in the United States, 1960–1992." Presented at the annual meeting of the American Sociological Association, Washington, D.C., Aug. 8, 1995.

South, Scott J., and Kim M. Lloyd. 1992a. "Marriage Opportunities and Family Formation: Further Implications of Imbalanced Sex Ratios." *Journal of Marriage and the Family* 54:440–51.

———. 1992b. "Marriage Markets and Nonmarital Fertility in the U.S." *Demography* 29:247–64.

Stack, Carol B. 1974. *All Our Kin: Strategies for Survival in a Black Community.* New York: Harper and Row.

Stampp, Kenneth M. 1965. *The Peculiar Institution: Slavery in the Ante-Bellum South.* New York: Knopf.

Steckel, Richard H. 1985. *The Economics of U.S. Slave and Southern White Fertility.* New York: Garland.

Taeuber, Karl E., and Alma F. Taeuber. 1965. *Negroes in Cities.* Chicago: Aldine.

Terrill, Tom E., and Jerrold Hirsch. 1978. *Such as Us: Southern Voices of the Thirties.* Chapel Hill: University of North Carolina Press.

Thompson, Warren S., and P. K. Whelpton. 1933. *Population Trends in the United States.* New York: McGraw-Hill.

Tolnay, Stewart E. 1980. "Black Fertility in Decline: Urban Differentials in 1900." *Social Biology* 27:249–60.

———. 1981. "Trends in Total and Marital Fertility for Black Americans, 1886–1899." *Demography* 18:443–63.

———. 1984. "Black Family Formation and Tenancy in the Farm South, 1900." *American Journal of Sociology* 90:305–25

———. 1987. "The Decline of Black Marital Fertility in the Rural South: 1910–1940." *American Sociological Review* 52:211–17.

———. 1989. "A New Look at the Effect of Venereal Disease on Black Fertility: The Deep South in 1940." *Demography* 26:679–90.

———. 1995a. "Class, Race, and Fertility in the Rural South, 1910 and 1940." *Rural Sociology* 60:108–28.

———. 1995b. "The Spatial Diffusion of Fertility: A Cross-Sectional Analysis of Counties in the American South, 1940." *American Sociological Review* 60:299–308.

———. 1997. "The Great Migration and Changes in the Northern Black Family, 1940 to 1990." *Social Forces* 74:1213–38.

———. 1998a. "Educational Selection in the Migration of Southern Blacks, 1880–1990." *Social Forces* in press.

———. 1998b. "Migration Experience and Family Patterns in the 'Promised Land.'" *Journal of Family History* 28:68–89.

Tolnay, Stewart E., and E. M. Beck. 1992. "Racial Violence and Black Migration in the American South." *American Sociological Review* 57:103–16.

———. 1995. *A Festival of Violence: An Analysis of Southern Lynchings, 1882–1930.* Urbana: University of Illinois Press.

Tolnay, Stewart E., and Avery M. Guest. 1982. "Childlessness in a Transitional Population: The United States at the Turn of the Century." *Journal of Family History* 7:200–219.

Tolnay, Stewart E., and Patricia J. Glynn. 1994. "The Persistence of High Fertility in the American South on the Eve of the Baby Boom." *Demography* 31:615–31.

Tolnay, Stewart E., Stephen N. Graham, and Avery M. Guest. 1982. "Own-Child Estimates of U.S. White Fertility, 1886–99." *Historical Methods* 15:127–38.

Tucker, M. Belinda, and Claudia Mitchell-Kernan. 1995. "Trends in African American Family Formation: A Theoretical and Statistical Overview." In *The Decline in Marriage among African Americans*, 3–26. Ed. M. Belinda Tucker and Claudia Mitchell-Kernan. New York: Russell Sage Foundation.

U.S. Bureau of the Census. 1902. *Twelfth Census of the United States, 1900*. Vol. 5: *Agriculture*. Washington, D.C.: Government Printing Office.

———. 1943a. *Sixteenth Census of the United States, 1940: Agriculture. Analysis of Specified Farm Characteristics for Farms Classified by Total Value of Products*. Washington, D.C.: Government Printing Office.

———. 1943b. *United States Abridged Life Tables, 1939. Urban and Rural by Regions, Color and Sex*. Washington, D.C.: Government Printing Office.

———. 1945. *Sixteenth Census of the United States, 1940: Population. Differential Fertility 1940 and 1910. Women by Number of Children Ever Born*. Washington, D.C.: Government Printing Office.

———. 1975. *Historical Statistics of the United States: Colonial Times to 1970*. Washington, D.C.: Government Printing Office.

———. 1983. *Census of Population. Public Use Microdata Sample. Technical Documentation*. Washington, D.C.: Government Printing Office.

———. 1985. "The Social and Economic Status of the Black Population in the United States: An Historical View, 1790–1978." *Current Population Reports*, special studies series P-23, no. 80.

———. 1990. 1990 Census of Population. *Social and Economic Characteristics. U.S.* Washington, D.C.: Government Printing Office.

———. 1994. *Statistical Abstract of the United States: 1994*. 114th ed. Washington, D.C.: Government Printing Office.

———. 1995. *Statistical Abstract of the United States: 1995*. 115th ed. Washington, D.C.: Government Printing Office.

———. 1996. *Statistical Abstract of the United States: 1996*. 116th ed. Washington, D.C.: Government Printing Office.

van de Walle, Etienne, and John Knodel. 1980. "Europe's Fertility Transition: New Evidence and Lessons for Today's Developing World." *Population Bulletin* 34:1–43.

Waite, Linda. 1995. "Does Marriage Matter?" *Demography* 32:483–507.

Watkins, Susan C. 1991. *From Provinces into Nations: Demographic Integration in Western Europe, 1870–1960*. Princeton: Princeton University Press.

———. 1994. *After Ellis Island: Newcomers and Natives in the 1910 Census*. New York: Russell Sage Foundation.

Weeks, John R. 1995. *Population: An Introduction to Concepts and Issues*. Belmot: Wadsworth.

Wilson, William Julius. 1987. *The Truly Disadvantaged: The Inner City, the Underclass, and Public Policy.* Chicago: University of Chicago Press.

Woodson, Carter G. 1918[1969]. *A Century of Negro Migration.* New York: Russell and Russell.

———. 1930. *The Rural Negro.* Washington, D.C.: Association for the Study of Negro Life and History.

Woodward, C. Vann. 1951. *Origins of the New South, 1877–1913.* Baton Rouge: Louisiana State University Press.

———. 1966. *The Strange Career of Jim Crow.* New York: Oxford University Press.

Woofter, T. J. 1936. *Landlord and Tenant on the Cotton Plantation.* Research Monograph 5, Works Progress Administration, Division of Social Research, Washington, D.C.

Woofter, T. J., and Ellen Winston. 1939. *Seven Lean Years.* Chapel Hill: University of North Carolina Press.

Wright, George C. 1990. *Racial Violence in Kentucky, 1865–1940: Lynchings, Mob Rule, and "Legal Lynchings."* Baton Rouge: Louisiana State University Press.

Wright, Paul, and Peter Pirie. 1984. "A False Fertility Transition: The Case of American Blacks." *Paper of the East-West Population Institute,* no. 90.

# Index

STEWART E. TOLNAY is a professor of sociology and the director of the Center for Social and Demographic Analysis at the University at Albany, State University of New York. He holds a Ph.D. and a master's degree in sociology from the University of Washington, Seattle.

## DATE DUE